WOMEN IN WONDERLAND

Lives, Legends, and Legacies of Yellowstone National Park

ELIZABETH A. WATRY

RIVERBEND
PUBLISHING

To my dad, Robert J. Lewry,
who unconditionally championed my independent spirit...
and
To my husband, Robert "Bo" Watry
who lovingly encouraged me to always follow my heart ...

If only you both could see me now!

Women in Wonderland: Lives, Legends, and Legacies of Yellowstone National Park
© 2012 Elizabeth A. Watry
ISBN 978-1-60639-029-0
Printed in the United States of America.

6 7 8 9 0 SB 20 19 18 17

All rights reserved. No part of this book may be reproduced, stored, or transmitted in any form or by any means without the prior permission of the publisher, except for brief excerpts for reviews.

Cover and text design by DD Dowden

COVER PHOTOS:
TOP: Marguerite Lindsley Arnold (FAR LEFT) and three unidentified women along with Judge John W. Meldrum (FAR RIGHT) posed in front of the Roosevelt Arch at Yellowstone National Park's North Entrance, circa 1908. (COURTESY BILL ARNOLD)

BOTTOM FROM LEFT TO RIGHT: Ida Christine Carlson Eagle (COURTESY EAGLE FAMILY); Marguerite Lindsley Arnold (COURTESY BILL ARNOLD); Beulah Brown Sanborn *(FROM My Winter in Geyserland)*; Herma Albertson Baggley (COURTESY BILL ARNOLD).

RIVERBEND PUBLISHING
P.O. Box 5833
Helena, MT 59604
1-866-787-2363
www.riverbendpublishing.com

FSC
www.fsc.org
MIX
Paper from
responsible sources
FSC® C014174

Acknowledgments

Thank you to Montana State University professor and advisor Mary Murphy for recommending me to Riverbend Publishing to author this book and for her advice in the early stages of this project that gave me a better sense of direction and focus.

Many thanks to Bill and Lou Arnold of Spokane, Washington who graciously hosted me for several days while I sifted through their family treasure trove of Marguerite Lindsley's memorabilia. Seeing letters, photographs, clothing, and even Marguerite's ranger hat, made her lifetime in Yellowstone take on a vibrant meaning to me, and significance that I hope resonates in this book.

Likewise, thank you to Ruth Ann Bennett, who generously sent me her mother Herma Albertson Baggley's photo album and then invited me to return it to her personally in Mill Creek, Washington! It was great fun to help Ruth Ann dig through her family archive searching for more puzzle pieces of Herma's life.

Thank you to Kendra Eagle for finding her grandmother's letters, photographs, and other memorabilia and arranging interviews with family members that allowed me to make Ida Eagle come to life. Kendra and all the Eagle family, thank you so much for your enthusiastic support!

Thank you to Ellie Povah for inviting me into her home and taking time out of her busy West Yellowstone summer to tell me about her long and often adventurous life in Yellowstone.

Muchas gracias to Loretta and Bill Chapman of Gardiner, Montana for reading each chapter and offering helpful suggestions as well as for their endless and generous support in so many ways.

I am grateful for the assistance of Lee Whittlesey, Yellowstone National Park Historian, who took me under his wing early in my writing career, and coached me on how to be a better writer. Because of his meticulous direction and rigorous editing, I have been able to realize my dream of becoming a published author. In part, his conscientious guidance and support of my writing have made me what I am today. I owe him a debt of gratitude that will be hard to repay.

Unending thanks goes to Jessie Gerdes, Jackie Jerla, Mariah Robertson, Bridgette Guild, Anne Foster, and Colleen Curry at the Yellowstone Heritage and Research Center for keeping a watchful eye for incoming pieces of women's history that might aid my research and for their ever attentive assistance with my multitudinous history research on Yellowstone in general.

Thank you to Laura McCarthy, curatorial assistant at Yellowstone Gateway Museum; Molly Conley, at the Yellowstone Research and Heritage Center; Emily Yost, editorial assistant for Yellowstone Cultural Resources; Becca Kohl, at the Montana Historical Society; Tamsen Hert, University of Wyoming Head of Special Collections; Kimberly Thomas, archivist of the Harley Davidson Motor Company Archives; Blair Davenport, museum curator at Death Valley National Park; Stacy Mason, archivist at Harpers Ferry; and all the archivists, librarians, and historians who helped me find photographs and historical documentation on my subjects.

A very special note of gratitude goes to Bob Goss whose ardent assistance and dedicated research efforts continually kept me on the trail of new and insightful examinations of my subjects. And whose thoughtful care guided me through a physical illness that could have stymied this project as well as my lifetime aspirations, goals, and desires. For these things and so much more, I owe him an eternity of appreciation.

Finally, thank you to everyone who helped me with this project and I apologize to those of you that my failing memory may have missed.

Contents

Introduction

Established in 1872, Yellowstone National Park at once became famous for its near supernatural landscape of hot springs, geysers, and geological formations. This fame actually began as early as 1871 when journalists from as far away as New York began touting the region as America's Wonderland.[1] Sporting its new magical moniker, Yellowstone became known as one of the country's most spectacular places and as such drew the interest of every sort of person, American and European, men and women, young and old, wealthy as well as those of modest means.

However, located in far-off corner of northwestern Wyoming, the Yellowstone Wonderland was not easily reached in its earliest years. Because of its remoteness and the lack of roads to and within the park, travel by horseback offered the only accessibility. And the park offered very few services for tourists save for a few primitive hostelries erected by a few hardy souls. Together with the arrival of the railroad in the mid-1880s and the construction of a road system encompassing the park's major attractions, Yellowstone developed an air of civility within a few decades as hotels and general stores sprang up at Mammoth Hot Springs, Old Faithful, Norris, Lake, and Canyon. Accordingly, visitation to Yellowstone increased and, over time, that influx of people from all points of the globe has contributed significantly to the expansion of the park's historical record.

With the publication of Peter Nabokov's *Restoring a Presence: American Indians and Yellowstone National Park*, the narrative of Yellowstone's cultural history has become more inclusive in recent years, but it is still missing an important component—the contributions of women. It is my sincerest desire, with this volume, to remedy that omission by giving the women of Yellowstone a voice that will be heard through the centuries. Like much of America's history, Yellowstone's historical narrative contains numerous stories of the adventures, heroics, and contributions of men, while the contributions of women have become invisible and largely forgotten. As there are far more women whose lives were influenced and shaped by their experiences in the park than *Women in Wonderland* encompasses, this book represents merely the beginning of reclaiming Yellowstone's women from obscurity.

No matter what her background, education, or life experience, each of these profiles of the *Women in Wonderland* resonates with the evocative voice of a woman who chose to follow the call of an avant garde life in the unconventional American West, specifically Yellowstone National Park. The individual narratives that follow reflect upon the variety of enterprising experiences and meaningful activities of twelve women who elected not to be bound by tradition and thus to pursue paths less followed by women in the late 19th and early 20th centuries. These women were spirited, ambitious, independent, and, most importantly, intent on becoming self-actualized on their own terms. Many of the stories reflect how some of them pushed the boundaries of traditional gender spheres and entered male-dominated fields, either out of economic necessity or to purposefully define themselves, while others reveal how some women chose to either blend into their workplaces or become more forthright in attaining recognition. While many of these women's paths were by design, some occurred by default, but all pursued their course of life with courage, conviction, and confidence.

In general, *Women in Wonderland* explores the intersection of women and place. The biographical profiles in this book bring to light the cultural, environmental, and social history of Yellowstone as reflected through the lives of women who became intimate with the park and its landscape. All of the women showcased here found their lives appreciably changed by their encounters with Yellowstone. The accounts also reveal how these women interacted with political, cultural, economic, and social events that sometimes threatened their lives as well as their freedom to evolve and flourish, and how through it all they struggled to remain true to themselves. Furthermore, these twelve women helped to weave a fascinating texture into the cultural and social history of Yellowstone as both workplace and play place.

Indeed, their contributions to Yellowstone were many. Rangers Isabel Bassett Wasson, Marguerite Lindsley Arnold, Herma Albertson Baggley, Frances Pound Wright, and Margaret Mary Meagher originated and fostered new interpretations of Yellowstone's multi-faceted geology, dynamic environment, stunning landscape, and distinctive wildlife. Concessioners Anna Trischman Pryor, Elizabeth Trischman, Eleanor Hamilton Povah, and Ida Carlson Eagle set the standard for supplying park visitors with necessities as well as cherished memorabilia. Behind the scenes caretakers Beulah Brown Sanborn, Willie Frances Bronner, and Jean Crawford Sharp became masters at providing good food and comfortable accommodations to thousands of park visitors. And rounding out the narratives, the fate of Mattie Shipley Culver and the ordeal of Emma Carpenter Cowan contribute tragedy and legend to Yellowstone history. To be sure, each one of these women left a notable imprint on the history of women in Wonderland.

Emma Carpenter Cowan

(1853–1938)

An Impress that the Years Cannot Efface

"Surrounded by hostile Indians, her husband shot and left for dead, their horses and equipment commandeered by the redskins and herself and others in the party taken captive, a resident of Spokane had a honeymoon, such as few women have experienced, dreamed about, or even read about in the most lurid fiction," reported the Spokane *Spokesman Review* in 1932.[1] "She is Mrs. George F. Cowan, Sr." The dramatic event that the newspaper was referring to had occurred fifty-five years earlier when Emma Cowan, her husband George, and several others were touring Yellowstone National Park in 1877. Even though she was not on her honeymoon as the newspaper erroneously reported, Emma's encounter with the Nez Perce Indians had made her a bit famous around the country and continued to garner her fame until her death, thus making her a legend in her own time. Today Emma Carpenter Cowan's story still captures the attention of readers who are intrigued by chronicles of legendary Western cultural conflicts.

Born in Wisconsin in 1853, Emma J. Carpenter delighted in outdoor activities and loved to read books on travel and adventure. On April 24, 1864, ten-year-old Emma and her family embarked on their own voyage—westward. She enjoyed "beyond measure the gypsy lifestyle of travel, journeying toward the setting sun, expecting in all probability to find a pot of gold at the rainbow's point. For the land of gold was the objective [*sic*] place."[2] The young territory of Montana had received its name and status within two years of its first major gold strike. As they journeyed toward Virginia City, Montana, and its Alder Gulch, the Mecca of gold seekers at that time, Emma relished "camping in the lovely

nooks where wild flowers grew, traveling on to other pleasant places...,
sleeping at night in the great white-capped wagons..., and the never failing
pleasure of appeasing prodigious appetites."

It was on this trek that Emma caught her first glimpse of Indians.
While most people feared Indians and ran for protection when the alarm
of "Indian scare" went forth, Emma's father Daniel D. Carpenter did not
subscribe to these hysterics, and always treated the Indians kindly when
he came in contact with them. Thus, Emma grew up believing that the
threats of Indian attacks were mostly contrived stories, "without much
real foundation for fear." Her father instilled in Emma a sense of level-
headedness when it came to dealing with Indians, which undoubtedly
saved her life later on. From an early age, Emma looked forward to her
adventures in the West with coolness and poise.

On August 4, after three months of traveling across the plains and
mountains, the Carpenter family arrived in the bustling and chaotic
community of Virginia City. There they found more than 10,000 people
who were employed either in mining thirteen-mile-long Alder Gulch,
or in its multiple settlements supplying the miners with life's essentials.
Emma's father chose the latter, and purchased a butcher shop shortly
after the family took up residence in the disorderly town. Although the
Vigilantes attempted to maintain their version of civil order with swift
justice, riots and shootings were common occurrences. For Emma and
her siblings, Virginia City proved to be an exciting place, which drew a
thrilling cast of colorful characters.[3]

While living in Virginia City, Emma's father befriended an old trapper
who entertained her with wonderful stories of a wonderful place where
"fountains of boiling water...were thrown hundreds of feet in the air" and
"pools of water within whose limpid depths tints of the rainbow were
reflected." While she thoroughly enjoyed his fanciful tales that even her
"fairy books could not equal," Emma speculated that the old man's stories
might be "merely the phantasy [sic] of his imagination." Even though her
family relocated to Helena in the spring of 1865, Emma was determined
to one day seek the old trapper's land of mystery for herself—present-day
Yellowstone National Park.

In 1873, only one year after Yellowstone was established as a national
park, Emma made her first trip to the place people were already calling
Wonderland. She found the Mammoth Hot Springs weird and wonderful.

Emma spent two weeks exploring the springs, meeting an acquaintance or two, and putting objects in the flowing mineral waters of the travertine terraces so that she could bring home beautifully encrusted souvenirs. But while she explored the Mammoth area, others continued on the one-hundred-mile round-trip horseback journey to the Upper Geyser Basin. They returned with exhilarating accounts of dazzling geysers and colorful hot pools. To Emma "words seemed inadequate to express or convey the wonders they had seen as one and all would tell her, 'You must see them yourself.'" At the conclusion of her first visit, Yellowstone had only become more fascinating, and she resolved to return again as soon as possible.

In 1875, Emma married Civil War veteran George F. Cowan. Born near Columbus, Ohio, on February 10, 1842, George grew up in Wisconsin and was studying law in of the office of A.B. Hamilton in Hartford when Fort Sumter was fired on in April 1861. He immediately enlisted in Company B, Fourth Wisconsin, and served for nearly four years before his honorable discharge with the rank of sergeant in 1864. After a short return to Wisconsin, George moved west to Last Chance Gulch, which became the city of Helena in 1865. He tried his luck at mining for a while before being appointed Assistant Assessor of Internal Revenue in 1867, and he resumed his law studies. In 1868 he was appointed Clerk of the Court at Radersburg, where he finished his legal reading. Upon being admitted to the bar in 1872, George began practicing law in Boulder, Radersburg, and Helena. For the first two years of their marriage, George and Emma lived in Radersburg, about fifty-five miles south of Helena.[4]

In late July 1877, Emma's 27-year-old brother Frank, who had not yet viewed the "curiosities of Wonderland," decided to make a trip to the park. He and an old family friend, Albert Oldham, made plans to rent saddle horses and a pack animal, gather provisions, and depart by the first of August. While they were making their preparations another one of Frank's acquaintances, miner

In August 1877, twenty-four year-old Emma Carpenter Cowan was captured by the Nez Perce as they fled from the military through Yellowstone National Park. (COURTESY U.S. FOREST SERVICE)

A.J. Arnold, inquired about accompanying the two men. Now with a party of three, Frank also obtained a buggy. On July 29, the trio departed Helena for Frank's father's residence near Deep Creek, about forty-five miles south of Helena, where they planned to gather more provisions for the trip. It was here that the small party added six more members.[5]

That summer in Montana had been exceptionally hot and dry which, combined with the irritation of a grasshopper infestation, made for a miserable existence in Radersburg. It took very little consideration for Emma and George to decide to join her brother on a trip to Yellowstone. Because Emma was the only woman in the party, she convinced her mother to allow her thirteen-year-old sister Ida to come along for female companionship. In addition, Charles Mann of Radersburg and William Dingee of Helena both expressed a desire to join the party. With a much larger party than originally planned, Frank borrowed a team from his father, and secured the services of a young man, Henry Myers, as teamster and to cook for the extended group.

On August 5, the party of nine, which included Emma and George Cowan; Ida and Frank Carpenter; family friends A.J. Arnold, William Dingee, and Albert Oldham; and local residents, Charles Mann and Henry Myers, departed Radersburg. The entourage traveled south, camping the first night near Three Forks, Montana. The following day they followed the Madison River to Sterling, a small mining town and stage stop six miles south of present-day Norris, arriving after dark. Emma and most of the party on horseback had made it to Sterling well in advance of their slower supply and camp wagon, and chose to take supper at the town hotel. Upon hearing where the Cowan and Carpenter party was headed, the townspeople warned them of possible Indian trouble and advised them not to travel any farther. Although they carefully measured that well meaning counsel, Emma and her party believed it to be just another "old time Indian scare." In the morning they journeyed south passing through Ennis, where they were advised that they would find "fine fishing" on Henry Lake. "Some of the pleasantest days of our outing trip were spent here," Emma fondly recalled. After several days of hunting and fishing, they concluded their time at the lake with a "rousing fire, good supper, comparing notes, telling stories, and singing songs."

On August 13 the group departed Henry Lake and traveled southeast. After crossing seven-thousand-foot Targhee Pass and passing through ten miles of pine barrens, the tourists entered the park near today's West Yellowstone, Montana. Following the Madison River east and then the Firehole River south, they arrived at the Lower Geyser Basin. After nine days of traveling from Radersburg Emma enthusiastically declared, "We had at last reached Wonderland!"

The travelers established a permanent camp near Fountain Geyser and made daily short excursions to various points of interest. As the group had traveled as far into the park as possible with their wagons, they opted to leave their camp intact and proceed by horseback to the Upper Geyser Basin. While they were packing a few days' supplies, George Huston, an old guide and packer, rode into camp with a small party from Bear Gulch, today's Jardine, Montana. After a short conversation with Huston, the Radersburg tourists discovered that he too was traveling to the Upper Geyser Basin and they decided to join him. Emma and the party enjoyed Mr. Huston's company and found him to be "thoroughly conversant with every area of Geyserland." En route, Huston relayed the disturbing news of the army battle with the Nez Perce Indians in Montana's Big Hole valley, which had occurred on August 9. He also advised the uninformed tourists that he had encountered General Sherman and accompanying troops touring the park earlier that month. Huston assured the now nervous tourists that Sherman was confident the Indians would not come into the park, reasoning that their "superstitious minds associate [it] with hell, by reason of its geysers and hot-springs." Even with Huston's contention that they were safe, Emma was not thoroughly convinced that they would see no Indians before they reached home.[6]

Nonetheless, Emma and others enjoyed the splendid display of geysers and hot springs in the Upper Basin, while Frank and some of the group traveled to the Lake and the Falls under the guidance of Huston. Party members, now divided, arranged to meet again in few days at their permanent camp in the Lower Geyser Basin. On Thursday August 23, with the parties rejoined, they made plans to depart for home the following day. They were also planning to celebrate Emma and George's second wedding anniversary on August 24. However, upon awakening the next morning, Emma heard the guttural tones of two or three Indians who had suddenly appeared in their camp. Emma immediately woke her husband, who scrambled out of the tent and began consulting with the Indians.

The Nez Perce had long been friendly with white Americans and hostility rarely surfaced. But the depredations that the Nez Perce had suffered through the 1870s seriously altered their previously peaceful attitude toward whites. In early June 1877 the Indians were ordered to leave their generations-old homelands in Washington, Oregon, and western Idaho, and relocate on a reservation in Idaho. Several young Nez Perce warriors became hostile to the idea of being confined to a reservation. Their elders also believed the treaty creating that reservation to be invalid. The anger spread quickly and the U.S. military sent troops. While he had struggled for many years to avoid war, Chief Joseph knew that the majority of his people had been "inflamed by the deeds of the young men," and he found that they were "in no mood to heed him." As their leader, Joseph could not desert them. With General Oliver O. Howard in pursuit, Joseph's renegade band of Nez Perce headed south and east in search of sanctuary. After several battles and skirmishes, the Indians arrived in a lush meadow near the Big Hole River in the second week of August, 1877. They made camp in a location on the south side of the river, which the Nez Perce had long ago become familiar with during their treks to buffalo country. Thinking that they had eluded the military, the group of about 750 Nez Perce men, women, and children decided to rest in this comfortable camp for a few days.[7]

Little did they know that Howard had telegraphed Colonel Gibbon in Montana to assist with the pursuit. Gibbon gathered seventeen officers and one-hundred forty-six enlisted men from various forts and began trailing the Indians up the Bitterroot Valley. A cavalry scouting party commanded by Lt. James H. Bradley discovered the Nez Perce camp. At 3:30 in the morning on August 9, Gibbon's force began their attack. However, the Indians discovered the soldiers before the whites could get into position and a volley of shots alerted the village. Nez Perce men, women and children ran for cover in the nearby willows, sloughs, and river. Two Nez Perce chiefs, Looking Glass and White Bird, exhorted the warriors to fight and the soldiers soon found themselves in a hail of bullets. After over an hour of fighting, Colonel Gibbon ordered his men back across the river and into the timber. Twenty or thirty Nez Perce warriors held Gibbon's forces on the other side of the river throughout the night and into the next morning while the surviving Indians escaped.[8]

Although the Nez Perce suffered serious losses at the Battle of Big Hole, they evaded defeat and capture. But the Indians also knew that the U.S. Army would be intensifying its pursuit. Under the guidance of chiefs Looking Glass, White Bird, and Joseph, the Nez Perce decided to continue traveling east in hope of finding refuge with the Crow Indians in eastern Montana. One of the Indians who appeared at the Radersburg tourists' camp was Yellow Wolf, a Nez Perce scout who was leading a small band of warriors to survey the safest route through Yellowstone. Luckily for the Radersburg party, Yellow Wolf was one of many Nez Perce who believed that the enemy was the United States Army, not civilians, and he renounced the indiscriminate killing of whites.[9]

The men of Emma's party determined it would be best to break camp and attempt their trek north as though nothing was awry. But by this time twenty or thirty Indians had come into camp and more seemed to be on the way. As George and the others began to gather their things and pack up camp, another party member, Mr. Arnold, began passing out sugar and flour to the Indians on their demand. Upon observing this, George became perturbed and ordered the Indians away. Emma immediately saw her husband's reaction as problematic and wrote later that "this materially lessened his chances of escape."

The party began its trek north, followed by forty or fifty Indians whom Emma assumed were just going the same way. They passed a band of women and children who had turned east toward Mary Lake. Traveling another mile or so, the procession of tourists and Indians encountered another group of sixty warriors who materialized out of the timber at the command of one of the Indians on horseback. Another Indian announced in good English, "Him, Joseph," pointing toward the Indian who uttered the command, thus revealing to the Radersburg group that they were in the company of the famed Chief of the Nez Perce. At this point the Indians ordered the caravan to turn around and follow the trail to Mary Lake.

After several miles, Emma's party was forced to leave their wagons behind due to excessive fallen timber and they were allowed to take with them only a few things that they could carry on their horses. They stopped for lunch after traveling nearly ten miles on the trail and one of the Indians named Poker Joe (Lean Elk)[10] acted as interpreter for the white captives. He informed the tourists that if they would trade their healthy horses for the Indians' worn out steeds, they would be released. Considering their circumstances, the group agreed and began the exchange. While the Indians were caught up in the horse trading transaction, William

Dingee and A.J. Arnold escaped unnoticed into the surrounding forest and headed west.

The remaining Radersburg travelers, unaware of Dingee and Arnold's getaway, promptly mounted their exchanged horses and began their retreat toward the Lower Geyser Basin. They were only about a half mile away when they discovered that they were being followed by warriors. Much to their dismay the Indians informed Emma, George, Frank, Ida, and the others that the chief wanted to talk to them again. Disheartened they turned around. As they passed the site of their noon time stop Emma hoped that they would soon catch up with the squaw camp, with whom she "fancied we would be safer." Her hope was soon shattered as:

> Suddenly, without warning, shots rang out. Two Indians came dashing down the trail in front of us. My husband was getting off his horse. I wondered for what reason. I soon knew, for he fell as soon as he reached the ground—fell headlong down the hill. Shots followed and all was confusion. In less time than it takes for me to tell it, I was off my horse and by my husband's side, where he lay against a fallen pine tree. I heard my sister's screams and called to her. She came and crouched by me, as I knelt by his side. I saw he was wounded by the leg above the knee, and by the way the blood spurted out I feared an artery had been severed....I think we both glanced up the hill at the same moment, for he said, "Keep quiet. It won't last long"....Every gun of the whole party of Indians was leveled on us three, I shall never forget the picture, which left an impress that years cannot efface.

Emma did not have long to survey the scene as the Indians tried to drag her away from her husband. Looking over her shoulder, she saw an Indian with an immense pistol trying to get at shot at George's head. Instinctively she wrenched her arm away from the endeavoring executioner and leaned over her husband. She was immediately yanked from her protective posture, while another Indian stepped up and took aim at George. A pistol shot rang out and Emma watched in horror as her husband's head fell back, and a "red stream trickled down his face from beneath his hat." Emma vividly remembered the "warm sunshine, the smell of blood," her sister's screams, seeing rocks being thrown at George's head, "the horror of it all." She felt a sick faint feeling and then "all was blank." The day that should have been a joyous celebration of her marriage had turned into a horrendous episode of bereavement.

In the melee, Charles Mann and Henry Myers slipped away, while Albert Oldham was not so lucky. Oldham, who had been shot in the left side of his face, lay slumped at the base of a tree. After regaining consciousness, Emma's first recollection was of a "great variety of noises—hooting, yelling, neighing of horses—all jumbled together." As she was gathering her senses, she heard someone calling her name and soon her brother was at her side. Frank told her that the Indians said no further harm should befall them. For Emma, that assurance had come too late.

George and Albert were left for dead, and the survivors were ordered to press on toward the Nez Perce camp in Hayden Valley. When the Indians learned that Frank was familiar with the trail, they ordered him to move to the front of the group. Emma recalled that the remainder of the day was a trying ordeal of wearisome uphill travel through dense timber on a narrow trail that was fit for a few tourists, but not five or six hundred Indians in exodus. Upon arriving at the camp Emma was met by her brother and collapsed into tears in his arms as thoughts of her dead husband haunted her. She was then led to the campfire where Chief Joseph was seated. He said nothing, but motioned for her to sit down. Frank spread a blanket on the ground, and she "sank down on it, thoroughly exhausted." She asked about her sister and was informed that Ida was safe at Poker Joe's camp a short distance away. Chief Joseph assured Emma that she could see her sister in the morning. He offered her food prepared by the Indian woman, but heartsick and distressed she could not eat. That evening she and Frank "sat out a weary vigil by the dying embers of the campfire, sadly wondering what the coming day would bring forth."

The next morning Poker Joe took Emma to see her sister. "Such a forlorn looking child I trust I may never again see," Emma later wrote. "She threw herself into my arms in a very paroxysm of joy. She seemed not to be quite certain that I was alive," Emma continued, "even though she had been told."

Poker Joe then began giving orders for the day's movement of the bedraggled group. Emma, Frank, and Ida, now the only remaining members of the original Radersburg excursion, and the assorted bands of Nez Perce traveled through Hayden Valley and forded the Yellowstone River near Mud Geyser. Here they stopped to prepare dinner and to hold a council. Emma watched with trepidation as the Indians sat in circle and spoke one by one to the assembly. After an excited and heated debate the council voted on the fate of the captives by passing around a long pipe. If a chief smoked from the pipe, the vote was for release, but if the pipe was passed, the vote was for death. When the council had ended its proceedings, Poker Joe reported to Emma that the Nez Perce had decided to release her and Ida, but Frank and John Shively, another man who had been captured later, would have to remain as guides. Even though she was weakened from lack of food, Emma stood her ground, refusing to leave without her brother. After deliberation, the Indians agreed to let Frank go, and preparations were made for the remnant party to depart.[11]

The Indians gave Emma and Ida two worn horses, a little bedding, and bread and matches. With Frank afoot, the trio was guided by Poker Joe to a trail that paralleled the Yellowstone River. Here their Indian ally turned and said, "Now my friends, good-bye. You go down river, way down. No stop. Go all night. No stop. You get'm Bozeman three days." He also advised, "Go quick now. Go quick." For the first few miles, they heeded Joe's advice as best they could. However, with Frank walking, and Emma and Ida riding exhausted ponies, their progress was markedly slow. Nevertheless, they held steadfastly to the hope of surviving.[12]

The following day, August 26, near Tower Fall they met a company of soldiers near Tower Fall led by Lieutenant Schofield who had been dispatched from Fort Ellis to track the Nez Perce. Frank informed the military men that they were "fleeing from the Indians and were the only survivors of their party, as he believed then." Overwhelmed by the seeming certainty of rescue, Emma declared, "Oh, such a feeling of relief!" After they had been in the soldiers' camp for not quite an hour, they saw a man running toward the camp. He informed Schofield that his name was Pfister and he was with a party of Helena tourists who had been camped near the falls. They were attacked by Indians around noon and he believed the rest of the party had been killed. After a quick supper and now supplied with fresh horses, Pfister, Frank, Emma, and Ida rode to Mammoth Hot Springs. Upon arrival Frank telegraphed his brother, George, in Helena:

> Emma, Ida, and myself alive; Cowan and Oldham killed. Saw Cowan and Oldham shot. Balance missing. I think all are killed, but don't know. Will send particulars when I reach Bozeman. Helena party all gone except one—all missing. Indians fired into their camp. Joseph, Looking Glass, and White Bird were the chiefs.—F. Carpenter[13]

MRS. COWAN   GEO. F. COWAN

CHIEF JOSEPH NEZ PERCE
IDA CARPENTER   FRANK CARPENTER

*This beautifully illustrated collage depicts the main members
of the Carpenter Cowan party that were captured or
left for dead by the Nez Perce in Yellowstone, 1877.*

(FROM CONTRIBUTIONS OF THE HISTORICAL SOCIETY OF MONTANA, 1904. VOLUME 4)

The three family members arrived in Bozeman on August 28. It had been nearly a month since they departed Radersburg and four days since their dramatic ordeal with the Indians began, but for Emma it seemed like years had passed. Emma, believing she was a widow, went to her parents' ranch outside of Townsend with Ida, while Frank prepared to return to Yellowstone to recover the bodies of his brother-in-law and friends. Little did he know at the time that all had survived.

On the afternoon of August 25, Charles Mann and Henry Myers, the second pair to flee from their Nez Perce captors, were found by General Howard's scouts near Madison Junction. The first of the group to break away, William Dingee and A.J. Arnold, now on foot, covered forty miles in four days, following the Madison, climbing over Targhee Pass, and arriving at Henry's Lake where they encountered General Howard's camp on August 28. After being seriously injured and lying in the timber for thirty-six hours, Albert Oldham somehow managed to travel twenty miles. He was found along the Madison road on August 29 as General Howard's full command entered the park and began their pursuit of the Nez Perce.

But, the most unlikely survivor was Emma's husband, George Cowan. After being first shot in the right thigh, then a second time at close-range with a pistol blast to his head, George eventually regained consciousness, only to be shot a third time. A rogue warrior coming down the trail spied George as he attempted to drag himself up the hillside, took aim and hit the already wounded man in the left hip. Regaining consciousness for the second time but now unable to walk, George began to drag himself back to the party's last campsite in Lower Geyser Basin. After four days and ten miles of crawling on his hands and knees, he managed to make it to the group's old home base. Finding a few matches, a discarded tin can, and a small quantity of coffee beans, George was able to supply himself with a fire and a bit of coffee. The next day on August 29, he crawled a few more miles to the edge of the Firehole River, where his strength gave out. Thoroughly exhausted George laid down under a tree near the road and gave himself up for dead. Later in life as George recounted this story on numerous occasions, Emma must have shuddered to remember how her helpless husband sat on death's doorstep underneath that tree.[14]

Later that day, George was discovered by two of General Howard's scouts, Captain S.G. Fisher and J.W. Redington. They were astonished when George told them who he was. The scouts told George they were heading to the scene of the massacre to find the bodies of the party and that they were expecting to bury him. Redington recalled that George "seemed to be in full possession of his mental faculties...although he was pretty badly wounded." George was more worried about Emma than his own wounds and anxiously asked the scouts if they had any news about his wife, but neither Fisher nor Redington had any information for the bereaved man. While Redington was astounded that the George seemed so aware after all he had been through, he was even more stunned by George's appearance. "Cowan had very black hair and had lost so much blood that his face was deathly pale," the scout remembered. "The contrast was so striking I shall never forget it." After being shot three times, left for dead twice, and crawling nearly fourteen miles in search of assistance, George Cowan thought he was finally saved and he would soon be reunited with Emma.[15]

But almost as remarkable as his survival of the harrowing ordeal with Nez Perce, was George's survival of what should have been an uneventful rescue. As soon as he was discovered by Fisher and Redington, George was given food and a blanket. As George's luck would have it, the scouts could do little for him and had to move on. They positioned George in a place where the main contingent of the General's company, following a day behind the scouts, would easily find him. Before the scouts departed they built a fire for him and George fell asleep only to awaken to yet another peril:

The ground on which he was lying was full of vegetable mold, very dry at that season of the year, and the fire burrowed through it with facility. Cowan was awakened by the heat and found himself completely surrounded by fire. With great difficulty and severe burns, he extricated himself from this new danger.[16]

The following day, August 30, Howard's command, containing Cowan's friends A.J. Arnold and Albert Oldham, found George, dressed his wounds and began taking him on the long, arduous journey to Mammoth Hot Springs and then north to Bozeman.[17]

Meanwhile, Emma had been notified of the astonishing news. "Cowan Alive," read the headline in the *Helena Daily Independent Extra* on September 6, 1877. However, it would be another week of worrying before she would receive a report that George was expected to reach Bozeman on

September 19. Emma immediately departed to meet her husband only to find upon her arrival in Bozeman that the fragility of George's health had warranted an extended stop for him at Bottler's Ranch in Paradise Valley, about thirty-two miles north of Mammoth. Once again, Emma wasted no time in procuring a double-carriage, and rushing to George's side. She found him in better condition than she had expected and anxious to set out for home.

After arranging a bed for George in the back of the carriage, Emma, A.J. Arnold, and a driver set out for Helena from Paradise Valley. All seemed well as they approached a road bed that was graded around a steep slope in a rocky canyon only seven miles from Bozeman, when a pole strap broke and startled the horses. In a frenzy they ran away and the tongue of the carriage snapped. Luckily, all the passengers including George were thrown onto the hillside. The carriage was not as fortunate; it continued to tumble down the ravine until it came to rest at the bottom of the canyon. Borrowing a horse from a passerby, the driver dashed off to Fort Ellis, about three miles outside of Bozeman, and returned with an ambulance to transport George to the city. When they arrived in Bozeman, Emma's husband was transferred to a hotel where his friend A.J. Arnold prepared to dress George's bleeding re-opened wounds. As Arnold seated himself on the edge of the bed, the bed collapsed. Emma recalled that "this sudden and unexpected fall, in his enfeebled state, nearly finished him."

Even Emma commented on the string of uncanny events that seemed to plague the hapless George: "Had I been morbidly inclined, I might have conceived the idea that some avenging Nemesis was following in his foot-steps, which nothing but the forfeit of his life would satisfy." It would be another week before she thought he was well enough to travel home to Radersburg. Remarkably, with the help of A.J. Arnold through the winter of 1877-78, George fully recovered from his wounds.

Emma's brother Frank spent that same winter in Wisconsin where he chronicled his family and friends' adventure in Yellowstone in the book *Wonders of Geyser Land*, published in 1878. From there he moved to Texas where he married. In 1881, Frank, his wife of four years, and ten month old baby moved back to Montana. The baby died that winter and Frank died in January 1882 in Helena.[18]

Emma remained in contact with Charles Mann who returned to his position as clerk of the district court in Radersburg for another two years after his adventure in the park. He was an artist and had drawn many pictures of the Radersburg party's camps and scenes in the park. In a reprinted edition of Frank's book published in 1935, Emma thought it possible that Frank had put some of Mann's sketches into his original pamphlet, but as the drawings were not signed she could not be sure. Mann returned to the East Coast in 1879.[19]

Emma's friend Albert Oldham, a violinist, lived in Helena for a time after his return from the misadventures of the Radersburg party. Emma had first become acquainted with Oldham when she lived in Helena and even after she moved from Helena, he would visit her often. "He was a fine violinist, "she fondly recalled many years later. "He and his violin were always welcome." In 1910 Oldham moved to Weiser, Idaho to teach music and died there in 1928.[20]

Emma's sister Ida, born on Christmas Day in Virginia City, was just thirteen-years old at the time of the park trip. A year later she remembered trembling with fear during her captivity by the Nez Perce, but she also recalled rejoicing that her fifteen-year-old brother Willie had not been with them. During her terrifying ordeal she remembered the sight of her brother as he stood at the door waving a farewell with his handkerchief. "At the time I felt sorry for him that he could not go with us, as he would have liked to have done," she recalled. But when they were taken captive and during the period that she believed they were all going to be killed Ida thought, "how fortunate that he [Willie] would be left for father and mother." Undoubtedly, Willie was at the door to greet his sister upon her safe return home. Ida married James Stevens in 1882 when she was nineteen, but she only lived for another two years and was buried in Deep Creek Cemetery, near Townsend, Montana.[21]

George Cowan returned to his law practice in Radersburg and Boulder, and in 1880 Emma gave birth to the first of their three children, Charles F. Cowan. In 1882, their second son George F. Cowan (Jr.) was born. In addition partnering with H.M. Parker, George F. (Sr.) served three terms as territorial district attorney and took his family to Boulder in 1885 after the county seat was moved there. Emma and George's third child, daughter Ethyl, was born in 1889.[22]

In 1901, Yellowstone Park road engineer and historian Hiram Chittenden asked Emma and George to guide him to the scenes of their experiences of August 1877. "His recollection of localities was

Emma and George returned to Yellowstone in 1901 (as pictured here) to identify the sites of their harrowing experiences in 1877 for historian Hiram Chittenden. (COURTESY YELLOWSTONE NATIONAL PARK MUSEUM COLLECTION)

astonishingly vivid and accurate," Chittenden wrote of George Cowan a few years later. The author of *The Yellowstone National Park* published in 1895, Chittenden revised his history of the 1877 Nez Perce campaign for the 1903 edition based on the Cowans' detailed stories at the sites of their adventures. Chittenden also erected wooden interpretive signs at each of the significant locations, one of which was rededicated in 2007.[23]

Emma, George, and their three children moved to Spokane in 1910. There sons Charles and George Jr. followed in their father's footsteps and became attorneys and daughter Ethyl married Ben Maxfield. On August 24, 1925, Emma and George celebrated their golden wedding anniversary. It was also the 48th anniversary of their capture by the Nez Perce. They returned to Yellowstone several other times before George died in 1926 from pneumonia at the age of eighty-four. Emma lived in Spokane for another twelve years before she died in 1938 at the age of eighty-five.[24]

Emma Cowan's journey into legend began soon after she and her family and friends became captives of the Nez Perce. Newspapers all over Montana as well as the entire country rushed to publish reports of the Cowans' misfortune. In their haste, those writers made errors that complicated Emma's already enshrined myth even as they perpetuated it and made it larger. As newspapers continued to reminisce about Emma's harrowing ordeal well into the 1930s, the misinformation ballooned. Several newspaper accounts proclaimed that Emma had been a new bride and that their trip to the park was a honeymoon. The newspapers were either confused about the real story that the Cowan's trip was to celebrate their two-year wedding anniversary or believed that a story of a new bride experiencing traumatic misfortune on her honeymoon was somehow more interesting, for several printed that incorrect version.[25]

But that seems to be the stuff of which American western legends are made. Although Dorothy Johnson's novel *The Man Who Shot Liberty Valance* is fiction, her story and the subsequent John Ford movie of the same title illustrate the conflict between revealing the fact and preserving the legend. In this classic western film, when a prominent U.S. senator from the West tells a reporter the truth about a fatal frontier event decades after it happened, the newsman records as he speaks, and then, because of what the senator reveals at tale's end, tears up his notes.

The senator is stunned, and asks in disbelief, "You're not going to use the story, Mr. Scott?"

"No, sir. This is the West, sir," explains the reporter. "When the legend becomes fact, print the legend."

That fictional reporter's response seems very fitting when it comes to many chronicles of the old West. Much like the book and movie senator, Emma Cowan became legendary throughout her lifetime because of her one big event. The popularized and accepted (but not actual) version of Emma's experiences convey the historical truth that legends are often far more lasting than facts. By the time of her death 1938, the legend of Emma's having been a captive bride had become so entrenched in the well known story of the Nez Perce Indians in Yellowstone that it has been impossible to erase.

❦

Martha "Mattie" Shipley Culver

(1856–1889)

Far from Home and Friends

Mattie Culver's legendary status in Yellowstone stems more from her untimely death and seemingly misplaced burial site than from her life. A lonely grave along the banks of the Firehole River is the only lasting reminder of her days in the park. The white marble tombstone there, graced with a single rose, proclaims the rudiments of a short life:

Mattie S., wife of E.C. Culver
Died March 2, 1889
aged 30 years
The pure of heart shall see God

For nearly a century Mattie's isolated resting place, deep within the confines of Yellowstone National Park, kept alive a trace of her life and death, but her complete story and legend fell into obscurity. In 1984, author Nan Weber happened upon Mattie's grave while she was working for the summer in West Yellowstone. She began asking questions about the burial site and found that while nearly every veteran Yellowstone employee and local resident knew of Mattie, no one really knew who she was. The standard response was that "she was the wife of the winter keeper of the old Firehole Hotel" and that "she died in childbirth."

Finding this explanation insufficient to satisfy her curiosity, Weber found herself on a decade-long search for Mattie's life story. Her quest wound through an accumulation of what she has termed "Mattie myths" that ranged from Mattie's dying on a westward bound wagon train to her body's being stored in a pickle barrel through the winter of 1889. Through skillful research and a bit of serendipity, Weber pieced together a factual version of this woman's short but full life that ended one snowy winter day in Yellowstone. But as with most legends, even Weber's well researched rendering of Mattie's true life, *Mattie: A Woman's Journey West*, published in 1997, has been unable to sway the tenacity of the "Mattie myths."[1] Perhaps the best summary of this enduring phenomenon was submitted by actress Helen Hayes (1900-1993) when she remarked, "Legends die hard. They survive as the truth rarely does."[2]

Martha Jane (Mattie) Shipley was born September 18, 1856, in Lowell, Massachusetts, to George and Elizabeth "Betty" Higgins Shipley. George and Betty, both cotton weavers in England, had married in 1843, and started a family while continuing to work in the booming British textile industry. In the mid-1840s, Betty's younger sister and her husband emigrated to the United States and by 1848, they had settled in the town of Lowell, Massachusetts. Encouraged by favorable employment reports from Martha, George and Betty left England the following with their first two children.[3] Mattie was born in the United States two years later.

But the economic ebb and flow of the American textile industry proved to be as unstable as its English counterpart, and the Shipleys continually moved from one textile city to another. On October 5, 1858, Betty gave birth to the last of her children, Eliza Adelaide "Lida" Shipley, in Clinton, Massachusetts. By 1860, the Shipley family had taken up residence in New York. For reasons unknown, Betty and Lida remained in Lowell, presumably living with Martha Platt, while George and the three older children—sixteen-year-old William, thirteen-year-old Millie, and seven-year-old Mattie—relocated first to Newburg and shortly after to Cohoes, New York. For the next few years, George and William worked in the cotton mills while the two girls kept hearth and home. In the summer of 1862, George, now forty years old, enlisted in the Union Army and was assigned to Company I, Seventh New York Volunteer Artillery. After serving less than two years, George was shot in the hip and died six days later on July 12, 1864. William, Millie, and Mattie were now on their own.[4]

By 1865, Millie had joined William working in the Cohoes textile mills, while Mattie provided a comfortable home for her brother and sister. Following William's marriage in 1873, seventeen-year-old Mattie entered the textile industry full time, and thus began exposure to the health risks that eventually took her life. Working twelve hours per day— for which she was paid $1.00—Mattie endured deafening equipment noise, putrid odors of machinery toxins, fabric fibers floating about, and poorly ventilated work rooms. Little did the two women know that their occupation was one of the leading causes of respiratory ailments, which in most cases led to tuberculosis. While miners often contracted black lung disease from ingesting microscopic particles of coal dust, textile workers commonly developed "brown lung" from inhaling textile fibers and machinery fumes. Mill workers could thus see their lifetimes cut in half even from only a few years of work, a reality that Mattie would discover all too late.[5]

While Mattie and sister Millie labored as mill workers, David Alston, a man whom Millie had met at the end of the Civil War and planned to marry, sought a better life for himself and his intended bride in the West. Taking up the government's offer of free homestead land, David and his brother Joseph began farming a parcel of land near Pease Bottom, Montana. Located just north of the Little Bighorn Battlefield, Pease Bottom offered David and Joseph favorable growing conditions for crops as well as the opportunity to sell their agricultural goods to nearby forts Keogh and Custer. By the spring of 1881, David sent word for Millie to join him. Mattie and youngest sister Lida accompanied Millie, probably seeing the West as their salvation from a lifetime of industrial drudgery. Mattie, Lida, and Millie boarded a train in New York and in a few days arrived in Bismarck, North Dakota, where David met them. Following David and Millie's marriage, Mattie and Lida accompanied the newlyweds to the Alston ranch at Pease Bottom. During the next year, Mattie and Lida helped David and Millie run the ranch when David's brother decided farming was not for him, and returned east.[6]

Working on a ranch was not easy, but it afforded Millie, Mattie, and Lida clean air to breathe, beautiful scenery to view, and a personal sense of production to take pride in. Although the ranch took up much of her time, Mattie found a few moments for herself to attend social functions in the nearby town of Kurtzville. And she also found a husband. On October 24, 1882, in David and Millie's home, Mattie married Eugene A. Gillette, a railroad construction contractor for the Northern Pacific Railroad. From Bismarck, North Dakota, Northern Pacific crews laid track through Glendive and Miles City, Montana, and reached the area of Pease Bottom by the summer of 1882. Apparently Eugene spent some time in the Pease Bottom area, where Mattie caught his eye and their relationship blossomed. The railroad continued westward and arrived in the newly established town of Billings in mid-August.[7]

Mattie settled into married life at Billings' Park Hotel, while Eugene left the railroad and helped to build the new city. Eugene became one of several independent contractors working on constructing a ditch to divert water from the Yellowstone River to provide water to Billings. But shortly after their marriage, Eugene's health began to fail from a respiratory ailment he had contracted during his Civil War service. He apparently believed that his condition had been remedied by the arid climate of the west, but that hope proved false and by late summer 1883, Eugene's affliction was confirmed by physicians as tuberculosis. Mattie took him to Pease Bottom to recuperate, but by the time he was diagnosed the disease had advanced into its final stages. Eugene died on October 30, 1883, just six days after he and Mattie celebrated their first wedding anniversary. Thus in a little more than a year Mattie had gone from being a happy bride to a mourning widow. But she was left little time to grieve as she became Eugene's estate executrix and spent the next several years following up on a lawsuit that Eugene had begun concerning payment due him from a dissolved business partnership. Not until 1886, when the courts finally ruled in her favor, could Mattie resume her life.[8]

By that time, Ellery Channing Culver had become the manager of the Park Hotel, where Mattie had resided for the past three years. Ellery also had served in the Civil War and was drawn to the West in high hopes for a new life after being mustered out in 1865. He was first attracted to the gold fields of Virginia City, where he found that providing livery services for the multitudes of miners was far more lucrative than the slimmer pickings of crowded placer mining claims. By the early 1880s he worked on construction of the Northern Pacific Railroad, before turning his sights toward the saloon business in Stillwater, Montana in 1882. Within the next three years, he married, moved to Billings, and was widowed two years later, lost a brand-new saloon to fire, and joined a partner in owning a hotel.[9]

After his wife's death, Ellery absorbed himself in the activities of city life, serving as a juror, judge of elections, auctioneer, and general solicitor for the subscription-published memoirs of Ulysses S. Grant. By October of 1885 he managed the Park Hotel, where Mattie lived. Mattie and Ellery, having lost spouses shortly after being married, probably found a consoling and understanding spirit in each other, which developed into something more. On April 6, 1886, Mattie Shipley Gillette became Mrs. E.C. Culver.[10]

With both their hopes of happiness renewed, Mattie and Ellery purchased a house in Billings, and began to settle into married life. Within a month of their marriage, Ellery became a partner in the saloon business with Eugene McKee. During the summer, he and Mattie enjoyed participating in the Billings Fourth of July parade, where Ellery served as marshal, as well as church socials and outdoor activities such as hunting and fishing. The winter of 1886-1887 proved to be one of the coldest on record, but Ellery and Mattie probably centered their thoughts on preparing for a new baby.

That spring Ellery was offered a managership in the Yellowstone Park Transportation Company, away to the west. One of his duties was to oversee delivery of construction materials to the several park hotels being built by the Yellowstone Park Association, which would bring him in close connection with a friend, named R.R. Cummings, from his early days in Glendive. Cummings was in charge of supervising the construction of the park's hotels and would prove to be Ellery's most devoted lifelong friend. However, Ellery's first commitment that summer was to attend the birth of his baby girl on June 22, 1887, whom he and Mattie named Theda after her father's sister and grandmother. Evidently, mother and baby were faring quite well by July 2, because Ellery departed on the train bound for the park's terminus in Cinnabar (today's Gardiner) to begin his new position in Yellowstone.[11]

One of the earliest "hotels" in the park, Marshall's, had been built in the Firehole Basin (in today's Fountain Flats area), in 1880 by George Marshall—as a small mail station that also offered primitive accommodations for the park's earliest travelers. After the arrival of the Northern Pacific Railroad to the north entrance in 1883 and the advent of a connecting road system, which brought in larger volumes of tourists, Marshall applied for and was issued a ten-year lease in 1884 to build a larger hotel near the site that he already occupied. Marshall operated the hotel with partner G.G. Henderson until spring 1885, when he sold out to Henderson.

This T.W. Ingersoll photograph reveals some of the remodeling of the Firehole hotel in the mid-1880s. Note the unfinished balcony on the second floor.
(COURTESY YALE UNIVERSITY BEINECKE LIBRARY)

Within a few months, Henry E. Klamer became Henderson's new partner and the pair operated the hotel together through the summer season. By 1886 the Yellowstone Association had assumed possession of the hotel, renamed it the Firehole Hotel, and begun plans to expand the hostelry. The expansion would include two cabins that flanked each side of the hotel. Each of the cabins contained eight rooms with living space of sixteen feet square, and ten-foot ceilings. Considered "modern" by park standards at the time, the new cabin accommodations featured outside windows that offered a view of the surrounding geyser basin. It was here that Mattie and baby Theda would join Ellery as he took on his duties distributing the cabins' construction materials.

On July 28, Mattie and five-week-old Theda left Billings and traveled to Livingston, where they transferred trains and headed south on the Yellowstone Park Branch Line. This fifty-three-mile extension of the Northern Pacific Railroad took them through the majestic Paradise Valley, past the rocky cliffs of Yankee Jim Canyon, along the rushing Yellowstone River, and deposited mother and baby at the end of the tracks in Cinnabar. Because Mattie was traveling with an infant, she most likely took a stagecoach from the railroad terminus into the park. With travel in the late 1880s moving at a slower pace than today and travelers subject to the schedule of the park's transportation systems, the trip from Billings to the Firehole Hotel could have easily taken Mattie two full days. Even so, those two days were filled with new sights, smells, and sounds that must have delighted Mattie's sense of adventure.[12]

Mattie and Theda's journey through the park would have followed the standard tourist route at the time, traveling around the travertine terraces at Mammoth Hot Springs, climbing through Yellowstone's Golden Gate Canyon and carrying them to picturesque Swan Lake Flats, which featured a kaleidoscope of mountain ranges in every direction. For the next several hours, Mattie and Theda would have traveled through huge expanses of lodgepole pine forests and past a dozen or more meandering streams and the smoking hillside of Roaring Mountain, before stopping for lunch at the Norris Geyser Basin. After lunch, their route would have toured through the steaming thermal features of Norris before heading south through Gibbon Canyon, where they likely viewed the eighty-four-foot Gibbon Falls before being happily reunited with Ellery at the Firehole Hotel.

Mattie's summer was very full with a new baby as well as a husband to care for, but surely she found time to explore the wonders of the park that were just outside her door. As with many summer seasons in Yellowstone, Mattie's probably passed too quickly and by October she and Ellery moved back to Billings for the winter. At this point in their lives, Ellery and Mattie were adept at adjusting to a constantly changing lifestyle, so they resumed their city activities as if they had never been gone. Even though Billings offered plenty of opportunities for a full life, the couple had enjoyed their time in the park and chose to return for the summer of 1888.

Of all the times to be in Yellowstone, the summer of 1888 was the probably one of the best. The world's largest geyser, Excelsior Geyser, erupted many times that year, throwing water three hundred feet high and three hundred feet wide, before it lapsed into its usually long dormancy. A more spectacular scene could hardly be imagined. Ellery and Mattie, who were living in the midst of this land of marvels, must have had a tremendous sense of awe while in the presence of this dramatic spectacle.[13]

Unfortunately, what should have been the best of times for Ellery, Mattie, and one-year-old Theda turned into the worst of times. During the summer, Mattie's health began to show signs that she too had become a victim of "consumption," by then known as tuberculosis. In 1882, Dr. Robert Koch had discovered the bacterium causing tuberculosis and determined that the disease was highly communicable, but it would be several more years before

Photographer T.W. Ingersoll was in the right place at the right time when he captured one of the spectacular eruptions of Excelsior Geyser in 1888.
(COURTESY YALE UNIVERSITY BEINECKE LIBRARY)

its spread could be contained by vaccination and better health conditions. Between working in crowded, poorly ventilated textile industry workrooms filled with coughing mill operatives, and her year of married life with the infected Eugene, Mattie's exposure to consumption had narrowed her chances of escaping the fatal disease. Even though the medical field had identified the causes for the respiratory disorder there was, as of 1888, no cure. Treatment for her symptoms until she died was the only future Mattie could anticipate.[14]

Why the couple opted to stay at the Firehole Hotel for the winter was not recorded, but conceivably Mattie and Ellery wanted to spend the last few months of her life together with baby Theda in the most intimate setting possible. Perhaps having witnessed the effects of tuberculosis in New York and having nursed Eugene through his last days, Mattie decided that she wanted to experience her final months embraced by the serenity of the park and not amidst well-meaning but sorrowful friends. Then again, Mattie may have been optimistic enough to believe that she would make it until spring. Being sequestered in the interior of Yellowstone by waist-deep snow would certainly insure the couple privacy and seclusion.

Whatever their reasoning for wanting to weather the winter in Yellowstone, Ellery accepted the winter caretaker position for 1888-1889. In September and October, presumably leaving Mattie and Theda in the park, he made several trips to Billings to assist the Republican party with its convention and the November presidential election. Two days after the election of Republican candidate Benjamin Harrison on November 6, Ellery returned to Yellowstone and settled in with Mattie and fifteen-month-old Theda for the long winter at the Firehole Hotel.[15] As winter in the park was an event experienced by only a select few, Ellery wrote a description of the winter scenery for the *Billings Gazette*, which appeared in print on January 10, 1889:

> The Yellowstone Park is certainly worthy of deep study at any time, and especially in...mid-winter. The ground at the present writing is covered at this place with twenty inches of snow, and we have less here than at any other hotel in the Park, except Mammoth.... It is a strange sight and very beautiful, to see the heavy frost that gathers almost every night on the trees, telephone wire, and in fact everything. It is the frozen steam from the almost countless hot springs in our vicinity. We often see the telephone wire as thick as a man's wrist. Usually this frost disappears by ten or eleven o'clock. We can see at almost any hour a great cloud hanging over Excelsior, and other large geysers...There have been four of the Association's teams through the Park this month putting up ice for use at the different hotels. They are under the supervision of R.R. Cummings of Miles City, who for the past two seasons has been master mechanic for the Yellowstone Park Association. They had pretty hard work coming from Mammoth Hot Springs to Norris Geyser Basin. It took them two days, and they were obliged to camp out one night.
>
> We are 7,150 feet above sea level at this place. Nearly one mile higher than Billings. There is quite a difference in the temperature between day and night time. On the morning of the 26th ultimo at half past seven it was 32 degrees below zero; at four P.M. it was eight degrees above. That was the coldest that we have seen so far this winter...[16]

While the summer in Yellowstone had been exciting for Mattie and Ellery, the winter stimulated their senses. Ellery's penned impression vividly expressed his enchantment with the winter wonderland as well as his sense of the extreme conditions that surrounded them. This article proved to be the last communication that he would send to the *Billings Gazette* until March.

On March 2, 1889, Mattie S. Culver died. She was thirty-two years old. One can only imagine how the sense of remoteness must have overwhelmed Ellery as both a blessing and a curse. Experiencing the death of a loved one, especially after not quite three years of marriage, can certainly play havoc with one's sensibilities. But with an eighteen-month-old daughter to care for, Ellery probably had little time to spend worrying about his broken heart.

With telephone access throughout the park, news of Mattie's death reached the outside world within the week. Apparently unaware of her illness and distrustful of the information, the *Billings Gazette* published this report of her death on March 7: "Rumor has it that Mrs. E.C. Culver...has died at the National Park, of quick consumption, while residing there with her husband...It is sincerely hoped that the report is without foundation for by the death of Mrs. Culver society loses a bright star, and her husband and family a true and loving wife and mother." From this report it seems likely that Mattie did not travel to Billings after she became sick, and therefore her death was a surprise to all.[17]

For immediate preparation of her remains, troops at the nearby Fountain Soldier Station brought two barrels that they set end to end to contain Mattie's lifeless body, and covered the makeshift coffin with snow. One can only imagine Ellery's turmoil until his dear wife received a proper burial. Conceivably Ellery knew that his friend R.R. Cummings would be

Mattie Culver's grave near the Lower Geyser Basin is the lone reminder of her short life. (PHOTO BY AUTHOR)

passing through on his routine inspections of park properties, and awaited his arrival for help in digging a grave.

Because the interior of Yellowstone was completely snowbound from November until April, these inspections required Cummings and his line man Joe Fossom to travel the forty-plus miles to the Lower Geyser Basin and beyond on skis. Just when Cummings arrived at the Firehole Hotel is unclear, but presumably it was shortly after Mattie's death as it was his "custom to visit the several hotels under construction at least once every two weeks." Cummings recorded that upon "finding the sick wife dead, we were compelled to remove a partition [from the nearby hotel] in order to secure boards with which to make a coffin. The grave was hewn down into the frozen lava formation and after two days' hard work, she was consigned to rest, far away from home and friends." Cummings admired Ellery's stalwart ability to cope with his deep personal loss and noted that "the wonderful character of this strong brave man, his Christian fortitude, and fidelity enabled him to remain and endure uttering no words of complaint, 'She's only gone to sleep and we will soon meet again.' "[18]

In April, when the clutches of winter had abated enough to get horses and wagons into the park, Ellery and Theda left the Firehole Hotel bound for Spokane, Washington. In 1886, Mattie's sister Millie and her husband David Alston had moved there from Pease Bottom when drought made farming impossible. More than likely, Mattie had felt that sending Theda to live with her sister would be the best environment for a growing young girl. Millie, who had always been a pillar of strength for Mattie when she was in need, surely would be an excellent role model for her daughter.[19]

While Theda grew up in Spokane, Ellery continued working in Yellowstone. During the summer seasons he worked as an agent for the Yellowstone Park Transportation Company, riding the rails between Livingston and Cinnabar and promoting the company's park hotels and tours. He also served as a part-time United States Commissioner from 1892, until 1894, handling unlawful activities that ranged from tourists' inscribing their names in hot pools to poachers' shooting game within park boundaries. After the enactment of the Lacy Act, which gave Yellowstone legal authority to prosecute poachers and other violators, Ellery was replaced in 1894 by a full-time Commissioner Judge, John Meldrum. Ellery served as the postmaster in Gardiner, at the park's north entrance, from 1897 until his heath began to fail in the spring of 1904. Resigning as postmaster, Ellery spent two months in Spokane with Mattie's sister Millie and sixteen-year-old Theda, who nursed him back to health.

By the end of May, Ellery was well enough to return to Yellowstone; the place that most seemed to soothe his disheartened spirit. From 1904 until 1907, Ellery worked at what he knew best, promoting tours of the park. In the winters he presented stereopticon programs throughout the country and in the summers he made daily trips on the park train to personally induce visitors to patronize the Yellowstone Transportation Company. Considered by many to be a "walking encyclopedia of park information" and a "prince of good fellows," Ellery earned the title of Captain E.C. Culver, a common moniker often bestowed on popular men of a certain social standing. Even though Ellery enjoyed his work and his surroundings, his shattered heart was sometimes difficult for him to conceal. In 1901, tourist Carl Schmidt sensed Culver's tormented soul and quietly noted that "while all know the story of his faded dreams, not even the roughest cow puncher or mountaineer will allude to it in his presence."[20]

But even with his distant and traveling lifestyle, Ellery remained very much a part of Theda's life. Theda apparently fared well under Millie's tutelage and, upon finishing high school, she planned to attend college. But tragically, the black cloud that hovered over the other two loves of Ellery's life would reappear in the summer of 1906. After a brief illness, nineteen-year-old Theda died on July 20 of pulmonary edema. However, unlike her mother's lonely grave site in Yellowstone, Theda's final resting place would be with family. She was buried in the Alston family plot in Spokane, next to her grandmother Elizabeth Shipley, who passed away in 1892.[21]

Ellery's thrice-broken heart took a toll on his health and well being, and by 1908, he was forced to retire from his position as a train agent for the hotel company. In 1909 he retired to the Sawtelle Old Soldiers Home in Los Angeles, California, where several other "old soldiers" who had once belonged to Yellowstone's workforce would spend their last days. Ellery's dear old comrade from his early Yellowstone days, R.R. Cummings was at his bedside the day before he died. Cummings optimistically remarked to his friend "the sun will soon be shining, so we can go out and talk over good times." With tears in his eyes, Ellery weakly responded, "Oh, no, Dick. I am going to a better home. God has pointed the way and I am ready to go and meet my maker and my beloved in heaven."[22]

Ellery Channing Culver finally joined Mattie and Theda in death on April 17, 1922. And like his beloved Mattie he was buried "far from home and friends" in the Los Angeles National Cemetery.[23] If there is a heaven, Mattie must have been overjoyed to see him.

Anna K. Trischman Pryor

(1884–1973)

and

Elizabeth "Belle" Trischman

(1886–1984)

Curios, Coffee, and the Devil's Kitchenette

A few scattered black and white photographs in the Yellowstone National Park Museum Photo Collection have served through time as the only lasting reminders of the Devil's Kitchenette, a simple, log, open-air concession stand that once perched within a stone's throw of an extinct hot spring cave on the upper level of the Mammoth Hot Springs terraces. This popular subterranean geological attraction, named the Devil's Kitchen, beckoned intrepid travelers to explore its depths by squeezing through a narrow slit of an opening and descending a nearly vertical, rickety wooden ladder into its dark labyrinth. Down below the surface, plucky travelers would be treated to strange underground formations, smelly gasses, and, occasionally, flying bats that were often stirred up by mischievous guides. Anna K. Pryor and her sister Elizabeth Trischman thought that this nearly mystical place would be the perfect spot to offer nervy and spirited adventurers a cool refreshing reward for braving one of Yellowstone's underground features.

Although Pryor and Trischman first petitioned park officials for permission to offer cold soft drinks and ice cream at this location in

1913, it was not until 1924 that they were given a temporary permit for a trial period. They promptly erected a small rustic log structure and began operating the Devil's Kitchenette. This long-gone and popular refreshment stand, which operated from 1924 through 1937, proved to be just one of the many success stories of these two sisters who managed to survive a lifetime of tragedy, trials, and tribulations in the unusual setting of Yellowstone of Yellowstone National Park.

Anna Kathryn Trischman, born July 18, 1884, was the first of five children of George W. and Margaret (Gleason) Trischman.[1] George W. had been born in May 1848 in Germany and emigrated to the United States aboard the passenger ship *Ericsson* in the spring of 1866.[2] Within five months of his arrival in New York City on May 3, eighteen-year-old George enlisted in the United States Army.[3] Army life probably seemed like a safe haven to this poor immigrant adolescent looking for work as well as food and shelter. Arriving in America a little more than a year after the end of its civil war, George, a carpenter and wheelwright, was a practical recruit for the army.

With the conflict that had threatened the solidarity of the United States behind it, the U.S. military cast its eyes upon securing western lands for white settlement, and the ensuing movement required many wooden wagons and even more wagon wheels. However, George's tenure as a military man was cut short by health problems, including a heart condition, and he was discharged from Fort Shaw, Montana Territory, on August 1, 1869.[4] His whereabouts for the next eleven years are elusive, but by the mid-1880s he was residing at Fort Custer, M.T. While George was no longer enlisted in the army, he was eligible to work for army posts as a civilian and was employed at the fort as a carpenter. Conceivably, it was there that he met his future wife, Margaret Gleason.[5]

Margaret Gleason's personal history has remained largely a mystery. The only clue yet found of her life has been in the 1910 U.S. Census, recording that her birthplace was Ireland. Where and when George and Margaret actually met has not been found, but census records indicate that the couple married in 1883.[6] Following Anna's birth in 1884, George W. and Margaret increased their family by two more. Harry and Elizabeth, a pair of fraternal twins, arrived on December 22, 1886.[7] George T. was born on August 10, 1890[8] and Joseph, the couple's fifth child was born on July 29, 1893.[9] Once the children reached school age, the lack of adequate educational facilities at Fort Custer required Margaret to reside in Billings, Montana, during the school year so the children could attend school.[10] When Fort Custer closed in the spring of 1898, George W. moved the entire family to Billings.

For unknown reasons, Margaret's mental stability snapped in late March 1899. In a cowshed behind their house in Billings she tried to commit suicide with a large butcher knife. With a poorly placed slash to her throat, she missed her jugular vein and her attempt rewarded her with a gaping wound in her neck. She claimed that some woman had power over her and could make her do anything. She was apparently sent home to recuperate, where George W. kept a continual watch over her. About three weeks after her suicide attempt George W. went downtown while Margaret was sleeping. When he returned Margaret was gone. A search ensued and she was found alive on one of the islands in the Yellowstone River near the Northern Pacific Bridge. A few days later, on April 14, 1899, Judge Loud and Drs. Armstrong and Rinhart judged Margaret to be suffering from melancholia, and committed her to the Warm Springs Hospital (asylum) for treatment.[11]

While she was hospitalized, George W. secured a new position at Fort Yellowstone as post carpenter. For reasons that are not entirely clear, but perhaps overwhelmed with the responsibility for five young children, George W. obtained Margaret's release from the mental hospital six weeks later. Dr. O.G. Warren's report on Margaret indicated that "there was no improvement in her condition" and that her husband had removed her from the hospital.[12] The *Livingston Enterprise* reported that George W., along with his wife and children, spent the evening of Monday, May 29, at the Park Hotel in Livingston. After taking the Tuesday morning train to Cinnabar, Montana, and then continuing to the park by stagecoach, George W., Margaret, and children Anna, Elizabeth, Harry, George T. and Joseph, began settling into their new home at Mammoth Hot Springs.

On Saturday, June 3, Margaret's "dormant impulse of insanity" gripped her once again, but this time she took the hunting knife to the throat of her five-year-old son, Joseph. After slitting his throat and nearly severing his head from his body, she tried to carry on the "wholesale destruction of her children." Dramatically, the *Livingston Post* newspaper described the tragic scene of her attempt to kill her other children: "The demented mother pursued them for a short distance, but they escaped from the house, and sought safety in the home of a neighbor." Shortly after the children's tragic ordeal was revealed, authorities found Margaret back at her home "insensible to her surroundings and in a condition of mind, which prevented her from understanding the awful deed she had done."[13] It was a deed so appalling that it made national news: the *New York Times* ran an article about the tragedy on June 5, declaring that "the woman, Mrs. George Trischman...is *undoubtedly insane.*"[14]

The army guards placed her under arrest and took her to the post guard house in Mammoth. Because she committed murder in the state of Wyoming, Judge Meldrum, the park's judicial authority, sent a telegram to U.S. district attorney T.F. Burke in Cheyenne on Monday June 5. Without delay, Burke traveled to Mammoth Hot Springs to conduct an investigation. By Wednesday Burke had "decided that there was no question as to the insanity of Mrs. Trieschman [*sic*]," and ordered that she remain in the guardhouse until arrangements for her care could be made.[15] Despite his judgment of her severe mental illness, she was formally charged with murder on June 7, 1899.[16]

Following the assessment of her mental instability and subsequent charge of murder on United States federal lands, she was ordered to be confined in a mental hospital in Washington, D.C. On the evening of July 8, Margaret boarded the train in Cinnabar escorted by her husband and Deputy U.S. Marshal James Morrison. But about sixteen miles from Cinnabar, somewhere between Point of Rocks and Dailey's ranch, Margaret "left the railroad car under some pretext and it was a few minutes before she was missed." Discovering that she was nowhere to be found, the train was stopped and backed up to the point where she may have left the railroad car. After railroad workers conducted a short but unsuccessful search in the darkness, the train continued on to Livingston. George W. and Morrison stayed behind to continue looking for Margaret. No trace of her was ever found. George W. as well as other authorities believed that she threw herself from the train into the Yellowstone River, which at that spot flowed next to the tracks, and drowned.[17] However, without a body, her death remained an open case. In January 1901, George W. was summoned to Glendive, Montana to look at the remains of a woman found in the Yellowstone River. Despite the decomposed state of the female body that had obviously been in the river a long time, George W. stated that he was sure the remains were not those of his wife.[18]

While denied the resolution of his wife's demise, George W. managed to get a sense of closure with his dead son. George W., or perhaps a friend (which might explain the misspelling of the Trischman name) erected a monument to his youngest child that still stands today. In the southwest corner of the Mammoth military cemetery, Joseph's small grave is protectively surrounded by a crib-style iron enclosure. Ornamented with little shoes and socks, his carved gravestone conveys a touching reminder of a child whose time on earth was all too brief. The etched letters on the marble ledger of life spell out the details:

Joseph
Son of
Geo and Margie Trieschman
Born
July 29, 1893
Died
June 3, 1899
Tis a little grave, but Oh take care
Fond hopes are buried there

At the end of the summer of 1899, George W. perhaps feeling pangs of guilt for his role in the tragedy and certainly devastated over the double loss of his youngest son and wife, chose to send all four children to Helena, Montana, to school. Harry and George T. were enrolled at St. John's Hospital and Anna and Elizabeth were sent to St. Vincent's Academy.[19] In light of the family tragedy that they had witnessed, George W. must have feared for their future mental health, and perhaps believed that the consoling environment of Helena's Catholic Hill would ease their troubled souls. While it was not recorded how long the children stayed in Helena nor what nightmares they might have suffered as they grew up, they all managed to evolve into apparently stable adults.[20]

After finishing her education in Helena, Anna returned to Yellowstone to teach grade school at Fort Yellowstone, and presumably lived with her father George W., who had quietly resumed his job as post carpenter. Schools at many army posts were hastily organized with the simple tools of learning: paper, pencils, books, and a qualified enlisted man who served as a teacher. But in the absence of a capable soldier, families of some garrisons such as Fort Yellowstone had to pool their money to pay for a teacher. If no teacher could be found, the children would have to be sent away to school. For several years, perhaps influenced by her own discomfort in attending boarding school, Anna filled the need for a teacher in Yellowstone until she married George R. Pryor.[21]

George Roger Pryor and Anna Kathryn Trischman arranged their June 5 wedding to be held at Gardiner's Protestant Episcopal chapel, and the small town at the park's north entrance was abuzz with the upcoming event. "The wedding will be a conventional church wedding and will have the distinction of [being] the first elaborate church wedding ever occurring at Gardiner," the *Anaconda Standard* claimed. According to the *Livingston Enterprise*, George R. and Anna followed Victorian principles for a sophisticated church wedding as the bride and her attendants were attired in white and the bridegroom and George's best man in black. After the ceremony the bridal party adjourned to the Park Hotel for a wedding breakfast before the newlyweds departed for a honeymoon from the train station amidst hearty congratulations and good wishes from a large number of friends.[22]

Shortly after their marriage, George R. and Anna found what seemed to be an opportune way to make a living in Yellowstone. In the spring of 1908, they began negotiations with Ole Anderson to purchase his long established business known as the Specimen House. Coating common objects such as bottles, pine cones, hair combs, horseshoes, toy cannons, and animal figurines in the mineral laden waters of the travertine terraces of Mammoth Hot Springs had long been a favorite activity of souvenir-collecting tourists. Within days, objects placed in the trickling water were covered with glistening white minerals and thus created delightful mementoes of one's trip to Yellowstone. Recognizing the economic bonanza of making and selling these sought-after trinkets, Anderson had set up a collection of wooden racks and began making coated creations in 1883. Selling his "coated specimens" to park visitors from a small tent store at the base of the Mammoth Terraces, Anderson became one of the park's earliest entrepreneurs. While permits to operate a business were ordinarily required from the Secretary of the Interior, Anderson's tent operation, perhaps because it looked transient, was apparently overlooked by the park's understaffed civilian administration. Even when the army took over management of the park in 1886, Anderson was allowed to continue his operation without a challenge.[23]

By 1894, Anderson's business had grown to the extent that he requested permission to erect a permanent structure, stating that "a neat cottage would look much better to the public [than tents]." The government agreed and his request was approved. By 1896, his newly constructed Specimen House was operational and the Department of Interior gave Anderson a ten-year permit. In order to prevent interference with the business of the nearby general stores, Anderson's permit continued to restrict the sales in his store to coated specimens and not general wares.[24]

Evidently the army thought his business satisfactory through the next decade, because Anderson was issued a ten-year renewal in 1906 and his new permit carried an added privilege. In addition to selling his coated objects, Anderson was also authorized to sell picture postcards, which had only recently become mass produced and had quickly had become a popular tourist collectible. Two years later, Anderson decided to retire after twenty-five years in the business. His timing was perfect for Anna and George Pryor. With them just beginning their married life and searching for a livelihood in Yellowstone, Anderson's Specimen House appealed to their entrepreneurial spirit.[25]

After making an agreement with Anderson, George R. and Anna began thinking about how to be more competitive in the tourist commodities market and decided that they wanted to expand the store's offerings. In addition to requesting approval for the transfer of Anderson's lease, George asked Acting Superintendent Major H.T. Allen on April 10, 1908, for permission to install a bakery and soda fountain that would serve ice cream, hot and cold drinks, and fresh pastries. His contention was that this addition to the business enterprise would "add materially to the comfort of everyone engaged in or visiting the park." While that may have been a convincing argument, probably the most important element that led to approval was that there was no similar facility in Mammoth, and therefore the additional offerings of the Pryors would not upset existing concessioner privileges.

The Secretary of Interior granted the Pryors government approval for the lease transfer from Anderson, with the stipulation that a new lease be drawn up. The new lease covered the remaining eight years of Anderson's original lease, but also included the additional privileges of the bakery and soda fountain. Provisions of the lease permitted Anna and George R. to use the Specimen House as a residence as well as a store. In the store

This unidentified couple is most likely Anna and George Pryor, who purchased Ole Anderson's Specimen House in 1908. Note the coated specimens for sale on the table. (COURTESY YELLOWSTONE GATEWAY MUSEUM YGM.2006.044.0639)

they were authorized to carry "coated specimens, bottled sand, postcards, spoons, and other curiosities." They installed a complete soda fountain that offered ice cream, coffee, tea, and other non-alcoholic drinks, and a bakery that supplied confectionery treats such as cakes and pastries as well as delicious breads. To celebrate the offerings of the new and improved store, Anna and George R. named their enterprise the Park Curio Shop.[26]

In addition to overhauling the store that year, Anna gave birth to her first child, Georganna, on April 18, 1908. It is likely that Elizabeth stepped in at this time to assist with the store and to help to care for the new infant. Elizabeth had been thirteen years old when she and Anna were sent to school at St. Vincent's Academy in Helena in the fall of 1899, and probably she returned to Fort Yellowstone with her sister when Anna finished high school in 1902. Elizabeth spent the school year of 1903-1904 in Livingston attending Park County High School and graduated on June 15, 1904. Both her father George W. and her sister Anna attended the graduation ceremony in which "Miss Belle" took a prominent part."[27] At the end of two successful seasons of business and with another baby on the way, Anna and George R. requested permission from the Secretary of Interior in late October 1909 to expand the physical space of their store and residence. With the Secretary's approval they doubled the size of their store and living quarters, just in time for the arrival of little Margaret B. Pryor in early 1910.[28]

Architectural plans called for a wood-frame two-story addition with a peaked roof that mirrored the original building. The addition afforded George and Anna a space that included living room, kitchen, dining room, and front porch on the first floor, with five bedrooms and a bathroom on the second floor. The store would occupy the first floor of the original building and the center extension with its huge floor-to-ceiling glass windows. In addition to expanding the size of their store, Anna and George increased their merchandise line. Along with their standard wares of "Magnesia Coated Souvenirs from the Mammoth Hot Springs and Bottled Variegated Sands from the Grand Canyon," their business stationery now advertised Indian moccasins, Navajo goods, Mexican serapes and rugs, and burnt leather novelties. Furthermore, the letterhead listed A.K. Pryor as lone manager, an endorsement that seemed to foretell the future for the Park Curio Shop.[29]

By 1912, Anna and George R. Pryor's marriage had failed, and on October 19, George assigned all of his "rights, privileges, and franchise" of the Park Curio Shop to Elizabeth, who had already been an active participant in the store operations for some time. The two sisters wasted no time in making the contract legal. They created the partnership of Pryor and Trischman and made appropriate changes to the lease filed with the government. In the meantime, George R. applied for a permit to operate a dairy herd at Mammoth to supply milk and cream to the military and the hotels. Even though he was granted permission to do so, George R. apparently changed his mind and left the park.[30]

With Anna and Elizabeth at the helm of the Park Curio Shop, the business flourished. They decided to expand their venture, and applied for permission to erect a refreshment stand on the upper terraces near Devil's

Kitchen during the summer of 1913. The Secretary of Interior denied their request, citing the law that prohibited building a concession nearer than one-eighth mile to "any object of curiosity."[31] While they were probably disappointed, Anna and Elizabeth put the Devil's Kitchenette idea on hold for the moment and pursued other avenues to increase sales. But the two sisters soon discovered that they were not without competition in their quest to boost profits.

In March 1913, George Whittaker—a discharged soldier, packer, and scout— purchased the Mammoth general store run by Alexander Lyall and Walter Henderson. Whittaker renamed his enterprise, the "Yellowstone Park Store," and advertised a complete line of tourist needs, which included souvenirs, postcards, groceries, hard;ware, sporting goods, tobaccos, clothing, and Kodak supplies. He even catered to the individual "sagebrush" traveler by offering hay and oats to keep their "weed-burners" (horses and mules) supplied with nourishment. Attempting to further his take of tourist business, Whittaker applied to the park's army administrators for permission to install a soda fountain in his general store. Rather than create a commotion by merely complaining, Anna and Elizabeth resourcefully countered Whittaker's application by requesting permission to sell general wares and Kodak film. Acting Superintendent Colonel Lloyd Brett diplomatically denied both requests.[32]

Even without being able to realize extra revenues from their proposed refreshment stand and the privilege of selling general wares, the two sisters ended their 1913 summer with the satisfaction that together they had achieved a successful season. But just before they shuttered the doors of their store for the winter, they experienced a calamity that could have been a serious disaster. On September 10, an outbuilding behind their curio shop, used as a laundry and store room, caught fire and was nearly destroyed. The cause of the fire was determined to be faulty electrical wires. Luckily for Anna and Elizabeth, there was no wind to spread the fire to other buildings. So at the beginning of the 1914, they replaced the building at a cost of $908.77, which was only partially covered by insurance. Even with the added expense of erecting a new building, Anna and Elizabeth managed to eke out a profit for the 1914 season and looked forward to an even better season in 1915.

The idyllic world of Yellowstone's horse and buggy era came to an end with the introduction of the automobile in 1915. Yellowstone, the last

This circa 1912 photograph shows the Park Curio Store as it appeared after George and Anna doubled the size of the building a few years earlier. The people in front are not identified but the individuals on the right are probably (from right to left): George W. Trischman, two-year-old Margaret Pryor, Elizabeth Trischman, four-year-old Georganna Pryor, Anna Pryor, and George Pryor.
(COURTESY YELLOWSTONE GATEWAY MUSEUM YGM.2006.044.5132)

vestige of stagecoach travel in the west, had fended off hordes of combustible engines clamoring at its gates for nearly a decade before finally succumbing to the inevitable. On April 21, the Secretary of Interior announced his decision to allow motorized vehicles into the park, beginning August 1. While many park residents mourned the old days, others sprang into action. George Whittaker jumped on the entrepreneurial opportunity and applied for permission to the Secretary of Interior to sell gasoline, tires, lubricants, oil, and other auto supplies. Anna and Elizabeth also wanted to cash in on the needs of this emerging breed of visitor, so they too put in their application for a permit to sell gasoline and auto supplies. In mid-July, Whittaker received approval for his application and became the forerunner in this new phase of park concessions.

Apparently the Secretary decided that controlling competition was a good thing, and he denied Anna and Elizabeth's request. His letter stated emphatically that, "Pryor and Trischman have the privilege to operate a store for specific purposes, which does *not* cover the sale of gasoline, oils, etc." Even though the two women may have felt thwarted by this missed opportunity to expand their line of goods, business at their store flourished that year.[33]

In addition to themselves, Anna and Elizabeth employed a staff of five, which included a cook, soda fountain girl, clerk, yardman, and artist who created colored sand paintings in decorative bottles for the tourist trade. At the end of the 1915 season, the Park Curio Shop tallied revenues of $757 for cigar sales, $7,483 for curios, and $2,880 from the soda fountain. After accounting for all expenses and wages, the sisters reported a profit of $3,167: a remarkable yield for a seasonal business in an era when one could purchase an ice cream soda for 15¢. Perhaps to Anna and Elizabeth the entry of the automobile into Yellowstone seemed to be a bonus for all the park's businesses. But with automobiles came a political controversy regarding the administration of the park. That issue would soon test the mettle of all of Yellowstone's concessioners.[34]

Nineteen-sixteen became a critical year for all concessioners in Yellowstone, with the formation of the National Park Service under the Department of Interior. Two major factors contributed to the emergence of this new agency: World War I was raging in Europe and the War Department deemed it necessary to recall all available troops, including those administering national parks, to assist that war effort; and, the national park system had grown to the point where a separate administrative agency was needed to oversee its management.

Stephen T. Mather, the agency's first director, believed that there were too many businesses in Yellowstone, all competing for the same tourist dollar. Mather's solution was a system of "controlled monopolies," which, in effect, would reduce the number of companies operating in the park. His logic was that fewer businesses would be easier to manage and would more efficiently divide the "pie," and that the government could therefore control excessive charges to the public. In theory, the remaining companies would generate enough income to build new facilities, upgrade existing buildings, and provide improved as well as additional services to park visitors. With these administrative changes in the air, Anna and Elizabeth received only a one-year lease for 1916; the NPS, however, now authorized them to sell newspapers, hats, veils, gloves, toiletries, cigars, tobacco, colored glasses, and boxed lunches.[35]

Mather began implementing his plan of reorganizing the commercial makeup of the park in 1917, but luckily for the two sisters and other store owners, he focused his reorganization not on retail businesses but rather on hotels and transportation. This was partly due to the Secretary of Interior's issuance of leases and permits for retailers through the past decade, which stipulated that each mercantile establishment was allowed certain privileges that were not shared with the other. While the various hotels, camping companies, and transportation operations were consolidated and reorganized, Anna and Elizabeth were spared the administrative scuffle and were issued a ten-year lease for the Park Curio Shop. With sighs of relief, knowing that their immediate future was somewhat secured, the two sisters confidently resumed their daily duties to business and life.[36]

The 1917 season finished somewhat disappointingly when the park closed twenty days earlier than usual due to a threatened Northern Pacific railroad strike that came inconveniently as the United States entered World War I. According to U.S. Commissioner (and the sisters' neighbor) Judge John W. Meldrum, "within fifty hours after it was decided to close[,] every employee and tourist had left the park. Tourists who had gotten part way on their trip were turned back and fired out, as the hotels were closing with a maddening rush." However, a few auto parties continued to enter the park until the usual closing date of September 15. For Anna and Elizabeth, this reduced tourist trade at the end of the season meant a loss of at least a thousand dollars in sales.[37]

Even though the season ended poorly, Elizabeth and Anna splurged by purchasing their first automobile. After buying their new Buick for $1,100, they invited the judge to join them, their father, George W., and the girls for a road trip in September. They drove to Livingston to attend the county fair and circus, and then soaked in the mineral waters at Hunter's Hot Springs just east of Livingston. When it was time to return, George W. decided that he would rather take the train back. Leaving George at the train station in Livingston, Anna, Elizabeth, Georganna, Margaret, and the Judge drove south toward Mammoth about 4:30 P.M. Four hours later they found themselves in the "middle of about the worst hill on the road with busted tire." Having lived most of his life during the horse and buggy era, the Judge confessed that little seven-year-old Margaret knew more about autos than he did. Describing the event in a letter to his niece he wrote sheepishly, "I could never tell you how cheap I felt as I asked them 'what are we going to do.' Put on a new tire, of course, was the reply; and if you could have seen those two hop to the task, in the dark, you would surely think them worthwhile." Within an hour, they were back on the road. Strong resilient women such as Anna and Elizabeth rarely let anything as simple as a flat tire disrupt the progress of their lives.[38]

Anna began spending winters in Great Falls, Montana so that her daughter, Georganna, could attend school. Margaret, too young to go to school, stayed behind in Mammoth with Uncle Harry (Trischman) and Aunt Hattie, and her grandfather, George W. Little Margaret visited the judge often which must have made him cheerful. She became especially fond of the judge's niece Nellie Jones and her husband Howard who lived in New York, but who occasionally visited the park. Apparently Howard made quite an impression on both of the Pryor girls by "playing bear," for they thought he was the "funniest man ever." One day as the judge was writing a letter to Nellie, Margaret told the judge to "tell Mr. Jones that he could not see any bears now, as they are all in their holes under the snow." In addition to sending her love to Nellie and Howard, she also asked the judge to tell them that she "misses you very much."[39] A widower and without any children of his own, the judge developed a grandfatherly fondness for his neighbors' little girls and Anna loved that.

While Anna was in Great Falls, Elizabeth began working winters as a clerk in the Legislature at Helena, Montana in 1912 where she made six dollars a day, including Sundays. By the fifth session she had become the chief clerk in the office of House of Representatives. But the family always gathered in Mammoth for the holidays, and Christmas 1917 was a particularly memorable one. To give her little girls a special treat, Anna had a full Santa suit made for their neighbor and U.S. Commissioner Judge Meldrum. They worried a bit that nine-year-old Georganna, who had been to school in Great Falls might be "wise to the Santy fake; but she was just as innocent of it" as seven-year-old Margaret. The two girls swallowed the whole performance and were thrilled when "Santa" presented them with several dolls, and a two-story doll house nearly five feet long and over three feet high with six completely furnished rooms.

The 74-year-old judge was equally elated to bring merriment to the family who had taken him under their wing following the 1908 death of his wife of forty years, Emmaline. Even nearly ten years later, the Judged remarked that "it seemed quite out the question for me to arouse the usual Christmas spirit, and but for the preparations made by Mrs. Pryor and Elizabeth for the delight of the kiddies, it would not have been Christmas to me." By the time Christmas Day came to a close, Georganna was curious about the man in the red suit. As they were going to bed she asked her mother if she did not think that "Santy's voice was some like the Judge's." According to the Judge, Anna fielded Georganna's question sufficiently, and Santa's secret was preserved for yet another year. With joy in their hearts and visions of retail prospects in their heads, Anna and Elizabeth rang in the New Year and looked forward to another prosperous season in Yellowstone.[40]

By 1918, the din and the dust of the NPS's reorganizing the park's concessions had settled. With a secure lease guaranteeing continuance of their small business, Anna and Elizabeth proceeded into the 1920s with expansive plans. For the 1922 season, the ladies reported yearly sales that topped $24,000, and a handsome profit of just under $3,000. With motorized travel through Yellowstone came the establishment of auto camps throughout the park and for Anna and Elizabeth more business opportunities. In 1924, the two sisters joined forces with their nearby retail colleague George Whittaker and opened "an experimental delicatessen stand" in the National Park Service's "free auto camp" in Lower Mammoth.[41]

The new auto camps had become instantly popular and proved to be a huge boon to travelers who wanted to tour the park on their own. Likewise, the auto camps, filled with campers in need of food, clothing, sundries, and other needs, could be an enormous success for astute retailers such as Whittaker and the Pryor and Trischman partnership. Indeed, the buzz of travelers in these open-air compounds prompted Judge Meldrum to describe the camps as "veritable beehives." With the hum of business surrounding them, Anna and Elizabeth decided to renew their request for a refreshment stand on the upper terraces.[42]

This time the Secretary of Interior approved the request on a trial basis and they were issued a one-year permit. Opening in 1924, the Devil's Kitchenette with its non-alcoholic drinks and ice cream became nearly as popular an attraction as the natural feature for which it was named. Following the success of its trial year, the sisters' government lease was amended to include the Devil's Kitchenette.

In 1925, George Whittaker decided to concentrate his efforts on his retail stores at Mammoth and Canyon, and thus sold his share of the deli to Anna and Elizabeth. They immediately expanded the offerings of the "deli" by installing a "range, steam table, and full equipment" so they could offer cafeteria style meals. By that time the sisters had doubled the

Bustling with activity, the Devil's Kitchenette appears to be a
popular respite for many weary visitors to Yellowstone in 1929.
(COURTESY YELLOWSTONE NATIONAL PARK MUSEUM COLLECTION YELL16909)

capacity of the Park Curio Shop for the second time and added "Coffee Shop" to their rooftop signage. With three different retail locations, the Pryor and Trischman partnership required a staff of sixteen employees for the 1925 season, including seventeen-year-old Georganna. That year Anna and Elizabeth each earned a salary of $12,000, a most respectable wage for women or men of that era.[43] Impressed by the business acuity of Anna and Elizabeth, Judge Meldrum wrote to his niece that "if you shouldn't think that these women are 'captains of finance,' you have another guess coming to you."[44]

Business for Anna and Elizabeth in the 1920s was good. So good in fact that the two sisters bought a house in Los Angeles, California and began to spend their winters there. In doing so, they joined a growing flock of migrating Yellowstone concessioners and personnel who made California their winter homes, a trend that continues today. Judge Meldrum drove to Los Angeles with Anna, her daughters Georganna and Margaret, and her sister Elizabeth at the end of the 1924 season and noted in a letter to his niece that "to say we went joy riding doesn't express it." Even though the judge had been going to Los Angeles for winters since 1918, his sojourn of 1924-1925 proved to be very special as he "met more old Wyoming friends here during the three months—two of whom I had counted dead for the last ten years—than I would see here [Yellowstone] in that many years." Indeed, while Yellowstone beckoned to many concessioners and employees for the summer, California seemed to call more and more of them for the winter. While the judge thoroughly enjoyed his winters in California, he equally enjoyed his return to Yellowstone each summer to resume his position as U.S. Commissioner, a position he held until the end of his life. He had decided long ago that it was far better to "wear out than to rust out." This was an assertion that was likely influenced by the entrepreneurial energy of his two women neighbors.[45]

In September 1927, Anna and Elizabeth honored Judge Meldrum with a birthday party at the park's majestic Grand Canyon Hotel. Actually there were several milestones for him to celebrate that year. In addition to turning eighty-four, Judge Meldrum, who had been appointed the park's first commissioner in 1894, was considered the oldest living resident of Yellowstone National Park. His thirty-three years of attending to the legal issues of the park had made him one of the most recognized United States Commissioners in America. Anna and Elizabeth treated the "grand old man" of the park to a celebration "which bordered on elaborate," reported one newspaper. The guest list included all the well-known Mammoth personages such as Superintendent and Mrs. Horace M. Albright, Mr. and Mrs. Jack E. Haynes, and Mr. and Mrs. Chester A. Lindsley. Anna and Elizabeth spared no expense for what was probably the biggest birthday bash the judge had ever seen—without a worry about their own futures.[46]

Throughout the 1920s, economic signs in Yellowstone as well as in the entire country had been pointing upward until one fateful day in 1929. Overly optimistic speculation in the 1920s had prompted people to buy stocks with loaned money and then to use those stocks as collateral to buy more stocks. Based on borrowed money and unrealistic optimism, the stock market appeared to be booming, but in reality was growing unsteady. On Black Tuesday, October 29, the New York stock market crashed and began the largest financial crisis of the twentieth century. The crash marked the beginning of a widespread and long-lasting economic depression that affected every citizen in the nation. While Anna and Elizabeth seemed to have escaped the economic fallout in 1930, their partnership showed a loss for the first time in 1931. Prudently, the sisters reduced their salaries commensurate with economic conditions for the next few years, with Anna drawing only $1,000 and Elizabeth $750. However, Anna and Elizabeth's business expertise, good judgment, and perhaps a little women's intuition, helped them to weather the financial storm clouds of the Great Depression.[47]

The disconcerted atmosphere of 1929 and 1930 brought more than just economic turmoil to Anna and Elizabeth. On May 12, 1929, their father, George W. Trischman died at the National Home for Disabled Volunteer Soldiers in Sawtelle, California. He had been admitted to the home earlier that year because of a heart condition that required constant monitoring. At the time of his death at age eighty, George W. had lived long enough to watch his daughters Elizabeth and Anna become successful entrepreneurs in a time when women rarely owned and operated their own businesses and he had lived long enough to be a loving grandfather to his now grown granddaughters Georganna and Margaret. His passing in 1929 spared him the heartache that Anna, Elizabeth, and Georganna would have to face a little over a year later.[48]

"The Flower Withereth," read the title line in the *Livingston Enterprise* on December 2, 1930, announcing the untimely death of twenty-year-old Margaret B. Pryor the preceding day in Los Angeles. A picture of health in high school, Margaret had won two cups for her ability in tennis. She graduated from St. Mary's Academy in Los Angeles in 1928 and was awarded an honors medal in athletics. Margaret was just "blossoming into womanhood" in 1929 when she was forced to leave her studies at the University of Iowa because of ill health. For nearly two years, Anna sought the best medical care that could be found for Margaret but it was to no avail. On October 16, 1930, Judge Meldrum wrote to park photographer Jack Haynes that "word received from Mrs. Pryor yesterday left Margaret 'not so well.' I fear she is facing another sojourn in [the] hospital, which means a second winter of worry for the other members of the family." A few days later Jack Haynes returned the judge's letter with an optimistic reply "She is going to have the best of care and I think she will out grow her trouble."[49] By the end of the October, Margaret had undergone surgery that confirmed the doctor's foreboding diagnosis. The newspaper noted the cause of death as "an unusual malady for one so young, that has baffled science for ages, had seized the young lady and could not be stopped."

Following a funeral service at St. Paul's church, Margaret was laid to rest in the Calvary Cemetery in Los Angeles. In June, the judge returned the kindness that the Pryor family had bestowed upon him for so many years. He ordered several eight by twelve enlargements of a photograph of Margaret Pryor from Jack Haynes, which he presumably presented to the family. No doubt this touching gesture helped Anna and Elizabeth deal with their grief and persevere through the trying days that lay ahead. Remarkably these two resolute ladies did more than just hold their own during the emotionally and financially disheartening days of the 1930s; they expanded their holdings and prospered.[50]

Early in 1932, Anna approached George Whittaker about purchasing his stores at Mammoth and Canyon. At age sixty-two, Whittaker had been working in Yellowstone for over forty years and was considering retirement.[51] He seemed receptive to selling his businesses to Anna and commented that "I would rather sell to her than a stranger who might be hard to handle." While the concessionaires in Yellowstone were in competition with one another, they generally respected each other and valued the balance of business that they had taken part in creating. Selling to a stranger could possibly upset the balance that kept business in the park running smoothly. Whittaker also knew it took a lot more than fortitude to deal with the government's regulations and felt that Anna and Elizabeth's favorable relationship with the administration would "suit the post bunch better than I do."[52]

Anna, Elizabeth, and Whittaker settled on a purchase price of $75,000 for his operations in Mammoth and Canyon, which included the store buildings as well as gas stations, inventory, equipment, and four automobiles. Amazingly, despite dismal economic conditions in 1932 and the fact that they had no male partners, the two women were able to secure a $17,000 loan from the National Park Bank in Livingston and a $13,000 loan from the Yellowstone Park Transportation Company.[53] Giving Whittaker a down payment of $5,000 cash, they made up the remaining $40,000 in notes from friends and family.[54] Anna then traveled to Washington, D.C., to negotiate the transfer of Whittaker's lease to Pryor and Trischman. One of the provisions of the new lease agreement stipulated that the sisters were prohibited from selling photographs of Yellowstone or photographic supplies and equipment. Jack Haynes of Haynes Picture Shops had acquired exclusive rights to sell those items in 1930. But Anna and Elizabeth hardly needed such rights. They now owned a curio store with a coffee shop and soda fountain; two general stores; two gas stations; a store, deli and cafeteria at the Mammoth Auto Camp; and a refreshment stand. Returning triumphantly with a new ten-year lease, the sisters officially took possession of Whittaker's Mammoth and Canyon stores on April 1, 1932. Anna and Elizabeth were now in control of all the general stores and gas stations in the northern end of the park.[55]

By 1934, the Pryor and Trischman businesses were all showing profits, returning upwards of fifteen percent. In financial language, they were back in the black. But beyond that, Anna and Elizabeth had paid off half of the $70,000 in loans and notes by the end of the 1935 season. By 1936, their general stores at Canyon and Mammoth produced over $110,000 in sales, the gas stations contributed $51,000, and the women's original Mammoth businesses—the Devil's Kitchenette, campground cafeteria, and Park Curio Shop—grossed around $50,000.[56] In 1941, the NPS gave Pryor and Trischman a new lease, this time for twenty years. However, there was a price to pay for the extra time. They had to invest over $50,000 during the next five years for additions and improvements to their facilities.[57] By this point, the National Park Service had a firm grip on its mission of maintaining an esthetically pleasing park for visitors. The NPS mandated that abandoned sites be restored to their original condition and insisted that new services be provided if that need existed. Apparently, Anna and Elizabeth agreed to the $50,000 expenditure. After all, they had invested their lives in building up a successful chain of visitor services and they took great pride in it. With a record 580,000 park visitors in 1941, the ladies probably did not regret their decision.

However, the ensuing years of World War II (1941-1945) took a toll on all of the park's businesses. Most operations were either severely curtailed or shut down completely. The Park Curio Shop in Mammoth closed and the store, deli, and cafeteria at the Mammoth Auto Camp suffered the same fate. The sisters opened the employee rooms near the

Pryor Stores
Yellowstone Park,
Wyoming

Every Need for the Motorist and Traveler in Yellowstone Park

WHERE—
Courteous Employes
Serve You

AND—
Prices Are Right

ENJOY—
A 5-Course Sunday Dinner 75c away from home, or a —la Carta Service at reasonable prices in our Coffee Shop

MAKE THE PRYOR STORES
A MEETING PLACE
IN THE PARK

AT MAMMOTH
The Curio Shop
The Coffee Shop
General Store
Gas Station

NEAR DEVIL'S KITCHEN
The Devil's
Kitchenette

MAMMOTH CAMP GROUND
Cafeteria
General Store

AT GRAND CANYON
General Store
Gas Station

Pryor's General Stores
Sell at Montana Prices
(In Original Packages Only)
Liquors — Wines — Ales — Beers
NO PERMIT NEEDED

You'll Feel at Home at Pryor Stores
Anna K. Pryor   Elizabeth Trischman

This newspaper advertisement touts all the offerings of the Pryor Stores in 1939.
(FROM LIVINGSTON ENTERPRISE JUNE 13, 1939)

shop for overnight lodging for sporadic park visitors, and served visitors meals in the employee dining room. They closed the store at Canyon and kept open only the Mammoth General Store and gas station. In 1944, only 64,000 people visited Yellowstone. But once again the sisters did not let an economic cloudburst dampen their personal spirits or business attitudes.[58]

By 1947, the sisters were beginning to feel their age. Anna was sixty-three and Elizabeth sixty-one, and they had been in business for almost forty years. They realized that if one of them were to die, their partnership would legally dissolve. In order for the surviving sister to continue the businesses in the park, she would have to go through the permitting process with the park all over again. On May 27, the Pryor and Trischman partnership incorporated as Pryor Stores, Inc., with Anna as president and Elizabeth as vice president/treasurer, and daughter Georganna on the board of directors. Shortly after resolving this legal issue, the two women began thinking about retirement. In a January 1948 letter to Oliver G. Taylor, the superintendent of concessions, Anna and Elizabeth confessed that "it's later than we think, and the extremely heavy work of the past few years has been a definite strain on us." But finding a suitable buyer was another matter.[59]

Several prospective buyers approached them, but Anna and Elizabeth did not believe that any of them would meet the stringent demands required by the National Park Service, nor meet their own personal requirements. One prospective buyer stood out, however. Trevor Povah, son-in-law of Charles Hamilton (who owned the general stores in the southern portion of the park), expressed interest in purchasing the business. While Anna and Elizabeth felt confident that Trevor and his wife Eleanor could run the businesses in a professional manner, Trevor made no actual offer. Evidently, it was one thing for Anna and Elizabeth to contemplate retirement, but another for them to be able to act upon it.[60]

Not only did tourism to Yellowstone resume in the postwar years, it increased substantially. By 1948, visitation in the park reached over one million visitors and, in 1952, Pryor Stores, Inc. tallied record sales of $383,406.26. With that exemplary level attained, Anna and Elizabeth decided it was definitely time to retire. They began negotiations with Charles Hamilton, and on September 23 he offered them $250,000 cash for all the Pryor holdings. Hamilton had several reasons for wanting the businesses. He was concerned that an outside buyer, especially one

Anna Pryor (on left) and Elizabeth Trischman (on right) looking happy to be retired in the mid-1950s. (COURTESY MONTANA HISTORICAL SOCIETY H-56532)

with deep financial pockets, could cause adverse financial havoc for his stores and gas stations in the southern portion of the park. But the most significant issue was the fact that his buy-out of Pryor Stores, Inc. would give Hamilton a monopoly of the general store business in the park. Being astute and judicious businesswomen for over forty years, Anna and Elizabeth undoubtedly calculated this into their counter offer of $300,000 on October 7. Hamilton accepted the offer and finalized the deal on January 5, 1953. Pryor Stores, Inc. was officially dissolved that same year on March 20.[61]

Anna, and Elizabeth finally retired to their winter home in Los Angeles. After a lifetime of surviving family tragedies, two world wars, and multitudes of business trials and tribulations, Anna and Elizabeth wanted to rest, or, as Charles Hamilton put it "start to enjoy life because as the second chapter of St. Luke says, you cannot take it with you."[62] The two sisters and lifelong business partners did their best to heed this advice because they had learned all too well how fragile life can be. That fragility would test their courage one more time.

On March 12, 1961, Georganna suffered a stroke. She was making satisfactory progress when she suffered another stroke on November 3, and she died on November 8 at the age of fifty-three. With neither daughter to see her into her old age, Anna spent the last years of her life as a patient in the home of her nephew Harry (Bud) Trischman and his wife in Los Angeles. She died on October 27, 1973, at the age of eighty-nine, and was buried in the Calvary Cemetery in Whittier, California. Elizabeth outlived her older sister by eleven years and died on November 20, 1984, at the age of ninety-seven.[63]

Sadly, the death knell tolled once more in 1984. This time it was for the sisters' Park Curio Shop. Structural deterioration and the NPS's detection of high levels of radon and carbon dioxide had caused the building to become unsalvageable. Late in 1984, the eighty-eight year old historic Park Curio Shop—beloved by generations of Yellowstone visitors—was torn down.[64]

Through the years, thousands of visitors to Yellowstone purchased mementos of coated specimens and sand art from the Curio Shop, sipped on malts and root beer floats from the soda fountain, savored fresh confectioneries from the bakery, and delighted in hot sandwiches from the lunch counter. For more than three quarters of a century the Park Curio Shop occupied a prominent position as one of the longest operating concessions in the park and represented the keystone of the two sisters' hard-earned legacy in Yellowstone. Indeed, Anna K. Pryor and Elizabeth Trischman had served Yellowstone well.

❀

Ida Christine Carlson Eagle

(1883–1962)

Mom Eagle

Family legend holds that, while the Eagle family was enjoying one of their traditional weekend outings in Yellowstone National Park, a park visitor curiously surveyed the multitude of children at play near Ida Eagle. "Hello, Ma'am," said the stranger. "Is this a picnic or are they all yours?" With the same forthright character that sustained her throughout her life, Ida stalwartly replied, "They're all mine, Mister, and believe me, it's no picnic!"[1] Indeed, raising ten children and assisting her husband, Sam, in the operation of a general mercantile store in the then frontier town of West Yellowstone, Montana in the early 1900s was no picnic for Ida Eagle. But it is doubtful that she would have traded her life for anything else. Throughout her lifetime as wife, mother, and business partner, Ida Christine Carlson Eagle quietly played instrumental roles in forging a community out of a wilderness, imparting important values to her children, creating solid family bonds, and becoming a key figure in the establishment of the famous Eagle's Store, a Yellowstone legacy that continues today.[2]

Ida Christine Carlson was born on September 11, 1883 in Long Lake, Minnesota, to John and Susan (Hukari) Carlson. What should have been an idyllic childhood for her in the pastoral environment of America's midwestern region turned into a real-life scene right out of "Cinderella." In 1892, when Ida was just nine years old her, mother was killed in a runaway horse-and-carriage accident, an all too common occurrence in horse-drawn America. It is unknown whether her father felt inadequate to raise a daughter or if he thought that she would be better off being raised with female influences, but for whatever the reason he sent her to live with nearby relatives. According to family chronicles, Ida was required to care for the relative's small children in return for room and board, and was generally treated like an unwanted stepchild. Whether Ida's father remained a part of her life has gone unrecorded, but if Ida entertained any prospect of a future relationship with her father that hope was dashed when he died in 1902 when she was nineteen.

Orphaned and on her own, Ida supported herself by working as a waitress in Spooner, Wisconsin. It was there in 1905 that she and a friend, Irene Taylor, read a newspaper advertisement offering waitress positions at the Fountain Hotel in Yellowstone National Park. With no family ties to hold her back, Ida wasted no time in leaving the unhappy memories of Wisconsin behind her and heading west with Irene. She arrived in Yellowstone with a hopeful heart and expectations of finding a more favorable life and she found them.[3]

Yellowstone National Park in the late 19th and early 20th centuries was an idyllic tourist place with stagecoaches arriving several times a day full of dressed-up, genteel tourists, very merry and all excited about their trip through what even then was one the world's most famous places. The Fountain Hotel, located about halfway between Madison Junction and Old Faithful, was built during the fall and spring of 1890-1891 and had opened in June 1891. The F-shaped two-story building contained 135 guest rooms, a "gents parlor" as well as a "ladies parlor," a large dining room that measured fifty-eight feet by forty-two feet, which likely doubled as a ballroom after the tables and chairs were removed, and offered guests luxurious amenities not generally found in a wilderness setting, such as electric lights, steam heat, and hot mineral baths. One lady traveler staying at the Fountain during its first season in 1891 was clearly impressed with the hotel and declared it to be "a most imposing lodge for so vast a wilderness."[4]

According to an article in the July 1893 issue of *Harpers Weekly*, Fountain was considered "one of the best [hotels] in the park." Perched upon a knoll overlooking the Lower Geyser Basin, the hotel offered visitors a panoramic view where one could take in a spectacular eruption of Fountain Geyser from a comfortable veranda seat. Or if guests desired, the hotel's location also offered the convenience of being within walking distance of Fountain Geyser and an assortment of other thermal features, such heart-shaped Evangeline Geyser, from which escaping steam created a heartbeat-thumping noise that harkened visitors back to Longfellow's poem, and hot springs such as White Sulphur Spring (today's Leather

Pool), which also supplied the hotel's mineral baths. A walk around the Lower Geyser Basin was so mesmerizing that one visitor claimed "only the promise of a natural hot-spring bath lured us back to the house." The availability of a large array of geysers and hot springs probably made a stay at the Fountain seem like living in a mystical land, if only for an evening. For Ida, working and living at Fountain Hotel for the 1905 season would prove to be an entire summer of enchantment.[5]

At Fountain Hotel, Ida almost immediately saw Sam Eagle eyeing her and commented to her friend Irene, "I'll bet he thinks he's smart." While she may have been wary of his "smart" look, it did not take long for Sam, whose fishing expertise supplied the hotel's dining room with its daily catch, to reel in Ida's attention. Even though Sam bartended all evening and fished all day, and Ida probably worked long hours as a dining room waitress, they managed to spend a little time together. Through the course of the summer, Ida and Sam became quite fond of each other. Sam may have even taken Ida to the Fountain Hotel employee's romantic rendezvous, Lovers Leap, to while away an afternoon, or to take in one of Yellowstone's beautiful sunsets. As the end of the season approached, each began to make plans for the winter, and Ida decided to go to California. Possibly because it sounded like a good place to spend the winter or maybe because Ida was going there, Sam also sent off an employment application to California. Ida left the Fountain Hotel near the end of September and headed to San Francisco. For a Wisconsin girl, the idea of spending a winter in California must have seemed like an exotic excursion. The expectation of adventure surely loomed in her head, even though she was going there to work. Perhaps the hardest part was leaving Sam behind. While Ida's seasonal position had ended, Sam opted to continue working until the first of November so that he could help close up the Fountain Hotel and the recently opened (1904) Old Faithful Inn, not far away. But Ida promised to write to him as soon as she got to California.[6]

In Sam's first return letter to Ida dated October 1, 1905, he wrote that he was happy to hear she was enjoying herself. He also revealed that his application in California had not been accepted and so he was unsure of where he would be spending the winter. Sam cautiously hinted at his affection for her with his closing salutation, "Your loving friend, Sam." By mid-October Ida was living in and probably working at the Ormond Hotel in San Francisco. Gainfully employed, she apparently wrote to

*Ida Carlson and Sam Eagle visiting Giant Geyser in 1905, the year
they met at the Fountain Hotel.* (COURTESY EAGLE FAMILY)

Sam suggesting that he join her there. Sam's response to her was one of
practicality. From his reply, it appears that Sam had previously been to San
Francisco and was well aware of the lures that could separate him and his
hard-earned money. His answer to Ida was as much sound reasoning as it
was a foretelling of his plans that might include her. He assured her that his
affection for her had not changed, but he believed "if I am lucky I can save
quite a bit in the next few years…we are both young…and what is a couple
of years compared to a whole life[?]" While Sam acknowledged that he
realized it was difficult for them to be apart, he hoped she understood his
practical way of thinking. Perhaps she did understand, but even so she was

no doubt disappointed that she and Sam were going to be separated for the entire winter.[7]

In mid-December, Ida decided to accept a waitress position at the Potter Hotel in Santa Barbara, no doubt seeking southern California's warm weather, palm trees, and flowers. Meanwhile Sam traveled east and found employment at the Commercial Club in St. Paul after a hunting trip in northern Minnesota. Once Ida was settled into the Potter Hotel, she must have sent Sam a letter relating her fears about their long-distance relationship. We can infer this, because in his January 10, 1906, letter Sam countered her qualms with, "Well sweet, you seem to see a change in me. If I had you here [for] a few minutes, I'd squeeze the life out of you and dispel those doubts." The next letter Ida received from Sam a week later was equally expressive on his affection for her as he wrote, "I miss you very much, which I hope is returned." Whether Ida became very busy or decided to play hard-to-get may never be known, but her letters to Sam after Christmas seemed to become fewer and farther apart.[8]

One reason could have been that she was not pleased with the unromantic Christmas present Sam sent her, which was a box of writing paper. By March 14, Sam took a guess as to why she was being unusually silent and wrote that he "just discovered a big mistake in regard to my Xmas present. Why didn't you turn around and send that box of paper right back...the idea of sending your sweetheart a box of writing paper for Xmas, it's a corker." Obviously his enticement to get more letters from Ida had backfired, and poking fun at the errors of his ways was one way of smoothing over his blunder. Apparently it worked, because Ida's letters to Sam resumed with weekly regularity.[9]

By mid-April Ida had moved farther north to Modesto, California. When the massive earthquake that leveled San Francisco struck on April 18, 1906, Ida was ninety miles away. Ida and Sam's friends from the Fountain Hotel—Alex Stuart and Laura (Larsen) Stuart—were much closer. Alex and Laura had married in the fall of 1905 and were also spending the winter in California. According to Sam's letter to Ida on March 8, 1906, Alex was managing a barber shop and working as a waiter in a restaurant in the downtown area of San Francisco. Sam wrote that he believed the Stuarts were not planning to return to the park for the upcoming summer. On that fateful day in April when the city of San Francisco was reduced to rubble, Alex and Laura narrowly escaped "with fire and destruction but a block away." Ida was lucky to be a good distance away in Modesto and not in San Francisco visiting her friends.[10]

Without the convenience of today's instantaneous communication network, Ida answered Sam's letter from April 14 with uncharacteristic speed as she sensed that he would be concerned about her safety. Sam was relieved to hear that she was not in San Francisco when the earthquake hit. He also relayed his anxiousness to get back to the park for the summer, as he was looking forward to enjoying the mountain air and Ida's renewed company. As a result of this catastrophic event, the Stuarts also chose to return to the park for the summer of 1906. Alex confided later in life that he "had been in love with the Yellowstone country for quite some time, but it took an earthquake to really make up my mind." To be sure, the earthquake completely altered Alex and Laura's outlook on their future aspirations. The Stuarts' change of plans would also contribute to Sam and Ida's future endeavors.[11]

Ida and Sam were assigned their old positions at the Fountain Hotel for the summer of 1906 and they were joined by their friends Alex and Laura Stuart. Since Ida and Sam worked and played at the same location for the entire season and did not need any letter writing, the record of that summer is silent. A fair assumption would be that they enjoyed another season of bliss at Yellowstone's Fountain Hotel. At the end of the summer, Ida chose to spend the winter in Helena, Montana, perhaps because that was where her friend Irene was going. Ida left Yellowstone in mid-September and settled in to Helena's Grandon Hotel. In October, Sam, still working in Yellowstone, sent several letters to Ida voicing his concern about her choice of accommodations in Helena. "By the way, Ida," Sam wrote, "get a room on the outside & don't think of sleeping in an inside room, because your health must be considered first." While Sam understood Ida's frugality, he scolded her for making her health a secondary priority behind money. "It's all right to be saving but never put money ahead of health," Sam counseled. He closed his letter with a loving sort of prodding, "Now if my little girl loves me, she will look for better sleeping quarters."[12]

In the early 1900s, physicians advocated that fresh air was beneficial for sufferers of tuberculosis, a respiratory illness that was the leading cause of death in America at that time. Medical specialists extended that premise to healthy people, and suggested that sleeping with a supply of fresh air was good for avoiding illnesses. The architecture of the Arts and Crafts

Movement addressed this idea by designing houses with sleeping porches on the front and/or back of the home, typically on the second floor and predominantly on the corner to facilitate cross breezes. Working in eastern cities early in his life, Sam was probably exposed to overcrowded living conditions where the air quality was less than favorable and the threat of disease was ever present. His concern for Ida's sleeping in an inside and thus a "closed" room seems to indicate that Sam believed fresh air was essential for good health, and that an outside room with a window Ida could open would be better. His keenness for fresh air may explain why he wrote to Ida that he felt "crowded" in St. Paul during the winter of 1905-1906 and why, a year later, when he wrote her about his congested lifestyle in New York City, Sam complained that he hardly had "enough room here to breathe." It seems that Sam wanted Ida to have a more healthful environment than he was experiencing. With Sam's expressed concern for her health and well-being, it is easy to see how Ida became captivated.[13]

Meanwhile, Sam finished his duties in Yellowstone and headed off for his annual hunting trip in northern Minnesota, writing letters to Ida along the way. After bagging a deer and a moose, Sam landed in St. Paul and began a winter-job search. His thoughts ranged from going to Florida to taking a train west to securing a job in New York. Then again maybe he should consider returning home to visit his family. When logic did not seem to help him make a decision, Sam tossed a coin to see if his winter was destined to be in East or West. "It came up East, so I guess I'll have to stick by it," Sam wrote to Ida on December 18. In many ways, Sam's early years of roaming around the country speak volumes about his lifelong desire to be on the move, whether it was serving as a fishing or hunting guide in the wilds of Montana or skiing seventy-plus miles for a mail run or jaunting off to Washington, D.C., to lobby for privatizing the town site of West Yellowstone. But in late 1906, visiting his family in Pottstown, Pennsylvania, became a priority for Sam and he decided that a surprise Christmas visit was in order. On December 22, he wrote to Ida that he was happy that he made the decision to return home, because his surprise arrival was greeted with a resounding "SAM!" by the entire family and, on a more serious note, because his father was "in bad shape & I know my being here will cheer him up."[14]

Sam spread Christmas cheer that season from Pennsylvania to Montana, and Ida's present from him was a marriage proposal. "You can tell Irene

& all your friends that we are engaged to be married next summer," Sam happily wrote. "I'll be pleased to have you wear my engagement ring... and I hope we will never be separated again." And just to be sure she understood his seriousness, Sam signed his letter, "your future husband, Sam." As the clock struck midnight on December 31, 1907, Ida must have looked forward to the New Year and her new life with joy.[15]

After Christmas, Sam went to New York City and found a position at the Knickerbocker Hotel located at Broadway and Forty-Second Street. The luxuriously appointed hotel, built by John Jacob Astor and opened for business in 1906, was considered a showcase of New York's economic prosperity. In addition to offering rooms decorated with paintings by artists such as Maxfield Parrish, James Wall Finn, and Frederic Remington, the hotel exhibited an opulent, three-story restaurant and bar that seated an after-theater dinner-crowd of two-thousand patrons. However, even working amidst all this splendor Sam was not impressed with his workplace nor with New York City. "I wouldn't make a home in New York for a mint," he complained to Ida. "By the time you pay for your room, food, and laundry, you haven't much left. I'm certainly through with the East." Clearly unhappy, Sam relied on Ida's letters as his only sense of comfort.[16]

Ida's frugality that had sustained her through her life apparently went beyond her own finances when she ignored Sam's frequent requests for things that he could bring her from the East. "A new trunk or suitcase?" he inquired of Ida. Not getting a response from her did not deter Sam, and he continued to implore her for a list of items she wanted from New York. Even though it appears that she never asked for anything, Sam bought her a new suitcase anyway before he left New York. More than likely the practicality of a suitcase suited Ida's thrifty nature.[17]

At the end of February, Sam accepted a job at the New Willard Hotel in Washington, D.C. The original Willard Hotel on the corner of Fourteenth Street and Pennsylvania Avenue was opened in 1847 and eventually hosted presidents Lincoln and Grant, as well as other notable guests including Charles Dickens and Buffalo Bill. By the time of Sam's arrival, the hotel had been completely remodeled and expanded by New York architect Henry Janeway Hardenberg, and it reopened in 1904 as the New Willard Hotel. Obviously much happier working at the New Willard, Sam excitedly wrote to Ida almost twice a week telling her about his life. Between spending time in the Capitol observing legislative sessions, exploring the

This stunning photograph of Ida Carlson Eagle was her wedding portrait in 1907. The locket around her neck contained a picture of Sam and today is a treasured family heirloom. (COURTESY EAGLE FAMILY)

city's attractions, and going to the library where he could read a newspaper from anywhere in the country, including Helena, Montana, Sam filled letters to Ida with his interesting activities.[18] Even though Washington was stimulating for Sam, he missed Ida and was anxious to get back to Yellowstone National Park. Ida was equally as anxious to leave Helena and resume her summertime life at the Fountain Hotel. While Sam's job there began in early June, the management decided to postpone hiring the rest of the staff until later in the season. Hence Ida was not scheduled to return to the park until after the first of July. While she was not happy about the situation, Sam advised her to not make trouble for herself by complaining and, in his typically practical manner, he advised her that July would come soon enough. Heeding Sam's calming recommendation, Ida waited out her time in Helena. As Sam predicted, July came around and so did Ida's summer position at the Fountain Hotel.[19]

At the end of yet another harmonious summer in Yellowstone, Ida and Sam were married on September 17, 1907, just two months before the first Oregon Short Line (branch line of the Union Pacific Railroad) locomotive steamed into what would eventually become West Yellowstone. Within ten days of the railroad's arrival on November 12, the newlyweds put in their application to lease land, from the Forest Service, for a store at Yellowstone's west entrance. In addition to Ida and Sam's application, the Forest Service received two others for special-use permits, one from Charles A. Arnet and the other from L.A. Murray, who, like them, also saw the railroad's entry at the west entrance to Yellowstone and the emergence of a new town as a lucrative opportunity. Ida and Sam then departed for what would become Ida's favorite winter getaway, California. The couple spent the winter of 1907-1908 working in San Diego and enjoying the company of their friends and Fountain Hotel coworkers, Alex and Laura Stuart. Sam worked as a bartender at the newly established Café Union located at 3rd and D streets. Believing that restaurants were good investments, Sam apparently invested in this one, a business owned by M.T. Farrow, a brother of T.E. Farrow, then superintendent of hotels for the Yellowstone Park Association.[20]

On March 27, 1908, Sam and Ida received approval from the Forest Service for their one-acre plot of land, which was located on West Yellowstone's corner of Second and Park streets, today's Yellowstone and Canyon streets. With this news, Ida and Sam's thoughts turned toward their new summer business venture. At the same time they became aware that, in San Diego, the Café Union's enticement of "Music and the Delicacies of Dining" was not drawing enough business to cover its operating expense. It is unclear whether Sam lost money in the financial debacle of the Café Union, but it is possible that he did. If that were the case, both Ida and Sam realized that any financial loss at this time could jeopardize plans for their future store. The failing Café Union could have been an underlying catalyst for Ida and Sam' bringing Alex and Laura Stuart into their store business as informal partners. Family speculation also holds that Ida herself may have provided some of the necessary funding to get the store started. If so, then Ida surely saved Sam's and her dreams from being waylaid.[21]

Whatever arrangements Ida and Sam made between themselves may never be known, but they managed to get building materials, showcases, and merchandise ordered and scheduled to ship on the first available train to the park's west boundary in the spring. Their new partner Alex

This rare 1908 image of Sam Eagle standing at the hotel bar, which he called his "office," is the only known photograph of the interior of the Fountain Hotel.
(COURTESY EAGLE FAMILY)

Stuart agreed to go to Yellowstone in early May to get construction started on the store while Sam settled his business at the Café Union. En route to Yellowstone, Alex left his wife Laura and their daughter Marguerite, and a very pregnant Ida Eagle, in St. Anthony, Idaho. On May 9, 1908, Henry Eagle, the first of Ida and Sam's ten children, was born there. In early June, Sam stopped in St. Anthony to hold his new son in his arms for the first time and to embrace Ida. He then continued his travels and joined Alex at the west-boundary townsite to help with the store construction. Although neither of the men had any construction experience, Alex and Sam managed to erect a 14' x 20' building with a typical western false front that would serve as the first Eagle/Stuart Store. Once the building was up, they installed the showcases and stocked the merchandise that had arrived from California on the same train as Sam. Then Sam departed to begin his supporting job at the Fountain Hotel, leaving Alex, Laura, and Ida in charge of the new store. All four of them must have been excited yet apprehensive in hoping that it would succeed. Through the next few decades Ida would frequently find herself in charge of the store, and it was a responsibility that she became quite adept at handling.[22]

That summer Sam worked his usual job as bartender and fisherman at Fountain Hotel, while Ida and the Stuarts ran the new store. The number of visitors entering the west entrance via the Union Pacific's Oregon Short Line that year was 7,172, which represented more than a third of the 19,452 total park visitors. With the welcoming railroad depot yet to be built, the Eagle/Stuart Store on the corner across from the railroad's arrival platform probably represented, for most arriving passengers, the only evidence of civilization on the edge of the Yellowstone wilderness. As one of only two stores then operating in the nascent settlement, the business no doubt kept Alex, Laura, and Ida quite busy with daily train arrivals and departures.[23]

Charles A. Arnet, one of the other recipients of a special-use permit from the Forest Service, opened his Yellowstone Store that summer. Arnet was also appointed postmaster for the new town, which had yet to be officially named. In those early days, it was often referred to as "Boundary" from its location on the west boundary of the park, and occasionally as "Terminus" due to the name of the railroad car that was initially used as a mail and passenger depot. But once he was appointed postmaster in October 1908, Arnet changed the town's name to Riverside. Evidently it did not matter to him that the Madison River was two miles away and that the new name did not adequately promote Yellowstone. But it did matter to the town's growing residential population and to the Union Pacific Railroad, and they began to rally for change. Meanwhile, Arnet had become disgruntled when he discovered that his proposed plan to sell liquor was going to be disallowed by the Forest Service. He left his business under the management of Bishop Williams and moved back to Clyde Park, Montana. Before the year was out, Arnet had decided to relinquish his appointment of postmaster of Riverside, Montana.[24]

Ever the opportunist, Sam Eagle began his campaign to be named postmaster of the new town even before he finished his season at the Fountain Hotel. As an established business owner with a wife and baby, Sam probably appeared to be a stable choice for postmaster, and he was awarded the appointment, which would officially take effect in November 1909 following the expiration of Arnet's term. F. Jay Haynes, official park photographer, wrote a letter to Sam expressing his support of Sam's commission as postmaster. Haynes, understanding that a postmaster's salary was based on the number of letter cancellations, also wrote that he planned to send as much mail as possible from the Upper Geyser Basin and Canyon to the Eagle's Store post office. In a vote of confidence, Haynes believed that Sam and Ida would provide better service than the post office at Mammoth.[25]

But before Sam began his position as postmaster, he and Ida, with six-month old baby Henry, worked as winterkeepers of the Fountain Hotel for the winter of 1908-1909. While Ida had grown up in Minnesota and Wisconsin and was aware of the rigors of life in a winter landscape, she probably encountered more than a few challenges while caring for an infant in a totally isolated region such as Yellowstone's Lower Geyser Basin. However, as winter residents, Ida and family were afforded the same luxury of using the hotel's hot water, supplied by Leather Pool, as the hotel's summer guests. Their closest neighbors were their friends and business partners, Alex and Laura Stuart, who worked as winterkeepers of the Old Faithful Inn with their young daughter Marguerite in tow.[26]

In summer 1909, Alex Stuart took his turn working at the Old Faithful Inn, while Laura, Sam, and Ida ran the store. On August 14, Ida added another son to the family when she gave birth to John E. (Ed) Eagle in St. Anthony, Idaho. At the end of that year, the Stuarts bought Arnet's Yellowstone Store. Sam took over as postmaster and renamed the growing community "Yellowstone." It would be another eleven years before the town would undergo its final name change to "West Yellowstone."[27]

By the end of 1909, Sam and Ida were the sole proprietors of Eagle's Store. While Sam's appointment as postmaster gave them a source of year-round income, it also meant that they would be have to remain at the store throughout the winter. Ida, with two small children, would spend her first of many winters in the town often classified as the coldest place in the country, with temperatures routinely dipping down to 30 or 40 degrees below zero. Family records declare that Ida was the only woman in West Yellowstone during the winter of 1909-1910. More than likely, Henry and Ed were the only babies, as well.[28]

As visitation to the park increased through the years, Ida and Sam expanded Eagle's Store in both size and merchandise. They installed a soda fountain in 1910, making it one of the earliest soda fountains in the West. Sam and Ida purchased the original fountain from the Liquid Carbonic

Fittingly, Ida Eagle posed for this photograph on Eagle Nest rock. The town of Gardiner can be seen in the distance. (COURTESY EAGLE FAMILY)

Company of Minnesota for $1,391.80, the equivalent of $30,000.00 today. At that time, Liquid Carbonic was the leading soda fountain company because of their heavy-duty and well constructed equipment, and their often-wise business advice to prospective soda fountain owners.[29]

Founded in 1888 by Jacob Baur, the Liquid Carbonic Company was essentially the creator of America's mass soda fountain phenomenon that began in the early 1900s. Baur perfected a process to liquefy and store carbon dioxide in pressurized canisters that he made available for sale. Prior to Baur's commercial production of liquid carbon dioxide, soda fountain owners had to purchase carbonated water, which was expensive and took up valuable storage space. By 1909, Liquid Carbonic Company supplied everything from marble-topped counters and back bars to syrup pumps made of a "secret process non-corrosive white metal" (today known as stainless steel.) The company also advised how to select the right size soda fountain for any business, which would increase profits but not create a heavy financial burden. Ida and Sam's original plan was to make the soda fountain area into a large U-shape, but with limited funds they (for then) heeded Baur's counsel that there should be "a happy medium between too little and too much money invested in a soda fountain," and constructed only half of that.[30]

The Eagles' new white-marble–topped soda fountain with a dozen wire stools was not the only addition to the Eagle Store during those early years. On September 25, 1910, Ida gave birth to the couple's first girl, who was named Helen (Sis) Eagle. Helen was followed by Samuel P. (Bud) Eagle born July 11, 1912.[31]

While Ida and Sam were very busy with the store during the summer season, and also with raising their children, they always reserved Sunday afternoons for a picnic in Yellowstone Park. On one such occasion, Ida must have shuddered in horror as the scene that took her mother's life when she was just nine years old replayed before her eyes. Ida and Sam were unloading the carriage at their favorite picnic spot when something spooked the horses, and the team took off with couple's four small children inside. Somehow the army soldiers in charge of the park at that time were notified, and heroically stopped the runaway horses. This time fate played a kinder hand for Ida. The children were returned unharmed to their waiting and very shaken parents. In spite of this heart-stopping event, Ida and Sam continued, for decades, their Sunday family picnic excursions into the national park.[32]

As their family grew, Ida's thrift and resourcefulness became a way of life for the Eagle household. She was an expert recycler long before it was popular. Ida saved anything and everything that could "serve a second term" such as socks and old clothing that she turned into braided rugs, or square wool samples from Woolrich and Pendleton that she crafted into quilts. With several children to keep dressed, Ida made most of their clothing by hand, which she also washed by hand with a simple washboard. According to son Ed, Ida's hopeful wishes for a sewing machine were dashed when Sam bought a new rifle instead. In a rare moment of emotional despair, Ida went to the woodpile and cried.

More than likely Sam found a way to get her a sewing machine before too long.[33]

In addition to changing diapers, making clothing, and feeding several hungry mouths, Ida assisted Sam with the post office they operated from 1909 until 1936. On many occasions Ida would run the post office and store by herself while Sam took his turn to make the two-day, seventy-six mile cross-country ski run to the train depot in Monida, Idaho, to pick up the mail. The massive amount of snowfall in West Yellowstone allowed train service to the town only between May (sometimes June) and November. Depending on the time of year as well as the year itself, mail would be delivered to West Yellowstone by wagon, skis, dogsled teams, and snowshoe. During the winter months magazines, newspapers, and catalogs were stored in a shed at Monida until spring, when those heavier items could be transported to town after rail service resumed.[34]

Substantial yearly increases in park visitation meant increased sales for Eagle's Store, and also meant more work for Ida. At the end of the season Ida earned a well-deserved rest. With four small children not yet of school age, Ida, Sam, and family began, in 1914, what would become their traditional, end-of-season sojourns to California It was there (in Long Beach) that Ida gave birth to fifth child William Arthur Eagle on November 11. Walter C. Eagle, Ida's tenth child would also be a Long Beach baby.

On August 1, 1915, the first automobile entered Yellowstone National Park and set in motion a complete alteration of park transportation. By 1917, the long lines of yellow, red, and green four-horse stagecoaches of the various Yellowstone transportation and camping companies awaiting the arrival of passengers at the West Yellowstone Union Pacific railroad depot were gone. In their place were auto-stages—the custom-designed, yellow-hued, White Motor Company tour buses of the Yellowstone Transportation Company—that sported roll-back roof-tops and drivers in jaunty caps. And the American public exercised their independence and drove themselves to and through Yellowstone in their own automobiles. Eagle's Store, located on the most prominent corner at the park's west entrance, was the ideal place for motorists to find what they needed for excursions into America's Wonderland. Ida and Sam responded to this new style by gearing their merchandise to the independent excursionist, including adding a gas station to the front of their store. The couple not only supplied the automobile movement, they participated. In June 1916, Sam Eagle was issued the first permit of the season for private automobile entry into Yellowstone National Park. That pass, "Season Ticket of Passage No. 1" for the family's five-passenger Ford touring car, was and still is proudly displayed on the counter of Eagle's Store.

Ida and Sam were not the only business owners intent on getting their share of the automobile tourist trade. Alex and Laura Stuart, their original partners before purchasing Arnet's Yellowstone Store, also expanded their offerings by establishing a vehicle repair garage. Wisely, Alex secured a service contract with the Yellowstone Park Transportation Company to repair and maintain the company's buses. For Ida, Sam, and the Eagle's Store as well as their friends the Stuarts, life in West Yellowstone had changed forever.[35]

Between 1927 and 1930, Ida and Sam expanded their store once more. Utilizing plans provided by Bozeman architect Fred Willson, Sam and his cousin Raymond Mauger built the three-story log structure that still graces the corner of Yellowstone and Canyon. Rough-hewn logs on the exterior gave a rustic western appearance, while the friendly character of the Eagle family provided the interior with convivial warmth.

While the store's soda fountain was never expanded to the full-sized

By 1942, when this photograph was taken, the Eagle's Store had expanded both in size and in the volume of merchandise carried to supply park visitors. (COURTESY EAGLE FAMILY)

U-shape that Ida and Sam envisioned, they did enhance it in the 1930s. They purchased a hardwood counter from a vendor in Long Beach, California, and decorated it with ceramic "pillow" tiles that today still grace the front of the fountain counter. These beautiful decorative tiles were manufactured by a variety of Southern California companies between 1923 and the mid-1930s, but from which one Ida and Sam purchased the tiles has remained a mystery. Today the Eagle's Store soda fountain remains one of a handful of soda fountains that continue to operate in the American West.[36]

Between 1908 and 1927, the Eagle family had grown nearly as exponentially as the store, with Bettie Eagle born November 23, 1917; Rose Eagle born September 27, 1919; Harold L. Eagle born August 24, 1921; Joseph G. Eagle born April 13, 1924; and Walter C. Eagle born February 26, 1927. Most of the (now) ten Eagle children resided on the second and third floors of the new store. Ida and Sam's second-floor room had a balcony that faced west and afforded them a majestic view of the rolling timbered hills of the South Fork of the Madison River and today's Two Top Mountain. Always practical and judicious, the couple's inclusion of a balcony off their bedroom was probably for more than just a view, and conceivably hearkened back to Sam's earlier advice to Ida that fresh air was the elixir of health and well-being. In either case, her second floor balcony must have given Ida some well-deserved solace at the end of her long and busy summer days.[37]

For much of the year during their first years in West Yellowstone, Ida and her family lived in semi-seclusion because the nearest substantial town, Bozeman, was eighty-nine miles away. Telephone service arrived in the town in 1926 and the following year a switchboard was installed in Eagle's store, where Ida served as telephone exchange operator. She would then direct her boys to deliver messages throughout town on their bicycles. When Sam became the first licensed fishing and hunting guide in the area, his skill and expertise in these areas made him a sought-after escort. For Ida that meant Sam was either out in a stream or in the woods a great deal of the time. Pragmatic and resilient, Ida became skilled at juggling the managerial duties of the store while she cared for her and Sam's ten children.[38]

Education for their children was a high priority for Ida and Sam, even if it meant they would have to sacrifice their time together. With no high

Mom Eagle and several children are loaded in the car for the annual trek to Bozeman for the upcoming school year in this 1930s family snapshot.
(COURTESY EAGLE FAMILY)

school in West Yellowstone for the children to attend, Ida and Sam made the decision in the early 1920s to buy a house at 623 South Third Street in Bozeman, Montana. For the next two decades, Ida and the children would live in Bozeman during the school year, while Sam stayed in West Yellowstone to perform his duties as postmaster and to maintain the store.[39]

After getting the children settled in the school routine, Ida would return to West Yellowstone to help Sam with the store until mid-November. She hired a cook/housekeeper, a nanny of sorts, to take care of the children in her absence. For the most part, the arrangement worked tolerably except for one season, 1934, when Rose couldn't wait for her mother to return to Bozeman. In a letter to her brother Ed, who was living in St. Regis, Montana, Rose related her experience with the hired housekeeper's culinary retaliation of the Eagle children's likes and dislikes of her cooking.

> Mom is not coming down for good until about the middle of November! We sure are anxious for her to get here as "Cooky" is getting rather unbearable. The kids are terrible! You know how us

Sunday afternoon outings into the park were an Eagle family tradition for decades, as this 1930's photograph illustrates. (COURTESY EAGLE FAMILY)

kids like wienies! Well, Mrs. Mehlburg decided to give us our fill of them! She'd have boiled wienies, wienies in brown gravy, and sometime she'd be good and give us wienies and some other meat in brown gravy! We'd have wienies and eggs and wienie salad! Well it happened that Betty was going to a church dinner and she was supposed to bring spaghetti and tomatoes with hamburger! Mrs. Mehlburg asked Betty a lot of questions concerning the dish and she wanted it be just perfect! Betty took it down to the church and she looked into get a peek of the delicious contents when low and Behold! Guess what she saw—spaghetti with tomatoes and wienies! Boy!

Although the boys' table at the church dinner thought the dish was grand and ate it all, Bettie was embarrassed. It would be a good guess that Bettie never asked "Cooky" to make a church dish for her again. Ida seemed to take this all in stride, and retained Mrs. Mehlburg's services for the following school year.[40]

Even though she was very busy raising ten children, Ida made time for each of them when the need arose. Daughter Rose apparently did not acquire her mother's sewing talents and on one occasion sewed her finger onto the machine in a junior high home economics class. According to Rose, "that ended my sewing career." So when Rose had to make a dress for her eight-grade class, Ida came to her rescue. After she brought home her less than acceptable creation, Ida quietly ripped out all of Rose's inferior stitches and replaced them for her.[41]

Ida was often "Mom Eagle" to more than just her own flesh and blood. Chuck Andersen arrived in West Yellowstone in the late 1940s, fresh from his first year of college, to work as a seasonal ranger at the park's entry gate. As he was looking around the store, perhaps looking a little puzzled as to what he should buy to supply the larder in his one-room ranger cabin, Ida pointed out a few grocery items and said, "This is what you should have." One of the things that Chuck liked most about Ida was that "she talked to me as a person, not as a ranger." For all of his long life, Chuck Andersen considered Ida a friend and never forgot how Ida "had a way of guiding you." (Chuck eventually became a member of Ida's extended family when he married Wally Eagle's wife's sister, Joyce Rowse.) [42]

Ida's own children were not the only ones in need of feeding and care. Eagle's store, like most of Yellowstone's summer businesses, relied on seasonal help, who had to be fed and housed. Ida's typical day during busy summer months revolved around breakfast, lunch, and dinner for family and staff. There were so many people to feed at Eagle's Store that meals were usually served in shifts, which made for a long day of cooking. Ida was an expert at cooking over a woodstove, and huge pots of soup were one of her staple menu items. She became quite practiced at making delicious soups out of most anything and then stretching it to serve a crowd of any size.[43]

Ida initiated a long-enduring family convention with the strong work ethic that she and Sam instilled in their ten children. *Idleness* was not a word in the Eagle family vocabulary, and Ida gave each of the children daily chores as soon as they were old enough to handle a broom or reach the counter. Youngest child Wally chopped wood and mopped floors until he was old enough to wait on customers and sell his favorite merchandise: fishing tackle. As an adult Wally would become the originator of "Wally's Feather Duster," a popular fly for fisherman in the West Yellowstone area. To assemble his creation, Wally used an ostrich herl from a feather duster. One might wonder if Wally conjured up the idea for his famous fly as a young man when he was using his mother's feather duster for its original purpose, as a cleaning tool. His brother Joe swept floors at age five, while his sisters tended to soda fountain customers. Another responsibility of the boys was to keep the soda fountain stocked with blocks of ice from the ice house in back of the store. Long before automatic ice makers, the Eagles cut their ice from nearby Hebgen Lake during the winter, hauled it to the store by sled, and stored it in a cabin, which was really "two cabins built one inside the other, with sawdust between the walls to keep it cold." And all the boys took a turn at cranking the ice cream that had to be made fresh every day for the soda fountain. Ida made sure everyone did his or her share of the work.[44]

Bettie Eagle seemed to be the sibling whose work ethic most closely resembled Ida's. So much so that her taskmaster-style management, which she conducted with an endearing mix of humor and seriousness, earned her the nickname "The Whip." Former Eagle's Store employees remembered that Bettie had a true gift for endearing herself to the staff by tempering her firm "instructions on how to clerk in the store" with her "quick wit that kept us shocked and laughing." While she helped oversee the whole store, she took special pride in the operation of the soda fountain and would sometimes even get down on her hands and knees to scrub a spot off the floor. Even though she worked long hours, Bettie was known to "always come into work happily singing." Working hard even rubbed off on unsuspecting spouses such as Margaret, wife of Harold Eagle. After

This label for Mom Eagle's Chocolate Sauce may reveal the ingredients of her signature treat but not the recipe, which is still a closely guarded family secret.
(COURTESY EAGLE FAMILY)

spending a week working at Eagle's Store, Margaret fell ill and went to see a doctor. Not finding anything physically wrong with her, the doctor summed up his diagnosis as exhaustion and commented to her, "What are you trying to do? Work as hard as the Eagles?" Indeed, keeping up with the Eagle family was a task all its own.[45]

Another element of Ida's productive heritage appeared in the form of "Mom Eagle's" homemade chocolate sauce, which has become regionally famous and which the store still carries today. Just when she created her namesake chocolate sauce has remained a bit of a family mystery—or perhaps that hidden information is as much an ingredient to the success of the chocolate sauce as her signature recipe. When the time came for Ida to hand down her wooden spoon, she passed her secret chocolate sauce recipe to only a few close descendents. Today Ida's special formula and undisclosed ingredients remain carefully guarded by the family. However, a clue to one element of the mixture—here not revealed—was discovered when an employee was once scolded for washing the pan and thus ruining a part of Ida's "secret." With her delicious chocolate sauce Ida provided her family with one of life's special treats.[46]

Ida also made sure that she provided her children with the essential ingredients that would help them create their own recipes for successful lives. Along with that strong work ethic, Ida taught her children some core values. Those included strong senses of family, business, and faith, as well as other important ideals such as education, perseverance, and adaptability to change. Ida not only taught this ideology to her children, she and Sam lived by it too.[47]

Wisely, the Eagle children's education did not stop with high school. All of Ida's ten children attended Montana State College in Bozeman (today's Montana State University). Henry graduated first with the class of 1930 and Wally graduated twenty years later in 1950.

Sadly, Ida and Sam's fourth oldest son Bill did not get to enjoy the fulfillment of graduation. At the age of twenty-two, Bill succumbed to affects of an infection and died in 1936 while he was a senior at Montana State. Ida had faced multitudes of life's challenges but this tragedy deeply tested her strength and she chose to deal with Bill's death in solitude. According to family members, she went to her room, closed the door, and did not emerge for several days. Many of her family believed that Ida's broken heart from Bill's death never really mended.[48]

As the children began to grow up and go off to school, college, and after-graduation employment, Ida's end of season time in West Yellowstone began to change. By the mid-1930s, she began to feel her nest emptying. "It sure seems lonesome with all you kids gone," Ida wrote to son Ed. But Ida also found that she and Sam had more time to spend together and she would frequently go with him when he went fishing. According to her letter to Ed, Ida must have gone with Sam quite a bit as she wrote that she had "done a lot of stocking mending." In addition to writing frequent letters to her far-flung brood, one of Ida's favorite things to do was to go for a leisurely afternoon drive. "Pop and I have been going out riding every afternoon," Ida wrote to their son Ed, "as Bess is working afternoons and [there] is no business." In the same letter Ida apologized for not writing to him on Sunday, explaining that she and Sam had gone to Bozeman and got home late because they had returned via the Madison road. "I had only been over that road once about nineteen years ago," she wrote, "and it was such a beautiful summer day that it was a treat to be out." Not surprisingly that nineteen-year span was probably the busiest time in Ida's life with the store, post office, soda fountain, and a growing family all in full swing.

And Ida always looked forward to her one or two week "rest" in Long Beach, California, which she and Sam usually took in February. In a letter addressed to "Everybody," meaning all the children in school at Bozeman and under the care of the hired housekeeper, Ida passed on her motherly instruction from afar telling Harold to be sure to "close the garage door as someone might get your toboggan and advised "you kids keep warm and keep your feet dry." Even from her rented California apartment Ida kept a watchful eye over her entire family, at least as much as she could from a distance.[49]

But some things were out of her control. When Sam died suddenly from a heart attack in 1950, Ida's youngest son, Wally recalled that Ida repeated her solitary retreat to her room just as she had done after Bill's death, and remained there for days. Following Sam's passing away, ninth child Joe took over management of the store. After returning home from World War II and completing his education at Montana State College, Joe would serve for more than fifty years as the manager of Eagle's Store. At different points in their lives and different seasons of the year, nearly every Eagle family member worked at the store. Bettie and Wally, employed in Bozeman during the school year as librarian and teacher respectively,

A lot of years and life had passed by before Ida posed for this elegant portrait in the 1940s, probably the first since her wedding photograph in 1908.
(COURTESY EAGLE FAMILY)

worked during the summer months. Joe's wife Kay, a former "Beanery Queen" (Union Pacific Railroad dining room waitress) and Wally's wife Frankie also became involved in the store's operation. And just as her children had been given daily chores, so too have Ida's grandchildren received them.[50]

As Ida's retirement approached, her children and grandchildren began to take over responsibility of the store, and technology brought television to West Yellowstone in the 1950s. From that point on, Ida's Saturday evenings were reserved for watching Lawrence Welk, sometimes with one or more of her granddaughters, Susan Eagle Reynolds, Delia Eagle Voitoff Bauman, Betsy Eagle Steadman, or Joan Eagle Goldstein.[51]

On August 17, 1959, the Eagle's Store, Ida, and the Eagle family weathered one of Mother Nature's most frightening convulsions: an earthquake. Fifty-four years earlier Ida had been spared the devastation of the San Francisco earthquake because she had been ninety miles away, but in 1959, she experienced the terror of a big quake in Montana. The epicenter of the 7.5 Richer scale earthquake that struck at 11:37 P.M. was just fifteen miles north of West Yellowstone. Carl Eagle, Ida's grandson, recollected that he had been trying to quietly creep up the stairs to his sleeping quarters after returning from a movie when the quake hit. The intensity of the tremors seemed to throw the stairs right out from under his feet. In a letter to his parents, San (Bud) and Jean Eagle, Carl wrote that "windows cracked, lights fell, and the building rolled" before the power went off and panic set in. The store he declared "looked right garish" with piles of "postcards, comic books, magazines, and broken Frankoma pottery ankle deep." Former employee Dick Post recalled that "every bottle of Pepto-Bismol broke and the contents covered everything." Dick and most of the other employees spent the night cleaning the store, while tensing in readiness for the next aftershock. Ida's son Wally remembered the aftershocks lasted for days, and those shocks turned the town's streets into waves of undulating pavement. Amazingly, the soda fountain endured the tremendous shaking without one broken "pillow tile." While the interior of Eagle's Store suffered minor breakage and damage, the Eagle family and Ida's heritage survived intact.[52]

When Ida Eagle died on September 24, 1962, she left behind six sons, three daughters, twenty-three grandchildren, and a sister, Helen Goss of Seattle. But she also left behind an impressive family legacy. Behind every busy man is usually an even busier woman, and Ida Eagle exemplified this rule. Performing multiple roles as business partner, wife, and mother, Ida was a major contributor in keeping Eagle's Store on a continual track of success. Bolstered by her steadfast character and her signature stoicism, Ida helped steer the store through multiple noteworthy events, which included the arrival of the railroad and multitudes of park visitors; the admission of automobiles that brought even more visitors; two World Wars and the Great Depression that nearly stopped all park travel; and the earthquake of 1959 that traumatized the town of West Yellowstone. No stranger to life's challenges, Ida persevered through it all with dignity and grace. To friends and family who saw her in good times and bad times,

Ida was stoic. To bachelor rangers in need of a grocery-shopping assistant, she was protective. To multitudes of employees whom she watched over, she was patient. To hosts of tourists in need of guidance, she was helpful. No matter the association, Ida Christine Carlson Eagle, "Mom Eagle," endeared herself in one way or another to nearly everyone who crossed the threshold of her store and her life.[53]

Today Ida's legacy lives on with those she left behind. Brimming with a touching love of family, the Eagles and their store continue to radiate a deeply-held sense of place that began with Ida, Sam, Henry, Ed, Helen, Bud, Bill, Bettie, Rose, Harold, Joe, and Wally, and which continues today with the even larger extended Eagle family. At 10 A.M. and 3 P.M. on any given day during the summer season, you will find an Eagle or two at the soda fountain having coffee or savoring the traditional family treat—ice cream with "Mom Eagle's Homemade Chocolate Sauce"—and keeping Ida's legacy alive.

Willie Frances Crawford Bronner

(1872–1948)

and

Jean Crawford Sharpe

(1900–1992)

Like Mother, Like Daughter

Jean Crawford Sharpe and her mother Willie Frances Bronner probably epitomized the many Yellowstone employees, including a good number of women, who lived and worked in Yellowstone National Park during stagecoach days. Many stories of these early "savages" were not recorded and their park memories unfortunately died with them. Jean's chronicle of working and living in the park for several years at various locations is a rare and vivid reflection of what may have been typical of life in the park from 1909 to 1917. Moreover, her forty-one-page narrative of recollections and entertaining anecdotes provides us with a unique opportunity to understand life for the park's lesser known workforce, to learn about early forms of leisure activities, and to re-experience the spirit of a bygone era that meant so much to those who lived it.

In her reminiscences titled "This Is Me and This Is What I Remember: A Yellowstone Story 1908–1917," Jean Crawford Sharpe vividly recalled watching her mother, Willie Frances Crawford, transform from a woman of "timid insecurity" to a "self-confident, independent person." After enduring nineteen years of marriage and bearing five children with William Denson Crawford, Willie Frances's world changed completely when the couple divorced around 1908. Confronted with the reality of earning her own living, Willie Frances was suddenly faced with being the sole provider for her eight-year-old daughter Jean, the youngest of her five children. In her daughter's eyes, Willie Frances's courage was enormous as she embarked on a new adventure of working in Yellowstone National Park in the summer of 1908. Jean believed whole-heartedly that the practical experience her mother gained while working in the park through the next nine years immeasurably helped Willie Frances to re-define and re-create her herself. Moreover, Jean believed that her mother's newfound ability to realize her capabilities, strengths, and talents enabled her to confidently navigate through her life.[1]

Somewhat invisible in Jean's memoir is her own development from wide-eyed child to blossoming adolescent under the spell of Yellowstone. Yet, Jean's picturesque glimpses into life in the vast landscape of Yellowstone, both cultural and natural, reveal the personal values that grounded her and reflect the sensory experiences that influenced her perspectives on life. For nearly nine years, mother Willie Frances and daughter Jean were charmed by the friendly, harmonious work and social life in America's last best place. Together, they experienced the last vestiges of Yellowstone's idyllic stagecoach era and witnessed the beginning of the clattering motor car era. And also together, they found what mattered in life: people, places, and special memories.

Born on July 4, 1872, in Independence, Missouri, Willie Frances was the fourth of six children born to William Henry Francis Marion (1835-1927) and Elizabeth Jan Van Hoose (1837-1926). Her father, a Tennessean by birth, and her mother, whose native state was Kentucky, were married in Washington County, Arkansas, on November 18, 1861. The couple began on married life at the onset of the Civil War (1861-1865) with William serving as an ambulance driver for the army and Elizabeth frequently accompanying her husband into the battlefields. At the end of the war, William and Elizabeth started their family in Arkansas, with Lena Annette arriving on September 20, 1865. Elizabeth delivered their first-born son Henry Monroe on January 23, 1868. Their third child, Lydia Louise, was born in 1870.[2]

William and Elizabeth's southern heritage probably influenced their decision to remain in Arkansas at the end of the war, but the economic instability of a failed government reconstruction program may have altered their life plans. The Civil War and its aftermath disrupted nearly every family in the United States, especially those in the South, and was largely responsible for the westward migration of thousands of southerners. William and Elizabeth likely deemed it prudent to find a more financially viable area for their growing family, and moved westward in the early 1870s. The Marion family eventually settled in Montana, where Willie Frances's two younger sisters were born, Mable Florence in 1875 and Anna Laura in 1878. An 1880 census confirmed that eight-year-old Willie Frances and her family were living in West Gallatin, Montana, and that her father was employed as a carpenter. Her parents relocated several more times through the next few decades, living in Kansas, Oklahoma, and Washington. In the mid-1920s they relocated one more time to California, where her mother Elizabeth died in 1926 and father William followed in 1927. Both were buried in a family plot in Santa Ana, California.[3]

At seventeen, Willie Frances Marion married William Denson Crawford in Fayetteville, Arkansas on October 31, 1889. By early 1900, the couple's family had grown to include four children: Linley Roy, age nine; Minnie Rose, age eight; Clifton Elizabeth, age six; and William Earnest, age four; with yet one more baby on the way. By the time she became a mother for the fifth time on August 13, 1900, with the birth of Ora Eugenia (Jean) in Cisco, Arkansas, Willie Frances had been married for ten years and was living in Prairie, Arkansas.[4]

After Jean's birth the family record became imprecise, but by 1908 the union between Willie Frances and William Crawford had dissolved, and Willie Frances along with youngest daughter Jean moved to Montana. Her other children, who by this time ranged in age from eighteen years to twelve years, apparently remained in Arkansas either on their own or with their father. William Crawford lived out his days in Arkansas and died in 1952 at the age of eighty-seven.[5]

In the summer of 1908, Willie Frances applied for a Yellowstone National Park job through a recruiter for Wylie Permanent Camping Company in Bozeman, Montana. When asked if she ever cooked for large groups, Willie Frances's reply of having supplied meals for crews of threshers in Arkansas secured her a position as an assistant to the head cook of Wylie's Swan Lake Camp. For Willie Frances, the opportunity to work in the serene seclusion of Yellowstone must have seemed like an idyllic reprieve from her disjointed life. She wasted no time in accepting.

Leaving Jean in Bozeman with friends, Willie Frances made her way from Bozeman to Gardiner, Montana, at the north entrance of the park and then into Yellowstone.

A seasonal Yellowstone touring operation, which included both transportation and accommodations, the Wylie Permanent Camping Company operated eight camps and lunch stations throughout the park. Swan Lake was the first camp on its grand tour that departed from the north entrance. The camp consisted of dozens of gaily striped sleeping tents, a large dining room tent, a fully-equipped kitchen tent, a sizable office tent complete with extra writing desks, and a store tent, where candy, gum, cigars, and postcards were sold.[6]

With the arrival of the railroad in 1883, Yellowstone initially became a vacation destination for the wealthy. As recreational tourism grew throughout America, Yellowstone became famous as a place that travelers from all income levels could experience. By the late 1890s, options for touring the park other than via stagecoach-hotel tour had become available. One such was provided by the Wylie Permanent Camping Company. This type of coaching and camping operation allowed middle-class Americans to visit Yellowstone National Park at a reasonable cost. A six-and-a-half-day tour with Wylie offered visitors great value at thirty-five dollars, and included a boat ride across to Lake Camp—as opposed to the five-day hotel tour that cost fifty dollars plus a boat fee. The operation made no pretense to elaborate services or elegant furnishings, but instead offered "low prices as a great convenience to thousands of people who hardly feel able to bear the expense of such a trip."[7]

According to hundreds of testimonials collected yearly by the company's marketing department, few travelers with the Wylie Permanent Camping Company were ever disappointed. Many of the company's guests could have afforded the hotel tour, but chose Wylie because of the company's attention to good meals, clean camps, and high-quality service.[8]

That was something the Wylie operation worked at attaining and valued very highly. Their hiring of middle-class employees became a notable and visible feature. Many Wylie guests were impressed by the caliber and refinement of the Wylie staff, which consisted of schoolteachers and principals, lawyers and doctors, college students, and others from various professional trades. The camping company held hiring fairs throughout the country and hired people from nearly every state in the union. As

Willie Frances discovered, nearly every employee was hand picked for his/ her ability as well as his/her talent to mentor newcomers to Yellowstone. That summer of 1908, she worked under the tutelage of Nell Schwartz from Red Wing, Minnesota. Nell took Willie Frances under her wing, and the two women developed a friendship that lasted well into their later years. As Jean was not there to observe the summer's events, most of her mother's day-to-day activities and other friendships were not recorded. However, at some point during the summer, Willie Frances met Wylie coach driver Charlie Hardenbrook and was smitten.[9]

Charles Clyde Hardenbrook, born on September 11, 1873, originally hailed from Bedford, Iowa. After finishing high school in his hometown, he attended college in Monmouth, Illinois, where he studied business. Around 1897, Charlie secured a position as transportation assistant and coach driver with the Wylie Permanent Camps Company, then run by its founder William Wallace Wylie. Many Wylie guests considered Charlie one of the most pleasant and obliging drivers of the company. At the end of a tour in 1901, one tourist wrote, "Here we took leave of our friend and driver Charlie; whose uniform courtesy, politeness, and accommodating disposition did as much to make our trip the unalloyed round of pleasure that it was."[10] Loving his job, Charlie continued working for the company after Wylie sold it to Livingston businessman A.W. Miles in 1905. By 1908, Charlie was the manager of the transportation department for the renamed Wylie Permanent Camping Company.[11]

Willie Frances and Charlie apparently met at the Wylie Swan Lake Camp and spent time together during the course of the short but busy summer season. At least one photograph in Jean's memoir depicted Charlie with Willie Frances as well as another unidentified man and woman enjoying a picnic. Charlie's agreeable character that always seemed to charm his tour patrons must have made quite an impression on Willie Frances. On December 30, 1908, she and Charlie were married. But sadly, Willie Frances's second chance on love and life proved to be short lived.

"A Sudden Death," announced the *Bedford Free Press* on April 29, 1909. Even though he was only thirty-five years old, Charlie had died suddenly from a heart attack on April 26, 1909, shocking his mother, father, sisters, brothers, and devastating his bride of only four months. Within the next few days, Willie Frances, now a 36-year-old widow, stoically made arrangements to transport his body and herself to his family's home in

Bedford, Iowa. Following the funeral service on April 30, Mrs. Willie Frances Hardenbrook buried her husband as well as her hopes and dreams of their future together in Bedford's Fairview Cemetery.[12]

Returning to Bozeman, Willie Frances again marshaled all of her courage and headed back to Yellowstone for the summer season of 1909. This year would be very different as she assumed the position of Matron of the Swan Lake Camp. Each of the Wylie camps hired women to serve as matrons, or hostesses, who catered to the needs or whims (as the case might be) of the guests, and supervised the staff of women assigned to her. In addition to attending to the comfort of all the camp guests, the camp matron was charged with providing a sense of security for unescorted female travelers. The matron would greet each incoming stage coach at the platform with an air of professionalism "dressed in her business-like shirtwaist and long skirt, high button shoes, and a sailor hat pinned firmly to her Gibson-girl pompadour." This welcoming presence became a characteristic feature of the Wylie camps' hospitality and was sincerely valued by thousands of tenderfoot travelers. After punching their tickets for the Swan Lake Camp, the matron dispensed assignments and assisted guests to their wilderness quarters. She then worked with the camp manager and helped direct the camp boys loading luggage from the canvas or leather "boot" on the back of the coach and delivering it to waiting guests. As the matron of Swan Lake, Willie Frances was beginning her life anew, but this time she shared it with Jean.[13]

Arriving at the beginning of the season, nearly nine-year-old Jean was amazed by the camp's hustle and bustle. Vast numbers of men and horses hauled in materials, food, and other supplies in preparation for the arrival of hundreds of tourists expected that summer. Jean watched with delight as the storehouses, constructed of huge logs without windows and secured with heavy doors and steel locks, were opened and stocked. The storehouses became some of Jean's favorite places, because they smelled deliciously of prunes, dried apples, and coconut.

Adding even more flavor to Jean's first summer in Yellowstone was the prospect of learning a new language, lingo actually. The Wylie Camps as well as the hotels began hiring countless numbers of college students for seasonal summer help as early as the 1890s. Living, working, and playing with their fellow college students in the remote environment of Yellowstone led these fun-loving young thinkers to believe that they were

This 1909 photograph of the Wylie Camping Company Swan Lake matron's tent does not identify the two women sitting inside. However, Willie Frances was the matron of the camp that year and the woman on the left bears a striking resemblance to the photocopied images of Willie Frances in her daughter Jean's memoir. (COURTESY UNIVERSITY OF UTAH)

part of a distinct social group and that they should have a specialized vocabulary. They developed terms for their work, recreation, tourists, and for Yellowstone itself.

One of the earliest monikers used to identify park employees was that of "savage." While most Yellowstone historians believe that the usage of the term began earlier than the 1890s and its origin is unknown, a linguistics researcher in the 1930s proposed an interesting idea for the name's origin. She postulated that these college students, who lived in tents during the season, felt a certain kinship with Native Americans and that they honored their summer lifestyle by calling themselves "savages." While this suggestion to date has not yet been proven historically accurate, it remains an entertaining notion nonetheless.[14]

In addition to naming themselves, the "savages," the employees also gave their work positions playful expressions. The laundry workers became "bubble kings and queens," maids were styled "pillow-punchers," waitresses turned into "heavers," and dishwashers were coined "pearl divers." Everyone in Yellowstone acquired a lighthearted nickname. Tourists, no matter where they hailed from, were "dudes," stagecoach drivers were "bos," and soldiers were "swaddies."[15] Becoming familiar with and in-the-know about these humorous terms was akin to a rite of passage for Yellowstone employees that continued well into the 1950s. Even though she was not yet an official "savage," Jean felt privileged to be part of this high-spirited linguistic novelty, which only added to her adventures.

Jean's summer was filled with outdoor adventures. She learned to ride "ol' Charlie," the aged white camp horse who pulled the garbage cart or hauled fallen timber down the hill for the nightly campfire. "Ol' Charlie" also expanded her Yellowstone playground and, on one occasion, Jean found herself farther down the road than she was supposed to go. Entranced an endless profusion of brilliant blue gentian wildflowers that blanketed the roadway and unaware that she had wandered several miles from camp, Jean slid off the horse to pick a few flowers. With bouquet in hand and ready to return home, Jean then realized she had forgotten she was too little to get back into the saddle without help. Not the least bit flustered, she walked all the way back to camp leading "ol' Charlie." Exhilarated by the crisp Yellowstone air and her prized posy of wildflowers, Jean felt that she "probably was the happiest child in the world."

Jean was not the only child at Swan Lake that summer. Mr. Miller, the camp manager, brought his small daughter, who was about Jean's age, for a visit. The Miller family invited Jean to join them on a tour of the park. She was thrilled with the opportunity to see Old Faithful, Yellowstone Lake, and the Grand Canyon of the Yellowstone River. Unfortunately, while at Wylie's Old Faithful Camp near Grotto Geyser where they stayed on the first night, both Jean and the Miller's daughter fell ill and were put to bed. In the middle of the night, they were awakened by someone announcing that Giant Geyser was erupting. Knowing that Giant only erupted once every ten days or so, the two little girls begged to go watch it. But Mrs. Miller, thinking their health was of greater importance, insisted that they stay put and consoled them by saying, "You will be sick of geysers before we are through." While staying in bed seemed prudent at the time, Jean lamented later in life that in all her eighty-five years she never saw Giant Geyser erupt.

The evening campfire in all the Wylie camps was the crowning glory of an eventful day for employees as well as guests. The Swan Lake campfire was formed in the center of the camp using tall scrub pines and fallen timber. The camp boys stood the trees on end, pointing them inward to form a tipi. Lastly, in preparation for the evening program, the camp boys placed benches in a circle around the campfire. As there was no one person specifically assigned to conduct the campfire entertainment, Willie Frances served as social director that summer. She inspired the singing of songs that most everyone knew such as "Suwannee River," "Dixie," Yankee Doodle," "My Bonnie Lies Over the Ocean," and "In the Good Old Summertime." Jean remembered that some of the singers would try and sneak in some of their "naughty" favorites such as "I Wonder Who's Kissing Her Now," and "Oh Gee Be Sweet to Me, Kid!" Whatever the songs and whatever the crowd, the evening campfire was a perfect banquet of fun.

In addition to jovial singers gathered around the campfire, there were also captivating storytellers. One tale about a freight wagon that had been loaded with meat and was torn apart by a grizzly bear sent hair-raising shivers up Jean's spine as well as those of the novice campers who later that night would go to bed concerned that they had only canvas walls to protect them. Then there were the more true-to-life tales such as the story about a bear cub that fell out of a tree and landed on a clothesline full of one of the waitresses' laundry. In his fright and surprise, the cub was last seen high-tailing it over the hill with his two front legs stuck in a pair of ruffled drawers.

Willie Frances even got in on the action of laundry-stealing bears. One night she was sure that she saw a big brown paw reach inside the back flap of her tent and take her flannel night gown. Several mornings later, the camp boys returned from firewood gathering and sauntered into camp flying Willie Frances's nightgown from the end of a long pole. Her nightgown, which was covered with hair, had been found flattened on the ground like it had been slept on. Jean confessed that, "Willie Frances never lived down the story that a bear had slept in her nightgown." This story undoubtedly was added to Wylie's repertoire of campfire tales.

Campfires, singing, and storytelling were not the only form of entertainment at the Swan Lake Camp. There also were dances. The dances were held in one of the storehouses, where a mix of tourists and employees would dance to the tune of a small portable organ (pumped by foot) or mouth organ or sometimes a fiddler. Willie Frances was the music maker and there was "many a night when she wore out both her arms and feet playing that terrible organ so that others could dance." Jean loved listening to the quadrille caller who could "always be counted on to the keep the dancers in a state of excitement." This entertaining scene mesmerized Jean as she listened to the music and watched dancing for the first time in her young life. The evening entertainment always ended with one final waltz followed by the time-honored farewell tune, "Good Night, Ladies."

In too brief a time, the shortened hours of daylight and the brisk breezes of September signaled the end of summer and the time for Jean and Willie Frances to leave Swan Lake. If Jean was melancholy about leaving, it was short-lived as she found the coach ride to the train station thrilling. She sat up on top with the driver and he taught her to drive. When it was safe to do so, he would let her hold the reins, and showed her which fingers went over and which ones went under when managing the eight lines of a four-horse team. While Jean had her own reasons for being fascinated by Yellowstone's stagecoach drivers, Willie Frances had also become charmed by one driver in particular.

Yellowstone stagecoach drivers were considered a breed of their own. Each driver brandished his unique character with his lively signature narrative of the park's history and explanation of its natural features. "Geyser Bob" Edgar believed that being entertaining during his five-day tour with the same group was more important than being factual. He became famous for his tall tale of falling into Old Faithful Geyser and being spit out five miles away, and another yarn wherein he claimed that his horses shrank down to ponies because they had been submerged in Alum Creek. Another stagecoach driver, Charles Van Tassell, soft-pedaled his yarns by insisting that he told only "truthful lies," and even compiled his commentary into a popular pamphlet of the day. Colorful and imaginative, the charismatic stage drivers of Yellowstone eventually garnered world-wide reputations as being original characters right out of the Old West. While Willie Frances never divulged what magical feature of driver Billy (Blondie) Bronner drew him to her, she evidently found him personally appealing and they married in Bozeman in 1910.

For reasons not revealed in Jean's memoir, Willie Frances did not work in the park during the seasons of 1910 through 1912. But, by 1913, the lure of Yellowstone prevailed, and both mother and daughter once again returned to the park. This time the whole experience would take a different turn as Willie Frances chose to work for a different concessioner. Instead of going back to work for the Wylie Company, Willie Frances accepted a new position with the Yellowstone Park Transportation Company (the largest transportation company in the park) as the manager of the Canyon Mess Hall. The mess provided meals for stagecoach drivers and presumably a few other employees as well, and required a crew of workers in addition to the manager. As this was a contract job, Willie Frances could choose her own staff, and so twelve-year-old Jean was employed to help take care of the dining room in the mess hall.[16]

A substantial new building, the Canyon Mess contained a sizeable dining room, a large kitchen and pantry, quarters for Willie Frances and Jean, and an additional room for other female workers. Nearby was a separate building that had a bath room and a large wood room, stacked high with split wood for the huge wood-burning kitchen range, as well as quarters for the male help. Although the mess hall was well equipped for 1913, there was no refrigeration. Large chunks of ice delivered every day from the Canyon Hotel were the only way of keeping any fresh food from spoiling. Primarily, food supplies consisted of ample quantities of canned foods and canned milk. Due to the length of time to transport grocery items by freight wagon into the park, it was not feasible to acquire fresh fruits, vegetables, and milk. Whatever they lacked in fresh produce, Willie Frances made up with loaves of bread kneaded by hand, great beef roasts, and piles of fluffy mashed potatoes with smooth brown gravy, whole hams and pans of escalloped potatoes, and fresh baked apple pies and berry cobblers. Willie Frances even made her own blackberry jam from gallon cans of berries because there just "had to be jam for the hot biscuits that she frequently made for breakfast."

The mess, which served three meals a day, kept Jean busy nearly all day long. At mealtime Jean was responsible for serving food in family-style bowls and platters, pouring coffee, and slicing home-made bread. After the satisfied drivers departed, she removed the dirty dishes and scrubbed the white oil-cloth, which was tacked to the tables, and set up for the next meal. At the end of the day, Jean recorded the menus that had been served that day and mindfully noted to herself that if anyone ever looked back on those menus, they would have seen some "mighty good meals."

Around midsummer, Jean's seventeen-year old brother, William "Paddy" Earnest Crawford, joined them at the Canyon. It is unknown whether his appearance was by chance or whether the shortage of employees that season had elicited an invitation from his mother to come and help out. Whatever the reason, Paddy was gratefully welcomed and immediately put to work keeping the wood range stoked and swabbing dishes for which he was paid thirty dollars a month. While she enjoyed her newfound summertime friends, Jean was thrilled to have her brother to pal around with for the rest of the summer.

Even though they worked hard every day, Jean and Paddy took advantage of their youth and enjoyed afternoon outings on horseback into the park whenever there was a slow day or a spare hour. On one occasion they packed a lunch, saddled up their horses, and headed for the top of Mount Washburn. With their well-shod horses picking their footing over washes and rocks, Jean and Paddy made their way up the steep and winding trail. The youthful excursionists were rewarded for taking this strenuous journey with a breathtaking view from the 10,000-foot summit of Mount Washburn, and a spectacular lunch spot. Returning they followed a different route and came across a "glorious field of flowers." The magnificent sight of acres and acres of bright-red paintbrush became so etched in their minds that, seventy years later, both Jean and Paddy fondly remembered that day.

One of Jean's other pleasures was to visit the new Canyon Hotel, a half mile away, and wander around the elegant structure. The third hostelry built at the Canyon and completed in 1912, the Canyon Hotel was a massive building of incredible proportions that was a full mile in circumference. The sprawling edifice awed everyone from guests to employees. From the high unloading platform with covered porte-cochere for arriving stagecoach guests, to the beautiful lobby and expansive dining room to the huge lower-level ballroom, Jean assessed the hotel to be "modern and new-fangled in comparison to the Inn at Old Faithful." Looking down the wide, divided stairway in the lobby, Jean gazed into the elegant ballroom, never dreaming that only four years later she would be there dancing the tango or the fox trot to the music of a live orchestra.

After a summer of keeping the mess dining room clean and waiting on tables, for which she was also paid thirty dollars a month, Jean beamed, "I felt rich when I left in the Fall." But she also left Yellowstone rich in experiences and friends. While she worked hard that summer and looked forward to the end of the season, Jean also noted that there was a sense of sadness in saying "good-bye to a few friends that you might never see again." But she vowed to come back. Like so many of today's employees, she explained that "there was something about working in Yellowstone that was addictive and by the next year we would be anxious to come back and do it all over again."

And come back they did! At the end of the school year, with Jean finishing eighth grade and Paddy completing his junior year of high school, the two youthful and loyal Yellowstone workers looked forward to embarking on another exciting summer in the park with their mother. Leaving from Missoula, where they now resided, Jean, Paddy, and Willie Frances boarded a Northern Pacific train bound for Livingston in the late spring of 1914. Their stepfather, Billy Bronner, who was employed full-time with Montana Power Company would join them later for a short time to do what he loved best, driving tours around the park. Arriving in Gardiner on the train the following morning, the threesome were met by Yellowstone Park Transportation Company coaches and within a short time were all on their way to their new assignments at the Norris Mess Hall.[17]

The Norris location was quite a change from the Canyon. As opposed to the new and bright Canyon mess hall that sat on a sunny hilltop, the Norris Mess Hall was an old, rustic, crudely built building that was dimly lit and cheerless. The geyser basin was an acidic thermal area of mud pots, geysers, steaming springs, and spouting holes that filled the air with a heavy scent of sulfur, to which—incredibly—through the course of the summer they grew accustomed. But according to Jean "they "were too busy to be anything but cheerful."

The summer season started out roughly with very little help. Nonetheless they never let their spirits dampen. They made new friends and within a short time, old friends began appearing. Jean said that "it was not long before the reward for all the hard work began" with the close-knit staff at Norris organizing dancing, surrey rides, campfires, singing, horseback riding, and exploring. In addition to those pleasures, Jean experienced one other additional reward, when she developed a "phenomenal relationship with a bear family that summer, which lasted through 1915."

One day early in the 1914 season, a mother black bear and her two new cubs ambled into the clearing behind Jean's mess hall. As with most wild animals, she cautiously kept herself between the cubs and Jean. Never approaching her, Jean stood in the doorway and quietly talked to the mother bear. Slowly she became braver and moved a little closer,

*These bear twins depicted on a popularly sold postcard could possibly be the
yearling bear cubs, Archibald and Percival that Jean became acquainted with
in 1914.* (COURTESY YELLOWSTONE NATIONAL PARK DIGITAL SLIDE FILE 11538)

but still maintained a safe distance from Jean and her other coworkers
who gathered near the doorway. However, as mama watched guardedly,
the two playful cubs pressed their fearlessness and romped toward Jean
looking for something good to eat. In time, the mother bear became more
trusting and came closer, even to the point of licking syrup out of a pan
while Jean held it for her. Now that they were on a friendly basis, Jean
named the two cubs Archibald and Percival and the mother Jenny.

It would be Jenny and her two yearlings, Percival and Archibald, who
greeted Jean and Willie Frances when they returned to Norris for the 1915
season.[18] While the cubs were less rambunctious than the year before,
their new helper Mabel Peterson took one look at the three bears in the

backyard and ran off screaming to the mess hall, where she remained for the rest of the season. "No bears for Mabel," a bemused Jean observed.

Typically, finding staff to work at Norris presented little difficulty, but upon occasion Willie Frances would find herself in need of an additional helper. One day a stranger appeared at the mess house door. He appeared neat and clean, wore dark pants and a white shirt, and announced the reason for his call: "Mrs. Bronner. I've heard you need some good help and I can do that for you. I am a baker and a good cook and I want the job." Willie Frances invited the young man in to discuss his qualifications over dinner. By the time he finished his plate, George Ray had a new job. He proved to be the best coworker Willie Frances and Jean ever had. In addition to being a fast worker and an expert cook, he took over the hard job of kneading the bread and shared other chores with Jean.

Jean was thrilled to experience the baking of huge batches of bread, sometimes ten or twelve loaves at a time. On the preceding night, Ray and Jean would set out the aromatic yeast in the pantry. Overnight the dissolved yeast, along with a small amount of flour, created the dough for their bread. The next morning they added more flour, which produced a huge pan of dough that thrilled them with a "heavenly aroma that permeated the air." After the huge pan of dough that had been set aside and doubled in size, Jean began to knead the dough. Then she formed the dough into loaves, placed it into greased loaf pans, covered the pans with towels, and set them aside to rise for one last time. Finally, she brushed the light and puffy dough with melted butter and placed the loaves in the oven. In this era, before the advent of heat-controlled electric or gas ranges, baking bread in a wood-burning oven demanded Jean's constant and watchful eye for twenty-five to thirty minutes to insure that the fire was kept at just the right temperature. When the glistening, crusty brown loaves came out of the oven, Jean thought that she had never smelled such a marvelous scent.

Jean's delicious loaves of bread were not the only things rising in Yellowstone that summer; so were the hands of visitors in the park's fifth stagecoach robbery. On July 9, 1915, the last of Yellowstone's stage holdups occurred about a mile south of Madison Junction. A twelve-mile string of Yellowstone & Western coaches had just departed from the west entrance after picking up passengers from the Union Pacific Depot in West Yellowstone, Montana. In order to keep Yellowstone's all-pervasive road dust from covering visitors and drivers alike, stagecoach departures occurred at timed intervals, leaving about a mile between each string. By this time, road agents were well acquainted with this procedure and used it to their benefit. Letting the first stagecoach pass by, an unmasked bandit stopped the second coach. After relieving the passengers of their cash and jewelry, the robber sent the coach down the road and awaited the arrival of the next one. The road agent had robbed only five coaches when his game was discovered by photographer F. Jay Haynes, president of the Yellowstone & Western Stage Company, who had been traveling the same route in his private surrey. Without alerting the highwayman, Haynes turned his surrey around and headed back to the Madison Junction road camp to notify army officials. At about the same time, a visitor, Mr. Rice, jumped from one of the stopped stagecoaches and ran back to warn oncoming coaches. The robber shot at Rice, but missed. Probably realizing that he was in danger of being discovered, the bandit disappeared into the forest with his measly two hundred dollars in loot and vanished into one of the mysterious pages of Yellowstone history. The famous financier Bernard Baruch, who was thrilled to be part of a outwardly wild west adventure, declared: "It was the best $50 I ever spent." Even though Jean was not a witness to the robbery and heard only the stories that abounded after the episode, she agreed that it was "the most exciting event in 1915."[19]

On August 1, 1915, private automobiles were legally allowed into Yellowstone National Park for the first time. For many automobile enthusiasts, gaining entry into America's first national park was the most exciting event of 1915. But for others, such as Jean, it signaled the end of an extraordinary era. She believed that it was real horsepower that made the park live and breathe, and found the transition to motor cars distressing. She feared for the wild animals that she thought would retreat deep into the woods in terror of the clattering motor cars. In Jean's view, it was the freight horses, stagecoach horses, saddle horses, pack horses, and buggy and surrey teams that made the whole park work in tandem with nature. While she knew intellectually that the wilderness would still be there, Jean believed that the entry of automobiles into Yellowstone disrupted the serenity and solitude of the park's forests and mountains.

Departing in September, Willie Frances and Jean cleaned up and locked the hut and boarded the company's four-horse wagon for one last coach ride. Both happy to be going home and sad to leave Yellowstone,

*The Gardiner train station, designed by Robert Reamer, architect
of the Old Faithful Inn, greeted arriving passengers in all types
of weather with its graceful, curved log portico.*
(COURTESY YELLOWSTONE NATIONAL PARK DIGITAL SLIDE FILE)

Jean took her seat next to the driver, a habit she had formed when she was
eight. But now, at age fifteen, the prospect of sitting next to the driver held
a different charm, especially if the driver was one of the "young ones that
had a special twinkle in his eye." While she had learned to hold the lines
at age eight, holding the lines as a teenage girl meant that the driver had to
"hold her hand as he put each line over or under her fingers and instructed
her to guide the horses by certain touches." For Jean, that was "doubly
exciting." By the time Jean and Willie Frances returned to Yellowstone,
bright yellow busses had replaced the yellow horse-drawn coaches and
the twinkling eyed coach drivers had been replaced with college-age auto
enthusiasts in jaunty caps.

In 1917, Willie Frances, now forty-five years old, decided that she wanted
to spend one more summer in Yellowstone, so naturally Jean accompanied
her.[20] Arriving at the Gardiner train station, mother and daughter were
met by the Yellowstone Park Transportation Company's official buses.
Specifically designed for Yellowstone, the long touring vehicles sported an
open canvas top with several rows of seats, each having its own access door.

The "gear jammers," or bus drivers, were mostly city boys who were fascinated with cars and relished the idea of getting paid to drive around Yellowstone for the summer. A few horsemen came back and tried their hand at learning to drive motor cars, but few made the transition successfully. One horseman who successfully made the transition to motor cars admitted later that his biggest challenge was learning not to yell, "Whoa" when he wanted to stop, and "Get up" when he wanted to go.[21]

That year all transportation in Yellowstone was motorized. In addition to busses that replaced stagecoaches, motorcycles replaced horses for National Park Service ranger patrols, and panel trucks replaced freight wagons. For Willie Frances and Jean, this meant faster delivery times and increased availability of fresh vegetables, fruits, and milk to enhance menu offerings at their new location.

Willie Frances and Jean were assigned to the Canyon Mess Hall for the summer, the place where Jean had begun her Yellowstone work life. Jean began her day rising early in the chilly dawn hours, slipping into cold clothes, and dashing to the warmth of the big, wood-burning kitchen range in the mess house. The fire was already crackling and heating the grill top where hot cakes would soon be cooked. She set about boiling coffee in enormous pots, frying bacon in large pans with long handles, and poaching eggs in bacon grease. After flipping hotcakes when they were golden brown and placing them on platters in the large warming-oven to keep them hot, Jean would run out the front door to the big steel triangle hanging from the eaves and bang it loudly with an iron bar. The clanging stirred the drivers and sent them "charging across the meadow, shivering from the cold, anxious for the hot coffee and hot cakes to start the day." Many of the friendly ones would crowd around the stove in the kitchen to warm up, but one driver in particular caught Jean's attention.

Jake Skjold was a tall, blond, young man from Fargo, North Dakota, where he taught dancing during the winter months. The mess-house dining room had an old portable Victrola, so Jake, with his own collection of records, offered to teach Jean some of the popular dance steps. Pushing one of the tables to the side of the room, Jake began her instruction with the tango. Jean was thrilled. She had attended dances at her high school and at Columbia Gardens in Butte, but no one knew how to tango. Once she felt confident enough, Jean and Jake went to the Canyon Hotel ballroom, where the orchestra would play their special music. In her mind's eye, Jean imagined that she and Jake were the only dancers in the world as they whirled around the beautiful ballroom. Jean lamented later that, after she and Jake went their separate ways, she never found another partner who knew how to tango.

Even though she was tickled with her new activities, Jean still enjoyed one of her old pastimes, horseback riding. Although most everything had been motorized in the park, there were still some saddle horses available for the occasional tourist desiring an old-fashioned horseback trip, or for employees looking for an afternoon ride. One day when the work load was light, Willie Frances allowed Jean and two other workers—Elton and Ray—to go off on an afternoon excursion. The trio packed a lunch and headed for the Grand Canyon. They rode down a seldom-used trail on the west side of the canyon, far below the popular north rim lookout called Inspiration Point. The rocky, rough trail "zigged and zagged" its way to the bottom of the canyon. When they arrived at the river, there was just enough space to hold three horses and three people. But the view from the bottom was spectacular, and Jean described it as such:

> The steep walls of Yellowstone Canyon came closer together as they trailed farther away from the Lower Falls. The roar of the falls took on a softer sound—a more distant sound, but never fading away entirely. That turbulent river was a green as emeralds as it crashed over huge boulders in that narrowed canyon. What looked like sparkling white crushed ice tossed high and became foam as it slid into quieter pools at the side.

Although their position at the bottom of the canyon was mossy and slick, they managed to rest their horses and eat lunch. The three canyon trekkers feasted on thick ham sandwiches and devoured an entire pumpkin pie that Elton had wrapped and carefully attached to his saddle. Somehow the pie survived the journey to the bottom of the canyon right side up, although it probably would not have mattered to these happy-go-lucky adventurers.

Following Jean's seventeenth birthday on August 13—celebrated with a bonfire, toasted marshmallows, and fruit punch—the summer season of 1917 ended. She and Willie Frances went about their closing procedures in a quiet manner, somehow sensing that they would never be back. The world had changed and so had Yellowstone. The war was escalating in Europe and several of the men leaving Yellowstone came to say good-bye, knowing that they were being called to the draft, and that they might never see Willie Frances and Jean again. Willie Frances was personally familiar with that sentiment as both of her sons were already caught up in the war effort and fighting in far-off places. The solitude and serenity of the park seemed to have somehow evaporated. The increase in business left little time for camaraderie and close friendships, and the simple things, such as singing and storytelling, seemed to be too old-fashioned to do any more.

With the spirit of a pioneer, Willie Frances forged ahead, meeting every challenge of life head on. In the 1920s, she and husband Billy Bronner lived in Butte where he worked for the Montana Power Company. Sometime in the mid-1920s they followed the route of many former Yellowstone-ites and moved to California. She and Billy spent at least a few years basking in the warm California sun before he died in 1936 at the age of fifty-eight. While Willie Frances may have worked out of necessity, she also seemed to enjoy the independence that earning her own living afforded her. After owning a small hotel and a millinery shop in California, and later working for the Medical Social Services Department for the County of Los Angeles, Willie Frances retired at age seventy-two. In 1944 she moved to Portland, Oregon, to live her remaining years with Jean and Jean's husband Olin Dayton Sharpe and her grandsons, Olin D. Jr., and Donald.[22]

Four years after she moved to Portland to be with Jean and her family, Willie Frances Bronner died at the age of seventy-six.[23] She was buried in the Santa Ana Cemetery in Orange County, California, near her mother and father and alongside her husband William (Billy) N. Bronner. The simple inscription on her gravestone today reads:

Mother Dear
Willie Frances Bronner
1872-1948[24]

Etched in granite these silent words will eternally speak of the loving and intimate bond between a dedicated mother and a devoted daughter.

Jean continued to visit Yellowstone with her husband and sons, even staying in the Yellowstone Park Camps Company tent-operation at Canyon one summer. For the boys it was an exciting time as they giggled and whispered loudly trying to convince each other that a bear was trying to break into the tent. For Jean there were pleasant memories filled with her own emotion. Nonetheless she recalled that it was gratifying to show her family all of her familiar spots throughout the park. Forty years after Jean began her work as a Yellowstone "savage," she encouraged one of her sons, Donald, to spend a summer working in the park. While his experience in 1949 was completely different from Jean's, she believed that he enjoyed his summer in America's wonderland just as much as she had. Throughout her life, Jean cherished her experiences in Yellowstone from 1909 to 1917 as an extraordinary encounter with family, friends, and a very special place on earth. Ora Eugenia [Jean] Sharpe died on December 13, 1992 at the age of ninety-two.[25]

For Willie Frances and Jean, the years in Yellowstone had been good. There were few real opportunities for women in the early years of the twentieth century and Jean believed that it took a stout heart and a lot of fortitude to persevere. Throughout the shifting patterns of her life, Willie Frances cultivated the qualities of an inner character, which served her well and made her a courageous, wise, and resolute woman well into the twentieth century. Admiring her mother for always being kind but firm, Jean rarely questioned her instruction and always looked to her for advice. With appreciation and love, Jean celebrated her high regard of Willie Frances throughout her mother's life and beyond. In turn Willie Frances not only re-invented herself in Yellowstone, but she also evolved into an extraordinary role model for her daughter Jean.

While typical views of western women range from the passive sun-bonneted Oregon Trail pioneer woman to vulnerable "soiled dove" prostitutes to sensationalized figures such Calamity Jane and Belle Starr, the writings of Jean Crawford Sharpe offer us a glimpse into a fuller view of Western women. Jean's narrative characterizes not only a chronicle of her and her mother's physical survival, but it also speaks for their personal psychological growth, which she believed enabled them both to become full, strong, competent, and independent women. More often than not, behind-the-scenes women like Willie Frances and Jean were more than just a part of Yellowstone's history; they made part of that history. While their significance has become obscured through time, Jean's written record stands as a lasting testimony to the contributions of Willie Frances Bronner and Jean Crawford Sharpe to Yellowstone and to what mattered most in their lives: people, places, and special memories.

❦

Beulah Brown Sanborn

(1888–1976)

Hostess Extraordinaire

"Wherever you go in the Yellowstone Park, you meet people from Ogden who are enjoying their summer vacation in the wonderland of the west," claimed Ogden Mayor Frank Francis upon his return from the National Park in August 1920.[1] However, the Utahans to whom he was referring were not tourists. Without a doubt, Ogden was well represented in the park during the 1920s, as nine to twelve young men and women [from the town] were selected each year to work there as guides, entertainers, and hostesses.

Beulah Brown, an Ogden school teacher, probably initiated this summertime exodus of Ogden's young people when she began working in the park in 1915. According to her account, she began as a "potato peeler" with one of the early camp companies, either the Wylie Permanent Camping Company or the Shaw & Powell Camping Company.[2] By the time of the mayor's trip in 1920, Beulah had become head guide for the Yellowstone Park Camps Company at Canyon.[3] With few qualms she routinely took tourists out over the cliffs and down the great flight of stairs on Uncle Tom's Trail where they could catch an awe-inspiring view of the canyon and experience the thrill of the 308-foot Lower Fall. "She is a remarkable girl in that she is as much as home on the brink of the gorge where a misstep would launch one into eternity as she is in a class room teaching oral expression," proclaimed Mayor Francis.[4]

Her ability to create a feeling of home wherever she worked became one of Beulah's most endearing characteristics as she rose from guide to recreation director to manager of the Old Faithful Lodge to management executive for hotel complexes in California and Kentucky. Whether directing employee pageants of tourist entertainment, concocting an eclectic holiday menu featuring filet of chuckwalla (an edible lizard), or managing a national park hotel, Beulah brought her own spirited style into all her lifelong endeavors.

Born on November 30, 1888, Beulah was the first of three children delivered to Rev. E. Winslow Brown, D.D., and Jennie Whitehead Brown. Beulah's father, Eliphalet Winslow Brown was himself born near Champaign, Illinois in 1859 to farmers, James Brown and his wife Lillis. After the death of his father prior to 1870, E. Winslow moved to Jackson, Coshocton County, Ohio with his nine-year-old sister Alice and widowed mother. There he attended school and the Presbyterian Church and entered studies for the ministry. By 1880, mother and son were living in Wooster, Ohio, so that E. Winslow could attend the University of Wooster (today's Wooster College).[5]

The University of Wooster, a college founded in 1866 by Presbyterians who wanted to contribute to the education of America's youth, opened its doors to everyone including women. (In 1882, Annie Irish became the university's first woman Ph.D. graduate.) As it was one of the few colleges in the area to admit women, it was likely that Winslow met his future wife and Beulah's mother, Jennie M. Whitehead, at Wooster. According to the 1880 census Jennie was listed as "attending college," and a newspaper listed her later as an alumna of Wooster.[6]

After graduating with a Bachelor of Arts and Master of Arts in 1884, Beulah's father continued his education at Princeton's Theological Seminary from 1884 to 1887. Upon completing his degree at Princeton, he married Jennie M. Whitehead, of Licking County, Ohio, on May 17, 1887. Following his graduation on June 7, 1887, E. Winslow Brown was ordained a minister by the Presbytery of Newton in the Greenwich church of Stewartsville, N.J. (near Bloomsbury) and was installed as the pastor of that church. It was into this family of solid educational and religious values, that Beulah was born in 1888.[7]

Three years after Beulah's arrival, the Brown family was blessed with another daughter, Gladys, born in June, 1891. Another sister, Dorothy, made her appearance nearly a year later in September 1892. After five and one-half years in New Jersey, E. Winslow Brown was assigned to another congregation, this time in Iowa. In January 1893, the family moved to the small community of Malvern, where Beulah's father took charge of the Malvern Presbyterian church. Within a short time, Rev. E. Winslow became renowned for his ability to deliver sermons in a "clear, well modulated voice of ringing quality," a talent that Beulah would inherit and draw on for her future musical and theatrical performances.[8]

On June 4, 1895, the *Waterloo* (IA) *Daily Courier* made known that "it has been decided to hold a Wooster Day at the Chautauqua" and "July 1 has been selected as the day." The newspaper also published a list of Wooster alumni that were expected to attend, which included both Rev. E.W. Brown and Mrs. Jennie Brown.

Three days after this announcement, Beulah's mother, Jennie, died suddenly of an unknown cause at age thirty-four. E. Winslow Brown now had the full responsibility of three motherless daughters, all under the age of eight.[9]

By 1897, Rev. E. Winslow Brown had met and married Emily (last name unknown), who became a valuable assistant to him in his church work. For Beulah, Gladys, and Dorothy, their new stepmother apparently provided maternal support during their most formative years as young ladies. In 1900, Rev. E. Winslow was called to preside over the Presbyterian congregation of Spirit Lake, a quiet community in northern Iowa. As the twentieth century began, life for the Brown family seemed to be on the upswing. But it was not to last.

In 1904, tragedy struck again. On Thursday, January 28, Beulah's twelve-year-old sister Gladys began feeling ill while she was at school. However, by Saturday afternoon her condition worsened and her father sought medical attention. Doctors performed surgery when it was discovered that she was suffering from serious appendicitis. On Sunday she seemed to be getting better. But sadly, the family's hopes for Gladys' improvement were short-lived. "Early Monday morning," reported the local newspaper, "while the father was keeping loving vigil, the child passed into eternal life so peacefully as to give no warning of the change that had been wrought by blood poison." Her funeral was held on February 2, presided over by Rev. Hugh McNich, a classmate and friend of the bereaved father. She was buried next to her mother in the Calvary Cemetery at Malvern, Iowa.[10]

Rev. E. Winslow and Emily, Beulah, and Dorothy resumed their lives quietly and through the next few years the two girls completed their education in Iowa.[11] After finishing high school, Beulah attended Denison University in Granville, Ohio. She graduated in 1909 with a Ph.B. (Bachelor of Philosophy) and secured a position as an English instructor at Muskingum College in New Concord, Ohio that same year.[12] Apparently, Beulah was not one to let any grass grow under her feet, so within a year or two she moved on to accept a teaching position in another Ohio school. According to Mabel Sipe Davis of New Middleton, Ohio, Beulah was her high school teacher in Canfield, Ohio in 1910 or 1911. Davis recalled that Beulah "had a cough she could not get rid of and her doctor advised her to go west into the mountains to get rid of it."[13]

In 1914 or 1915, Beulah apparently heeded the advice of her doctor and moved to Ogden, Utah. There she secured employment as a high school teacher in dramatic speaking and elocution and also began working at Canyon in Yellowstone during summers. "Better Speech Week will be observed Wednesday afternoon at the Ogden high school," stated the *Ogden Standard Examiner* on February 26, 1918. "A program has been arranged under the direction of Miss Beulah Brown...commencing at 1 P.M." A few months later the newspaper reported that Beulah had also organized an extemporaneous speaking contest. The contest, held in April, allowed the participants one hour to prepare a speech on the subject assigned to them. The winner would then compete against a contestant of the Weber Academy. The ultimate prize for the contestants was to be selected as the regional representative speaker on High School day, May 3 at the University of Utah.[14]

Following the end of her teaching duties in June 1918, Beulah again headed to Yellowstone National Park to work for the Yellowstone Camping Company in the seasonal position of Canyon guide, a position she had held since 1915. But the summer of 1918 would prove more than just a routine break from the school year. That summer Beulah cut her Yellowstone season short and resigned her teaching position at Ogden high school to take on a new adventure: a trip to France related to the U.S.'s entry into World War I.[15]

"Local Girl Will Go Overseas For Red Cross Work," announced the Cedar Rapids *Evening Gazette* on August 26, 1918. Beulah, an accomplished vocalist and pianist, had put in her application for war work the year before, and in early August was selected to participate in the Red Cross "hospital hut program" of entertaining convalescing soldiers. After spending several months in Yellowstone, Beulah returned to her parents home in Cedar Rapids, Iowa, for what was supposed to be just a few days to prepare for her international assignment to work as a "cheer maker," apparently a job in an army hospital to lift the morale of wounded soldiers.[16]

The newspaper concluded the article by informing the community that Beulah would be at home on Tuesday evening, and anyone wishing to call might do so.

But shortly after this story appeared in the newspaper, Beulah was struck with a sudden illness that would cancel her trip. That illness turned out to be appendicitis, the same affliction her sister had died from fourteen years earlier. Surely her father was beside himself as he was faced with yet another daughter's life being threatened by a perilous ailment. The only consoling factor for E. Winslow at the time might have been that she was with family and not two thousand miles away in Utah or in Yellowstone at the time of the onset of her sickness.

The medical profession, which by 1918 had become a little more skillful at treating appendicitis, advocated that early detection and immediate surgery greatly increased survival rates in patients. After having gone through this ordeal with Gladys in 1904, Beulah's father apparently sought medical attention for Beulah immediately upon the discovery of her symptoms. His quick action proved prudent. "Miss Beulah Brown... who was operated on for appendicitis in St. Luke's hospital Tuesday afternoon is resting easily," reported the Ogden *Evening Gazette* on August 28. Alas, her overseas tour of duty would have to wait until another time. But she was not long in recovering from her illness and surgery, and by the following year Beulah was back in Utah and back in the park.[17]

In the summer of 1919, Beulah began the fifth of her eventual twenty seasons in Yellowstone. While spending her winters in Ogden, she helped recruit hundreds of young people from Ogden to work as "savages" in Yellowstone. They hardly fit the moniker of "savage" that was applied to all Yellowstone concessioner employees because these young workers were from colleges and good homes of refinement. The savages were hand-picked by camping company agents, probably by Beulah herself, who carefully investigated the scholastic and personal record of each applicant. Journalist Rufus Steele revealed in his *Outlook* magazine article "Summer Savages" (May 12, 1926) that "every candidate is asked whether he or she can sing, dance, tell a story, or make a musical instrument perform classically or in jazz. He also noted that "artistic ability goes a long way in landing a job." If offered a position the students understood that they were going to the park to work and to work hard. After spending the day serving up meals or making beds or guiding visitors to the canyon, Beulah and her coworkers were well aware that their service would not end at dinner. Each evening of the summer, after the last meal was served and the guests had taken a seat by the campfire, the savages swung into lively performances of music, dance, and comical skits. One visitor marveled that these savages, who worked as housekeepers, waiters, waitresses, guides, hostesses, and general help during the day and as entertainers at night, were "one of the real sources of pleasure in the park."[18] By the same token, a summer working and playing amidst the wonders of Yellowstone reigned high on the pleasure scale for the 1920s savage as well.

"Ogden Girls To Entertain in Yellowstone, Miss Beulah Brown Will Direct Program of Pageantry," proclaimed the *Ogden Standard Examiner* on June 4, 1922. While Ogden girls and other young women from various states had been participating in visitor entertainment for several years, this particular year was surely going to be special because 1922 marked the fifty-year anniversary of Yellowstone's establishment. The park was abuzz with all sorts of arrangements for the semi-centennial as everyone prepared for the arrival of notable guests such as President Warren G. Harding, Secretary of Interior A.B. Fall, Director of the National Park Service (NPS) Stephen T. Mather, and Assistant Director of the National Park Service A.B. Cammerer. In addition to distinguished public figures, the estimated number of tourists visiting the park that year was expected to reach 100,000. Up to that time, the park record for visitors was 80,000, set in 1921. In honor of the occasion, Beulah, now the general amusement director for the Yellowstone Park Camps Company, arranged a special program of pageantry that dramatized the history of Yellowstone in tableau, song, and dance. At each one of the locations—Mammoth, Old Faithful, Lake, and Canyon—employees staged a theatrical presentation of a particular time period of the park's fifty-years of tourism.[19]

Yellowstone's anniversary pageant in 1922 began at Mammoth Camp with the stories of John Colter, Jim Bridger, and Truman Everts, depicted in pantomime. Colter and Bridger represented some of the earliest white explorers to Yellowstone prior to its establishment as a national park. While Colter and Bridger were experienced mountain guides and routinely traveled through the West on their own, Everts, a member of the 1870 Washburn expedition, was not a practiced outdoorsman and nearly met his doom while lost in Yellowstone.

The Washburn exploring party had entered the present day park from the north in early September, a time when the fall weather could be cold, wet, and even snowy. On September 9, Everts found himself separated from the group and became lost in the wilderness of Yellowstone for over a month. The story of his survival with only the clothes on his back, a knife, and an opera glass became one of Yellowstone's most dramatic tales of courage and perseverance. Without a doubt, the Mammoth Camp's drama of Everts's "thirty-seven days of peril" began the series of pageants by presenting the audience with an experience of high adventure, but one that they could safely encounter from their amphitheater seats.

At Old Faithful, a cast of historical characters played by Upper Geyser Basin employees recounted the idea of setting aside the park as a national playground while the Washburn party sat around a campfire near Madison Junction. In one highly imaginative scene, an allegorical figure— the spirit of greed—appeared as the members of the expedition argued over whether the natural wonders should be turned into commercial endeavors or preserved for their beauty for future generations. The spirits of beauty, represented by young girls in filmy gowns, vanquished the spirit of greed with their artistic dances. Even though this famous campfire scene in recent years has been proven to be not historically accurate, allegorical scenes of Yellowstone's history like this one nonetheless enchanted visitors throughout the 1920s and well into the 1940s and 1950s.[20]

Lake Camp was the scene of a clever pantomime touting the legislation that dedicated Yellowstone as a National Park. The play portrayed President Grant signing the bill and the general rejoicing of an ecstatic American public that followed.

The last production to showcase the progressive history of the park was presented at Canyon Camp, under the personal direction of Beulah Brown. Dramatizing fifty years of tourism from stagecoach days to the advent of the automobile, the performance began with a stagecoach hold-up followed by a minuet illustrating the spirit of the park's yesteryears. Then several of the up-to-date yellow buses appeared on the scene and a jazz dance took over the log amphitheater. After an exciting summer of performance, song, and dance, Beulah probably wondered what could possibly top that. Maybe a winter in Yellowstone.

Winter in Yellowstone in the 1920s meant different things to different people as it does today. To some it was a snowy season full of skiing and

My Winter in Geyserland

By Beulah Brown

George and Morris Musser on Framework of a Tent

Copyright, 1924, by Beulah Brown

The two Musser boys sporting their long skis posed for Beulah during their winter at Old Faithful in 1922-23. (FRONTICEPIECE IN MY WINTER IN GEYSERLAND)

sleigh rides, to others it was a pretty season full of sparkling icicles and snowflakes, and to still others it was a quiet season full of restorative stillness, contemplation, and reflection. For Beulah Brown, a former Ogden school teacher and summer camps and lodges employee, the winter of 1922-1923 was filled with all of those sensations. It was a magic season.

After working seven summers in Yellowstone, Beulah yearned to see the park covered in a blanket of snow. Since the only people afforded that seasonal luxury were typically park rangers or winter keepers, Beulah supposed there was little chance that she would experience a winter in the park's interior. But when Mr. and Mrs. M.K. Musser, who were beginning their twelfth winter in the park as winter keepers, asked Beulah to tutor their three boys, ages seven, nine, and eleven, at Old Faithful for the winter of 1922-1923, she jumped at the chance.[21]

As summer waned and winter drew near, Beulah observed and noted the park's seasonal changes, and in a sense, prepared herself for a new Yellowstone adventure. "Some time in November, usually, the first heavy snow comes and this is a signal for the men who are doing post-seasonal work to hurry to Mammoth so as not to be caught in the interior of the Park," she recorded in a letter to a friend.

> Train service to West Yellowstone is then discontinued, and the roads of the Park become highways for only the people who can travel on snow shoes or skis. The rivers do not freeze over, as they are either too swift or fed by warm springs. The thermometer may drop to fifty below, but the days on the average are warm enough so that one may enjoy a few hours of the outdoors. Telephone service is maintained throughout the Park in order that the rangers and winter-keepers, who are now the only inhabitants, may keep in touch with one another. As for mail, once a month is considered good service.[22]

Once Mr. Musser left his car in West Yellowstone at the end of November, Beulah knew it was just a matter of time before the snows that bound them would arrive. Although she looked forward to a winter of hibernation in America's wonderland, she admitted that it gave her a queer sensation when the snow began to fall for ten days straight, and she realized she was there to stay. In contrast to Mr. and Mrs. Musser's calm mood, Beulah's frame of mind bordered on exhilaration. The thrill of isolation was exactly why she had wanted to be a winter dweller at Old Faithful.

That type of seclusion confounded many people's sensibilities then as it does today. Many of Beulah's friends were perplexed as to how she would be able to maintain a normal existence for four months and asked incredulously, "Where will you spend Christmas?" and "Will any of the people at Mammoth come up to see you?" She pragmatically informed her inquirers that a trip from Mammoth required skiing for three to four days, which meant visitors were unlikely, and that in order for her to go anywhere she would need to become more of an expert on skis than she was.[23]

Beulah did not have long to wait for the magic of winter to begin charming her at every turn. Capturing a special image of the season's enchantment, she wrote, "The Inn, which is beautiful in the summer, when covered with snow was much more so; its many angles and gables were decorated by an artist who used white luster and diamonds, and who changed his design at the will of the winds."[24]

The house that she and the Mussers lived in, located southwest of the Inn was heated and supplied with water piped from a geyser. This meant that upon returning from a long, cold ski trip, they found the house delightfully warm and no one had to rush down to the cellar to put coal in the furnace! Beulah especially enjoyed her baths of the "softest water," which were supplied by Yellowstone's natural hot water system. In addition to luxuriating in the geyser water bath, she and the Musser family made use of the water to wash their clothes and dishes. Beulah noticed that the only problem of using the natural hot water occurred when the geysers played. Following that eruptive activity, the water had a strong smell of sulphur and tarnished the silverware. But those annoyances seemed a small price to pay for its many rewards.

A root cellar, chicken house, and greenhouse also utilized the warm geyser water. Beulah reasoned that the mineral laden water must be why the chickens laid nearly two dozen eggs a day and the greenhouse produced lettuce, tomatoes, onions, and radishes were "supernaturally delicious."[25] By the time of Beulah tasted the geyser garden in 1922-23, this building at Old Faithful had already become famous. Built in 1897 by the hotel company, the 25' x 50' glass-roofed "hot house" sat directly on top of a hot spring that kept it constantly heated with 195-degree geyser water. A writer for the *Scientific American* magazine in 1898 was astonished "that splendid garden products can be grown" year round, even when the "mercury in winter is exceedingly low." In his article, he concluded that "the rich soil, the sun's light, and the condensation from the hot water make an ideal combination for the growth of vegetables."[26] Even so, the magazine writer would have been quite surprised to see the two-foot cucumber that Mrs. Musser presented to park superintendant Horace Albright in the spring of 1923.[27]

While geyser water seemed to be beneficial for plants and animals it was not considered the best for human consumption. Beulah and the Mussers relied on a reservoir behind the Inn for drinking water. The reservoir also provided water to operate a small electric plant, which enabled the winter dwellers to have electric lights with which to enjoy the evening hours. For Beulah, the long evenings were a luxury, with time to read, sew, or practice the piano. Even being in the midst of a snow-bound wilderness, Beulah and the Musser family enjoyed a civilized winter existence.

In preparation for her winter at Old Faithful, Beulah read about cross-country skis and skiing. "Skis," she explained to her readers, "are usually made of ash or hickory, six or eight feet long and about at that center is leather rigging into which your shoe fits, your heel being free to move up and down. Most people wear rubber and leather packs on their feet, the packs being large enough for a moccasin or several pairs of socks on the inside." Even though she read explicit directions on how to ski, Beulah found that she learned more from watching the Musser boys than by trying to recall the instructions. It was not long before she discovered that her two ski poles, which were designed to help push her along, came in handy for saving her from a fall. In addition to skiing around the geyser basin and riding down the Wylie Camp hill near Grotto Geyser, Mr. Musser guided Beulah and the family on full-day ski-excursions to places such as Lone Star Geyser and Spring Creek Canyon, places that today remain desired destinations for skiers. On one trip Mr. Musser took Beulah to a backcountry waterfall located four miles southeast of the Old Faithful Inn. Like many waterfalls in Yellowstone, there was not a trail to the spot and the fall was in such a secluded area that Beulah commented "you could pass within a few hundred yards and never discover [it]." Traveling over frozen swamps and up and down heavily forested hills, Beulah thought at one point that Mr. Musser had to be going in the wrong direction. But upon arriving at the one-hundred foot waterfall that seemed to "tumble out of the sky," Beulah realized that with "Mr. Musser as a guide, one is safe and will land always at the intended destination." After twelve years as the Old Faithful winter keeper, Mr. Musser most assuredly knew the area well.[28]

As far as she knew, Mr. Musser had been the discoverer of the hidden waterfall and to a certain degree he was. The only notation of this waterfall's existence prior to this time had appeared fifty years earlier in the report of the 1872 Hayden Survey. The exploration party camp was located near the fall and Dr. Bradley included a description of the feature in the report as a "fine cascade," but left it unnamed. With a bit of an ironic historical twist, Beulah called it "Unnamed Falls" when she first spied the magnificent, one-hundred foot, plunge-type fall in 1922. It would be another eighty years before the fall would be re-discovered and finally named Lone Star Cascade.[29] If Mr. Musser would have named the fall and officially reported it, he most likely would have been recognized as the discoverer. Perhaps just knowing that there was such an exceptional place in Yellowstone that only a few special people ever saw was celebratory enough for Mr. Musser.

"Christmas time was not a bit lonesome, even though I had not received any mail since the first day of the month," Beulah wrote to her friend and coworker, Margaret McCartney. Regardless of only being able to gather a small audience of Mr. and Mrs. Musser, herself, and few nearby rangers, Beulah helped her three pupils prepare and present a program at "school" on the Friday night before Christmas. To add a little extra thrill to the holiday, Beulah went to the ranger station on the afternoon of Christmas Eve and called the boys pretending to be Santa Claus. When she returned to the house, the boys were brimming with excitement. "Santa," they exclaimed, "has said he would come that very evening." And as promised, Santa surely did.

While the boys enjoyed frolicking in their winter playground, Beulah and Mrs. Musser passed much of their time planning their multi-day ski trip to West Yellowstone, Montana, a round trip journey of sixty miles. Mr. Musser and eleven-year old George had traveled to West Yellowstone with an overnight stop at the deserted Madison ranger station in late December to pick up the mail. They returned after a two-day stay in the town with forty letters, some cards, and nine packages for Beulah. Ecstatic over her mail bonanza, she proclaimed, "that was the best day I had seen for some time." As it was a multi-day excursion to retrieve mail, the Mussers only made one trip per month. The next outing to town would be Beulah and Mrs. Musser's. They scheduled their trip for early February and Beulah could hardly wait. Thoughts of skiing down Madison Junction hill, spending a night in a deserted ranger cabin, and greeting the fifty

Beulah models her two modes of transportation for the winter at Old Faithful, snowshoes and skis. (FROM MY WINTER IN GEYSERLAND)

inhabitants of West Yellowstone all loomed on her horizon as big calendar events. "My anticipation of the trip to West Yellowstone knew no bounds," she wrote to Margaret McCartney, a fellow camps company worker then living in Livingston, Montana. "For weeks it worked upon my imagination, and I was so enthusiastic that every time I skied down past Giant geyser, I dreamed of the time when I would go on to Madison Junction."[30]

Their day of departure (February 6) finally arrived, and they planned to get an early start, but when Beulah "consulted the thermometer" she found to her dismay that it was twenty below zero. While they waited for the sun to warm things up a bit, she and Mrs. Musser had plenty of time to try on their packs, which they quickly found were too heavy. After lightening their packs and rechecking the thermometer, which now read only twelve below, Beulah and Mrs. Musser began their adventure at 10 o'clock. With Mr. Musser breaking trail and also carrying the ladies' packs, the trio made the first two miles in forty minutes, a speed Beulah mistakenly expected that they would be able to maintain. The trail across the Fountain freight road slowed their progress, but not their spirits. "A more beautiful morning I never saw," Beulah recalled. "The steam had given the entire geyser basin the appearance of fairyland." About a mile from the Fountain ranger station, Mr. Musser pointed in the direction of the station and handed Beulah and Mrs. Musser their packs as a parting gift. It did not take Beulah long to figure out that even a lightened pack was not a pleasant thing to carry. But in a short while they reached the station where they built a small fire and refreshed themselves with hot coffee and sandwiches.[31]

At 3:30, they set out for their overnight destination, the Madison ranger station, with the sun still shining brightly. Even so, Beulah's enthusiasm started to wane as it became her turn to break trail and her pack seemed to get heavier. As they entered the Firehole Canyon all seemed beautiful, until they realized that they were now in the shade. It also seemed to be getting dark. The milepost indicated that it was three miles to the Madison Ranger Station and that they had come thirteen from Old Faithful. Beulah suddenly felt like she was a million miles from anywhere. Mrs. Musser tried to cheer her by pointing to the sun on the distant mountain tops as they continued on through the canyon. They passed what seemed like endless miles of curves and after each one Mrs. Musser would say, "the station is just around the next curve." By the time they arrived at the station the sun was completely set and the darkened building seemed cold. But within a few moments, the golden glow of lighted candles gave the place an appearance of home.

Reaching the station was a relief, but before they could get settled Beulah and Mrs. Musser needed to obtain drinking water from the river. Despite their "combined gymnastic efforts and ingenious devices," they found the bank too high to safely reach the water. Resigned, they filled their buckets with snow and patiently waited to quench their thirst when the snow melted. After building a fire in the stove, they dined heartily on a good supper of eggs, potatoes, bread, and jam. Fatigue soon superseded Beulah's plan to write letters, and her only thought after supper was going to bed. Even though she was exhausted, queer noises and weird shadows combined with thoughts of rats and mice kept her from sleeping peacefully for most of the night.

The next morning, one of the Riverside (near West Yellowstone) rangers, Clifford Anderson, telephoned Beulah and Mrs. Musser saying that he was on his way to meet them. Breaking trail seemed almost harder than it had been the day before, and two ladies had only covered four miles when Anderson met up with them. He had managed to break trail and travel nine miles in the same space of time. After refreshing themselves with a thermos of hot coffee, they followed Anderson to the Riverside ranger station arriving about five o'clock. Ranger Eivind Scoyen then guided them to West Yellowstone where they stayed and dined with the Harness family. The physical exertion of the ski trip had apparently worked up an appetite for Beulah because she recalled that she "just ate and ate and started in again," and astonished her hostess.

Beulah and Mrs. Musser were thrilled to have their first day in West Yellowstone to rest and prepare for one of West Yellowstone's social gatherings, a masquerade dance being held the next day. On their second day in West Yellowstone the thermometer registered forty-two below zero, but this was a big day for them and Beulah was not going to miss a thing in the big city! They were invited out to lunch and to dinner at the Teepee Inn, and then to the dance, which was held in the summer dance hall. Beulah felt like she was making up for all fall and winter and could not remember when she felt better or had as good a time. After all she had traveled thirty miles to a dance. They attended one more party on their third day in West Yellowstone at the home of the school teacher before they began skiing back to Old Faithful.

When Beulah and Mrs. Musser departed West Yellowstone, they found that the rangers had broken trail for them to the Madison Junction ranger station, which made their first day back on the trail very pleasant. Upon their arrival at the station, they were surprised to find the fire burning, candles lit, and supper ready. Ranger Roy Frazer had cooked a meal for them that was so fulfilling Beulah claimed it "took the tire off tired." They thoroughly enjoyed their evening.

The next morning they slept late, and started out for Old Faithful about ten-thirty a.m. After spending an hour and a half climbing the hill two miles from the station, they realized that it was storming. The wind and snow whipped their faces. Only occasionally could they find the trail and mostly they just trudged through the snow, content to make any headway at all. It became worse when they reached the open country outside the canyon, and they realized they were in a terrible blizzard. Often they could not even move forward and were only able to dig in their ski poles and stand with bowed heads until the wind briefly subsided. At times, snow and wind blew so fiercely that Beulah and Mrs. Musser could not even see each other. It had snowed over eighteen inches since they came through only a few days before, and to make matters worse the wind had created massive drifts. Beulah kept thinking that if only they could reach the timber that they would find shelter from the wind, but that proved to be a thin protection. The last half-mile to the Fountain ranger station proved to be an unremitting fight against wind and snow, with the final two hundred feet being the worst of all. Upon reaching the station, they practically fell from a big drift onto the front porch of the welcoming ranger station.

Safely inside, away from the wind and snow, the two weather-worn women collapsed into bed by seven o'clock. That was just in time for a mouse and a rat to begin their acrobatic acts. According to Beulah's letter to her friend, "when that rat jumped from the chair to the table, he almost shook the room." Beulah was not taking any chances with a monstrous rat on the loose and slept with an axe next to her bed "ready to deliver the fatal blow" should the varmint venture too close.

Mercifully, Mr. Musser telephoned in the morning to announce that he was on the way to meet them with sandwiches and apples. As they set out they discovered that the wind had erased any trace of a trail. The two ladies also found that as they tried to break a new trail, they sank farther into the deep snow than Beulah thought a person on skis could. After struggling for a mile or so Mrs. Musser thought they had arrived at a point where they could leave the road and take the shortcut that Mr. Musser had showed them on their outbound journey. As they wandered through the area that they believed to be the shortcut, they seemed to sink even deeper and Beulah began to notice that the snow had queer cracks in it. Just then, she heard Mr. Musser calling from the road. He urged them to hurry back to the road. He informed them that they were not on the shortcut and more exactly that they were on top of Goose Lake, a treacherous bog of warm springs and deep water. The shortcut they soon discovered was another mile down the road, and there they met up with Mr. Musser. Having braved darkness, wind, snow, a monster rat, and a wrong turn into a thermal area, the women found the rest of the journey back to Old Faithful appreciatively uneventful. Regardless of losing five pounds and "ruining her complexion," she believed that her sixty-mile trip on skis had given her "memories that a hundred years could not efface." All things considered, Beulah felt lucky to have had the opportunity to spend a winter in geyserland, and declared that she "wouldn't have missed it for anything."[32]

Just where in the park Beulah worked the summer of 1923 is unclear, but it was most likely at Canyon where she had been working for the preceding nine or so years. This was probably the year she left a piece of herself in the form of a place name, on a point on the south rim of the Canyon east of Artist Point. According to photographer Jack E. Haynes's personal files, Sublime Point (today's Point Sublime) was named by Beulah Brown in 1923 or 1924. A few years earlier, Horace Albright had formed a committee with Haynes, Marguerite Lindsley, and himself to sort through the massive history and jumble of Yellowstone place names in order to consolidate duplicate names and to create new ones where none existed. Evidently Albright liked Sublime Point and he accepted it as an official name with Beulah as the originator.[33] According to historians such as Roderick Nash author of *Wilderness and The American Mind*, the term *sublime* has played an important role in the history of wilderness in America and likewise Yellowstone. David Folsom, one of Yellowstone's earliest explorers described the canyon from that point as "pretty, beautiful, picturesque, magnificent, grand, sublime, awful, terrible." Originally used in connection with something to be feared, places like Yellowstone altered that meaning in the late 1800s to denote something to be revered and adored. For Beulah and nearly every traveler to Yellowstone the canyon was indeed a place that inspired awe and stirred reverence.

For the 1924 season Beulah became more involved with managing and overseeing the company's park-wide camp operations and was assigned for the first time to Mammoth Camp.[34] That year president of the Yellowstone Park Camps Company Howard Hays had become ill and upon his doctor's advice decided to sell the business. Hays, who originally came to Yellowstone in 1905 for his health, began working for the Wylie Camping Company as a surrey driver and worked his way up to becoming a trusted promotional agent for the company by 1910. His personal acquisition of the Yellowstone Park Camping Company in 1919 created quite a stir in the seemingly well-ordered hierarchy of Yellowstone's concession world.

The Yellowstone Park Camping Company, then headed by Livingston businessman A.W. Miles, was offered for sale in the spring of 1919 with a price tag of $150,000. Harry Child, the park hotel tycoon who had his eye on controlling all of the park's transportation and lodging concessions, thought the cost was too high to buy it himself and decided to wait for the price to come down. Howard Hays, Roe Emery, and Walter White of the White Motor Company pooled their resources and purchased the camping operation in the spring 1919 for $70,000 in cash and a $70,000 note. Needless to say, Harry Child was dismayed.

So when the camping operation was again offered to Child in 1924, he wasted no time in buying it. But in five years the price had gone up, considerably. To come up with the $660,000 price tag required by Hays and his partners, Child enlisted Vernon Goodwin, a former Los Angeles hotelier, as partner and manager of the park-wide camping operation. Beulah, a long-time employee of the Yellowstone Park Camps Company, was suddenly a valuable member of the staff that Goodwin counted on to assist him with his successful management goals and he gave her charge of the Mammoth Camp.[35]

But before Beulah took on too many managerial responsibilities, she made plans to expand her life's adventures internationally once again, applying for a U.S. passport to tour several countries in the fall of 1924. Her application documented that she had previously acquired a passport in 1918 and explained that it went unused due to illness. This time Beulah took her trip around the world. In December she sailed out of Los Angeles, embarking on a three month journey that took her to Hawaii, Japan, China, the Philippines, Sumatra, Ceylon, Egypt, Italy, France, and England. On March 21, 1925, she boarded the U.S.S. *Aurania* in Liverpool, England and sailed for New York, arriving on March 31. While it is unclear whether she was on a pre-arranged expedition, on a missionary tour, or on her own escapade, Beulah's trip around the world was quite an adventure for a thirty-five-year-old single woman in the 1920s.[36] After a brief visit with family in Iowa, Beulah headed back to Utah just in time to resume her seasonal mission of gathering her Yellowstone summer work-force of talented collegians.

This is one of the rare booklet covers for the Songs of the Yellowstone Park Camps that identifies Beulah Brown as the compiler and publisher.
(COURTESY YELLOWSTONE NATIONAL PARK LIBRARY)

"Miss Beulah Brown, manager at Mammoth Camp, has been the friend and confidant, as well as the director of many hundreds of girls during her years of devoted service in the park," observed a journalist in 1925. "In fact she has had a good deal to do with developing the finished form of nightly entertainment that has brought fame to the [park] camps." The campfire performances at all the camps began with the employees leading the audience in rounds of singing, including various state songs vocalized by traveling residents. "As might be expected, new songs and parodies are constantly emanating from the active minds of the savages, and 'Lady Beu' has frequently been the judge of whether a new song should be perpetuated in the camp anthology or go into the discard," explained writer Rufus Steele. Several years earlier Beulah had begun collecting an assortment of songs sung

*Herma Albertson, an Old Faithful camp employee, included this image of
Beulah in her photo album of friends and events for the summer of 1926.
She entitled it "Beulah Brown Our Camp Manager."*

(COURTESY YELLOWSTONE NATIONAL PARK ARCHIVES)

at each of the camps and by 1925, she had compiled the most popular ones
into a leaflet to be sold in the gift shops. Printed by J.O. Woody Printing
Company in Ogden, Utah, and authored by Beulah Brown, the forty-page
booklet contained songs such as "Take Me Back to Those Yellowstone Days,"
"Underneath the Yellowstone Moon," and Beulah's personal inclusion of
"Canyon Land," penned by her father, E. Winslow Brown, D.D., and sung
to tune of "Beulah Land," an 1876 gospel hymn. Singing songs around the
campfire with people from every state in the union followed by entertaining
performances of the camp savages undoubtedly created lifelong memories
for thousands of visitors to Yellowstone during the 1920s, and Beulah
Brown took pride in being at the heart of their experiences.[37]

By 1926, Beulah had made her way up the company's administrative ladder and she was beginning her eleventh summer in Yellowstone as the manager of the Old Faithful Lodge.[38] That was Herma (Albertson) Baggley's first summer in Yellowstone and to record her memories, Herma (see her biography in this volume) compiled a photo album of her friends and experiences. One of those images included a picture of Beulah Brown with Herma's handwritten caption, "Beulah, our camp manager."[39] While Beulah oversaw the daily duties of housekeepers and kitchen and dining room staff in Yellowstone during the summers, her future for the next few winters would ultimately be set in California.

The Pacific Coast Borax Company, which owned extensive land in Death Valley, took notice of interest in the public's potential for spending winters in the moderate desert climate in the mid-1920s. Observations of the successful resort facility of H.W. Eichbaum at Stovepipe Wells, along with waning borax mining operations in Death Valley, prompted officials of Borax Company to venture into the tourism business in 1926. Their mining infrastructure gave them a usable railway system already in place to transport guests, but they needed a comfortable inn. After wrangling over location and expenditures, the Borax board of directors hired Los Angeles architect Albert C. Martin to design a mission-style luxury hotel to be constructed at the mouth of Furnace Creek Wash. The location offered spectacular views of the valley and mountains. Moreover, there was a good supply of fresh water nearby at Travertine Springs. Construction began in September 1926, with adobe bricks made on site by local Panamint Indians.[40]

According to Ron Miller in his *Fifty Years Ago at Furnace Creek Inn*, it was Yellowstone Superintendent Horace Albright who recommended Beulah as "just the right person" when Borax executive Frank Jenifer remarked that he needed a competent manager for the new hotel. Mr. Jenifer's visit to Albright and Yellowstone in the summer of 1926 proved to be advantageous for both Beulah Brown and Jenifer. In hiring Beulah as manager of the hotel, Jenifer also got an entire staff of employees. For the next two years, when the summer season in Yellowstone ended, Beulah and her crew of capable help from the Old Faithful Lodge headed south for the winter season to work in Death Valley.[41]

Even though Death Valley would not become a national monument until 1933, it was one of many places that National Park Service Director

Stephen T. Mather and Yellowstone Superintendent Horace M. Albright were keeping an eye on as American tourism began to expand. In suggesting Beulah for the position of manager of the Furnace Creek Inn, Albright was most likely insuring that the resort would be run with the same standards of operation that the Park Service expected of national park hotel operations. And she delivered.

The new Furnace Creek Inn opened on February 1, 1927, with Beulah at the helm. The inn featured an airy lobby, appealing dining room, and ten or twelve finished guest rooms. Its daily rate of ten dollars included a room with a private bath and meals. Because the resort was only partially completed, the Borax company maintained a low profile for the Inn's first season, and thus not even the Automobile Club of America knew of the existence of the new hotel in Death Valley. Construction continued through the winter as the hotel grew under Beulah's watchful eye, and by the 1927-28 winter season Furnace Creek Inn boasted over twenty wonderfully appointed guest rooms. For many guests the facility there seemed more like a luxurious European hotel than a resort in the California desert. In addition to offering wonderfully comfortable accommodations in an area that many considered an inhospitable environment, Beulah stylishly added to the Inn's sense of elegance with staff members who wore smartly starched uniforms. She worked hard at making impressions, including surprising guests with an innovative holiday menu.[42]

"Lizard Filet Delicacy for Thanksgiving: Former Ogden Teacher Announces Death Valley Menu," proclaimed the *Ogden Standard Examiner* on November 23, 1927. Beulah obviously believed in making an imprint on the tourism world as well as on her guests with this non-traditional Thanksgiving menu. Incorporating the flora and fauna of Death Valley, the menu options consisted of cholla cactus cocktail; nectar of wild turnip soup; Death Valley crackers-baked-in-the-sun; Death Valley–grown celery hearts, radishes, onions, miners lettuce and cactus-hearts salad; fried antelope steak; filet of chuckwalla (an unlovely looking, but edible, monster lizard); baked Panamint mountain grouse; sweet tack (cookies sun-baked, cactus-shaped and flavored); Death Valley pumpkin pie; and ice cream frozen at Death Valley's frozen desert factory. The newspaper was quick to add that the menu claimed the foods "have been tested, tasted, tried, and declared excellent." Even so, one wonders how many orders of filet of chuckwalla they actually sold!

The Furnace Creek Inn in Death Valley provides a charming backdrop for Beulah and Henry Sanborn in the late 1920s.
(COURTESY DEATH VALLEY NATIONAL PARK PEO25)

On May 2, 1928, Beulah married Henry S. Sanborn. Henry was the accountant for the Furnace Creek Inn, but according to a later newspaper article he and Beulah actually met in Yellowstone around 1924. As stated by the State of California Certification of Vital Records, this was a first marriage for both Beulah, age thirty-eight and Henry, age thirty-five. Their marriage license from the County of Inyo, State of California indicated that the couple was married in a simple ceremony with G.J. Benefiel as the officiating clergyman and Harry P. and Pauline F. Gower serving as witnesses.[43]

The Gowers had been and continued to be long-time Death Valley residents. Pauline was another of the Borax Company's women hotel managers. She first managed the short-lived Death Valley View Hotel, a complex of employee housing turned into tourist accommodations in the early 1920s. Pauline later took over operation of the company's twenty-three room Amargosa Hotel, located about thirty miles from Furnace Creek. Her husband Harrison Preston Gower worked for the U.S. Borax Company from 1909 until the mid-1960s as a geologist. When a new hydrous calcium borate was discovered in the Furnace Creek deposits in 1959, the U.S. Geological Survey named the mineral, Gowerite, in honor of him.[44] He penned his recollections and antidotes in a one-hundred and forty-five page book in the late 1960s. The Death Valley 49ers, a non-profit organization founded in 1949 to honor the hard-scrabble miners of 1849, published Gower's compilation in 1970, titling it *50 Years in Death Valley: Memoirs of a Borax Man*. The book, which is still in print, remains a popular account of the history of Death Valley. For Beulah and Henry, 1928 would be their last winter season in the company of the Gowers and in the employ of the Furnace Creek Inn. Apparently, Beulah's reputation for quality management had made her a sought after hostess and hotel manager.[45]

In October 1929, the *Los Angles Times* announced that "Lake Arrowhead's South Shore European plan hotel, the Village Inn, built in the Norman-English style opens its autumn and winter season under the personal management of Mrs. H.S. Sanborn....who will be remembered as Beulah Brown before her marriage." The newspaper praised her loyal tour of duty in Yellowstone claiming generally correctly that "the new hostess has just returned to the Southland after her fourteenth summer as manager of Old Faithful Lodge in Yellowstone National Park." Beulah extended that loyalty of service to Lake Arrowhead as well, working at the lodge on the shores of that lake for the following five years. In fact, for the 1935 summer season, the resort succeeded in luring her away from Yellowstone to manage the upscale Arlington Lodge at Lake Arrowhead. "The summer season was ushered in at Lake Arrowhead last Thursday with the opening of the Lodge," the *Los Angeles Times* reported on May 19. "The Lodge will be operated under the direction of Beulah Brown Sanborn and will offer guests the finest in accommodations and appointments." Ever the professional hostess, Beulah could now manage anything from rustic lodge cabins to upscale lakefront hotels.

The half-million dollar Arlington Lodge had opened its doors on June 23, 1923, entertaining nearly a thousand wealthy guests. Situated just ninety miles northeast of Los Angles in the San Bernardino National Forest, the Lodge was considered a masterpiece of design. Created by Santa Barbara hotelier A.L. Richmond and architect McNeal Swasney, the building had been constructed on a high terrace and utilized native materials. The massive lobby, called the "Great Hall," welcomed guests with its spacious forty-five foot ceiling that towered above the sumptuous carpeting beneath their feet. The massive fireplace at one end of the grand lobby glowed with inviting warmth while the curved, grand staircase at the other end beckoned guests to ascend and explore the elegant bedchambers that featured exclusive hand-crafted furniture and private baths. The opening extravaganza concluded with a midnight champagne party and orchestra dancing. In 1923, guests to the fashionable Lodge could obtain round-trip transportation from Los Angles, one night of room accommodations at the Lodge, and three meals for fifteen dollars. For many guests the Lodge was more than a hotel, it was a place where ambiance blended with hospitality to create a luxurious retreat, a philosophy that Beulah strove to uphold as she took over its management in 1935.[46]

While Beulah was busily managing the various operations at Lake Arrowhead, Henry had also worked his way up the ladder at the same California resort. In 1932 he held the position of Café Manager and by 1936 he had been promoted to Resort Superintendent. Through the years Beulah and Henry honed their individual management skills and together they made an effective management team.[47]

As a successful pair of hospitality professionals, Beulah and Henry apparently captured the attention of the Mammoth Cave (KY) Operating Committee in the mid-1930s. Or perhaps because officials at Mammoth Cave were still working on trying to establish the place as a national park, Horace Albright was consulted and he may have recommended the Sanborns. Either way Beulah and Henry found themselves in the mountains of Kentucky in the summer of 1936.

Mammoth Cave in Kentucky had been authorized by Calvin Coolidge to become a national park in 1926. However, the authorization was contingent on the NPS's acquisition of the required amount of local property. A group of private citizens formed the Mammoth Cave National Park Association in 1926, and by 1934, the minimum acreage was secured. Later legislation empowered the National Park Service to administer and protect the area that included Mammoth Cave. In 1941, while the entire United States remained in the stranglehold of the Great Depression, Mammoth Cave National Park was so designated by Congress. Fortunately, the Civilian Conservation Corps (CCC) had already been working on constructing telephone lines, picnic areas, hiking and cave tour trails, water lines, an up-to-date sewer system, utility buildings, and park housing at Mammoth Cave for eight years. The CCC, an inter-agency cooperative government program created to provide jobs for young men during the depression years, began its historic labors with

Camp One in Mammoth Cave in 1933. By the time that the cave was officially established as a part of the national park system in 1941, the CCC had built a significant infrastructure for park administration and visitor services.[48]

In 1935 as Mammoth Cave drew closer to becoming officially declared a national park, the Mammoth Cave Operating Committee began looking for experienced hotel administrators to manage their hotel operations. The committee found exactly the right combination they were looking for in Beulah and Henry. On February 28, 1936, the *Middlesboro* (KY) *Daily News* announced "the appointment of Mr. and Mrs. H.S. Sanborn, two experienced National Park hotel operators as manager and assistant manager of the Mammoth Cave and New Entrance Hotels, and the Cavern Coffee Shop." The article continued with a listing of all the Sanborn's previous positions from Yellowstone to California.

The main Mammoth Cave Hotel that Beulah and Henry would oversee for the next twelve years was built in 1925, replacing an older building that burned down in 1916. In 1930, ten small wood cottages had been constructed a short distance from the hotel on top of a timbered knoll, which expanded the hotel's capacity to two hundred guests. The hotel's dining room could seat one-hundred and twenty-five people. The New Entrance Hotel, built at the only hard-surfaced entrance to the caves in 1923, offered simple accommodations and dining until 1945 when it was torn down. However managing the hotels and dining room was only one of the operations that Harry and Beulah would become involved in at Mammoth Cave.[49]

When the National Park Service took over management of the national parks, Director Stephen T. Mather advocated that the park concessions would be more effective and efficient if run by privately-owned monopolies regulated by the National Park Service. He succeeded in getting this plan into action beginning in 1917 in the larger, more heavily visited parks that contained numerous concessionaires, but some of the smaller parks were not yet forced to adhere to this business scheme. During the 1930s depression and the New Deal years, Secretary of the Interior Harold Ickes, apparently frustrated with run-down visitor accommodations and unsatisfactory visitor services offered by concessioners, tried to ban all private enterprises in the parks. Ickes believed that the government should take over all of the concessions and visitor services. While he failed in that idea, Ickes succeeded on a smaller scale with the establishment of National Park Concessions, a board of overseers for some of the agency's smaller parks.[50]

Henry Sanborn and several other incorporators founded National Park Concessions, Inc. to act as a non-profit corporation to operate and regulate concessions in these parks where major concessioners could not be secured. In the early 1940s, National Park Concessions was incorporated to handle marginal park concession operations in parks such as Olympic, Isle Royale, Big Bend, Blue Ridge Parkway, and Mammoth Cave. The concessions now run under the umbrella of National Park Concessions, Inc. were and still are under contract to the National Park Service and thus subject to NPS control. In 1944, Henry Sanborn was named president and general manager of National Park Concessions, Inc. and by 1947 Beulah Brown Sanborn as secretary.[51]

On February 20, 1958, the *Park City Daily News* of Bowling Green, Kentucky announced the retirement of the Sanborns from Mammoth Cave. Beulah, aged seventy, and Henry, aged sixty-six, were ready to enjoy a bit more of life before, as Henry put it, "they both arrive at the twilight age." Even though he stepped down from being president and general manager, Henry continued to serve on the board of directors of National Park Concessions for another twenty-three years, until his death in 1981. However, he would conduct most of that business from Arizona.

Many years earlier, a guest at Lake Arrowhead had suggested that Beulah and Henry should try Soda Springs Ranch, near Sedona for their vacation in 1934. Driving from Flagstaff to Oak Creek Canyon, they were instantly smitten with the beautiful red rock desert and vowed to come back there one day to live. Throughout their careers, Beulah and Henry had lived in everything from tents to motel cottages to fine hotel suites, but never their own house. More than twenty years after first visiting Arizona's Verde Valley, they built their first home on a wooded, green hill near Bear Wallow overlooking the colorful mountains of Sedona, Arizona. Designed for comfort, privacy, and relaxed living, the house reflected their lifelong experience in planning livable facilities for others and Beulah declared it "absolutely satisfactory." In fact, their house was considered more than satisfactory by the Verde Valley Association who selected it to be one of four homes shown during the third annual Sedona House and Garden Tour on April 19, 1962. Their inclusion of environmentally sensitive features, such as Thermopane windows, double insulation, and a heating and air-conditioning system that utilized the same duct work, and the presence of Beulah and Henry's office-at-home, made their house a perfect fit for the tour's theme "Living and Working in Red Rock Country." They even designed the doors to be able to accommodate wheelchairs, whenever that time should come, if ever. But in the 1960s, Beulah and Henry showed no signs of slowing down, let alone stopping.

An article on April 5, 1962, in Sedona's *Verde Independent* stated that a homes tour would include the Sanborn home, which was filled with fascinating souvenirs of their trips to the Orient, Central and South America, Europe, Africa, Canada, and Alaska. Following the Verde Valley Association's House and Garden Tour, Beulah and Henry, who had been just about everywhere else, were off to Australia and New Zealand. Retirement for Beulah was a more of a calling to a deck chair on steamships bound for some exotic destination than to a restful rocking chair.

Beulah Brown Sanborn died on February 11, 1976 in Sedona, Arizona at the age of 87. It is unclear if she ever slowed down long enough for the proverbial rocking chair, let alone a wheelchair, but considering her adventurous spirit and zest for life, that seems doubtful. A thoroughly modern woman for her time, Beulah fashioned her own success as a vibrant guide, an amusing entertainer, a congenial hostess, and an accomplished hotel manager in a hospitality career that spanned three states and more than forty years of her active life, a career that she had unassumingly begun in Yellowstone.[52] Even though her presence has faded from most books of Yellowstone history, Beulah's memory is still alive in the park folklore she left behind. Her booklets *Songs of the Yellowstone Camps* became cherished memorabilia for hundreds if not thousands of families who recalled sitting by one of the camps' or lodges' crackling fires singing songs such as "Underneath the Yellowstone Moon" and "Till We Meet Again." Adding those to her coordination of numerous pageants and programs to celebrate historic events or simply to entertain visitors, her naming of Point Sublime, and her chronicle of a *Winter in Geyserland*, it is clear that Beulah left us an amusing treasury of Yellowstone memories and carved herself a memorable if modest place in women's history in national parks.

✤

Isabel Deming Bassett Wasson

(1897–1994)

Ideal for Teaching

Isabel Bassett's trip to Yellowstone with her parents and a Brooklyn
Daily Eagle tour group in August 1919 not only changed her life, it also
changed park history. Yellowstone Superintendent Horace M. Albright
accompanied the New York entourage as they toured the park, and
listened to Isabel explaining Yellowstone's geology to the tour members.
Albright was so impressed with the aspiring geologist's knowledge of
Yellowstone's geothermal features and volcanic history that he offered her
a position for the following summer to present lectures to park visitors. She
accepted Albright's offer and, upon taking her oath of office in July 1920,
Isabel became Yellowstone's first seasonal woman ranger naturalist. In this
appointment Isabel Bassett discovered her love of teaching, which eventually
became her lifelong passion and she established a pioneering milestone for
the future of women ranger-naturalists in Yellowstone National Park.

Born as the third child of Edward Murray Bassett and Annie R. Preston
Bassett on January 11, 1897, Isabel Deming Bassett entered into a family
accustomed to upper levels of college education and high standards for
success. Following his graduation from Amherst College in 1884, Isabel's
father Edward attended Columbia University Law School. Completing
his law degree and passing the New York state bar exam in 1886, Edward
began his career in Buffalo. He married Annie R. Preston in 1890, and
two years later, they moved to New York City and began their family of
five children with son Preston Rogers Bassett, born on March 20, 1892.[1]

While Isabel was growing up her father became an eminent figure in
both national and local politics. From 1903 until 1905, Edward served in

the U.S. House of Representatives, but at the end of his term he declined to run again, preferring instead to attend to the needs of his community. Serving on a multitude of committees and councils, he was instrumental in developing the New York City subway system, and authored the first in-depth zoning ordinance in the United States. Credited with originating the term "freeway" to designate controlled-access highways, and with other urban planning concepts, Edward Murray Bassett was eventually recognized as a monumental figure in the development of city landscapes.[2]

Isabel's brother was also a great role model for her. Following in his father's footsteps, Preston attended Amherst College, graduated in 1913, and furthered his education at Polytechnic Institute of Brooklyn in 1913-1914. Ascending to a prominent position as an engineer and inventor in the aviation industry, Preston ultimately became recognized as one of aviation's pioneers. Holder of thirty-five patents for his engineering inventions such as carbon arc lights used in anti-aircraft searchlights, he was awarded honorary M.A. and D.Sc. degrees from Amherst, and an honorary L.L.D. (Doctor of Law) from Adelphi College. Preston's lifetime list of accolades nearly matched his father's by the time of his death in 1992. It is not surprising that Isabel Bassett chose to advance her education and pursue a career in geology.[3]

She greatly admired her father and brother, who introduced her to the marvels of earth science on their summer vacations. They filled Isabel's early life with outdoor excursions and, accordingly, she developed a passionate sense of wonder about the world that surrounded her. Even though she suffered a slight physical disability from polio suffered at the age of three, Isabel scrambled around quarries with Edward and Preston as they collected fossils. These summer excursions stimulated her interest in brachiopods, cephalopods, and crustaceans. Later in life, she attributed her continuing enchantment with science and geology to her father and brother.[4]

Upon her graduation from New York's Erasmus High School in 1914, Isabel entered Wellesley College. While her degree program was in history, she also enrolled in several science classes. One of those, the study of fossils taught by Margaret Parker, proved to be a turning point for Isabel. She became fascinated with Parker's collection of fossilized specimens and often helped her instructor transport samples to the classroom. Walking the paths of Wellesley with a pocketful of fossils was a thrill that Isabel fondly remembered all of her life. With Phi Beta Kappa honors and a Bachelor of Arts degree in history, Isabel graduated in 1918. But her interest in geology prompted her to seek more earth science education and experience.

That summer she enrolled in graduate geology classes at the University of Chicago, and studied under two renowned geology professors, Dr. Thomas C. Chamberlin and Rollin D. Salisbury.[5] In addition to a summer of graduate classes at the University of Chicago in 1918, Isabel took a class in index fossils with Professor Hervey V. Shimer at the Massachusetts Institute of Technology. In the fall, she returned to Wellesley to work as an assistant in the Geology Department during the school year of 1918-1919. With her goal now intently set on an advanced degree in geology, she returned to the University of Chicago for the summer of 1919.[6]

After she finished summer classes, she joined her parents and a tour group from Brooklyn on the aforementioned cross-country excursion to Yellowstone. The special tour had been arranged by a family friend, and editor of the *Brooklyn Daily Eagle*, Hans V. Kaltenborn. As the group traveled west, Kaltenborn invited Isabel to share her scientific knowledge of the country they were crossing by being a tour .guide. In Yellowstone, she talked about geological topics such as the origin of the Mammoth Hot Springs, the travertine terraces, the erupting geysers, the history of Yellowstone's Grand Canyon, and the volcanic flows on Specimen Ridge with an explanation of its layers of plant fossils and petrified forests. Park Superintendent Horace Albright listened attentively to Isabel for several days while the group traveled around the park. He thought her a "splendid public speaker" who possessed the "ability to hold a large audience while discussing scientific problems." For Albright, Isabel's lectures embodied his ideal concept of an informative blend of science and instruction for park visitors, and he invited her to join his nascent educational staff for the summer of 1920.[7]

Albright was Yellowstone's first official National Park Service Superintendent and he held strong convictions about the park's educational value. Stephen Mather, first director of the National Park Service, supported Albright's idea of making education one of the focal points of the NPS canons. In his 1918 report, he stated that "classes in science are to be afforded special opportunities to study in the national parks and museums containing specimens of their flora and fauna are to be established as funds are provided for this purpose." Albright believed that

Isabel Bassett (standing far right) made quite an impression on Brooklyn Daily Eagle *editor and trip coordinator, Hans Kaltenborn (center), with her ability to explain the various geographic regions that the tour group was viewing and experiencing. The woman on the left is not identified but is probably Kaltenborn's wife.* (FROM WESTWARD HONK)

in order for visitors to truly enjoy the park they needed to understand its flora, fauna, culture, and history and, especially, its geology. Both Mather and Albright felt that the educational mission of the NPS should do more than merely hand out informational pamphlets and maps. Making the national parks available as field laboratories for schools, universities, scholars, and scientists became an objective for both men. In accordance with this vision, Isabel's alma mater, Columbia University, broadened its curriculum offerings with a national parks course in 1919.[8]

While Isabel was finishing her degree at Columbia, Albright had hired Milton Skinner, appointed him chief park naturalist, and assigned him the task of organizing an information bureau and an educational plan for

Yellowstone. Skinner, who had first came to the park in 1896 as a college student, was well suited for the position because he had served many years as a guide and lecturer for the hotel company at the Upper Geyser Basin. Skinner's first order of business was to prepare and post monthly bulletins on birds, animals, flowers, and geology throughout the public areas of the park. These bulletins began as "Yellowstone Letters" and eventually became the popular periodical *Yellowstone Nature Notes*, which supplied park information to rangers and tourists into the late 1950s. Skinner provided the Mammoth information office—an early equivalent of today's visitor center—with photographs, ground relief maps, a wall display of wildflowers, and exhibits of geological specimens, and he placed free circulars, maps, and pamphlets there for the public.

The public responded enthusiastically in 1920 as 10,000 visitors utilized the information bureau and "appeared very much pleased with the service rendered." Equally valuable to the public that summer was the information bureau's moving into the field, via free half-hour lectures, presented three times daily, at Mammoth. Albright was delighted with the public's reaction to this new department, and declared the response completely "astonishing."[9]

After taking her final courses at Columbia University, Isabel graduated in May 1920 with an M.A. in geology. But that spring proved to be even more eventful for her. In addition to obtaining her graduate degree and embarking on a new job in Yellowstone, Isabel married fellow graduate student Theron Wasson.[10]

Theron, ten years her senior, had graduated from the Carnegie Institute of Technology in 1911. His continuing education was interrupted by the entry of the United States into World War I in 1917. After his enlistment, he was commissioned in 1918 as a Second Lieutenant of Engineers in France, and participated in several military campaigns including the march to the Rhine. In 1919 he enrolled in the geology program at Columbia, where he met Isabel. Theirs was a whirlwind courtship and they married on June 11, 1920.[11]

Following her marriage, Isabel Bassett Wasson began her first working summer in Yellowstone in the dual role of wife and ranger-naturalist. Isabel's daily lecture schedule as ranger naturalist began with an afternoon talk on the porch of the Mammoth Hotel at 4 P.M., followed by another at 7:30 P.M. at the cabins in the Mammoth Camp (later called Mammoth Lodge), and finally a campfire talk at 9 P.M. in the Public Auto Campground. She varied her lectures with three different talks each day, so that visitors who were staying for several days would not attend the same lecture twice. Her lectures were so well received that some visitors staying for only one day followed her from one to the next. In her presentation titled "How the Yellowstone Came To Be," she used her background as a geology teacher to discuss the geological formation of the park in less scientific "non-technical" language that was geared toward the general public. According to Albright's 1920 Report to the Secretary of Interior, this lecture and others that ranged from the history of the park to the care of its wildlife, was well attended by a fascinated public. Albright's boss, NPS Director Stephen Mather, believed that "an intelligent study of nature is greatly assisted by direction" and the favorable response to Isabel's presentations seemed to confirm Mather's philosophy.[12]

In addition to giving evening talks, Isabel worked in the National Park Service Information Office in the morning, and in the afternoon guided hotel bellmen on walks around Mammoth to teach them how to conduct educational tours. She observed that "these boys were good-natured and cooperative, but they had no background for the geological material I tried to impart to them. They spent most of their time with the tourists saying, 'See that formation, it looks like a camel lying down,' or having the children run around the hot spring basins, while they threw coins into the steaming water, which later would be gradually coated with lime."

Isabel reported to Albright at the end of the season that she believed that "it was useless to try to use these boys as guides, and that it would be much better to employ college youth as naturalist-guides, and give them brief specific training for such work." That recommendation, a new concept for the National Park Service and for some hotel concessioners, was an idea that had been originally used by William Wallace Wylie in his Wylie Camping Company. Wylie believed that college students could become enthusiastic students of the park's scientific phenomena, and so employed them as his primary force of educational tour guides beginning in the early 1890s. Thus, through the years, hiring college students has become a tradition for the National Park Service and park concessioners, and has brought thousands of young employees to Yellowstone. In some families, such summer work became a tradition handed down from mothers and fathers to daughters and sons to grandchildren and great-grandchildren, through several generations of Yellowstone aficionados.[13]

Lest that it be thought that Isabel's summer of 1920 was all work and no play, note that she was invited at least once a week to join excursions into other areas of the park. Often, she accompanied coworkers from the National Park Service Information Office while they observed animals and birds in various areas. On one occasion Isabel and a fellow ranger climbed Specimen Ridge, and Isabel experienced the "famous thirteen forests" of petrified trees. Discovered and brought to the attention of the scientific community by E.C. Alderson, of Bozeman, Montana, in 1887, Specimen Ridge represented one of the park's most remarkable geological features.[14]

As they do today, the "fossil forests" of Specimen Ridge covered an extensive area in the northeastern section of the park, stretching for nearly twenty miles along the Lamar River. These forests of well-preserved, upright tree trunks had been formed when a succession of growing forests was entombed by massive flows of various volcanic materials. As the first forest grew and was buried, there was a long enough period (200–300 years for pine trees, to 500–1,000 years for redwoods) without volcanic activity to allow a second forest to grow on top of the first. Alternating forest growth, and new outbursts of ash, mud and other materials spanning thousands of years, created more than 2,000 feet of fossil-forest beds on Specimen Ridge, which today contains at least twenty-seven such layers of petrified forests. It was here that Isabel became further enthralled with Yellowstone's geology as she discovered small specimens of fossil ferns and the largest of the petrified trees, a giant redwood that was twenty-six feet in circumference and twelve feet high.[15]

On another outing she accompanied a commercial movie crew to film the park's remnant herd of buffalo in Lamar Valley. In the early 1920s, with the American frontier essentially gone for thirty years, people across the country began to feel nostalgic about the vanished days of the American West. Movie directors capitalized on this trend and produced films to restore the public's memory of the Old West on Hollywood's silver screen. Commercial motion picture studios produced countless films filled with cowboys and Indians, saloons and dance hall girls, gunfights and cattle drives, and of course, stampeding bison. Isabel actually experienced the making of one of these electrifying scenes of the "Wild West." As she took a position safely inside the photographer's automobile, a ranger, located

Thundering bison heading toward the photographer's lens made a for a breathtaking postcard in the 1920s. (AUTHOR'S COLLECTION)

farther east in Lamar Valley, started a bison stampede. With heads down, the herd charged full force toward Isabel and the car that carried a tripod and camera mounted on its hood. This scene of a thundering herd of buffalo in the park must have seemed surreal to this 23-year-old New Yorker. As the stampeding herd reached the camera vehicle with Isabel inside, the rumbling column of buffalo parted, and two flanks of snorting animals swept by them. Afterward, she claimed that, "for a few minutes, we were in a sea of heaving, charging animals. I shall never forget it." That must have been the most heart-stopping experience of Isabel's summer. A few years later park superintendent Horace Albright would receive public criticism for allowing Hollywood to film such a Yellowstone buffalo stampede to make Gary Cooper's 1925 movie *The Thundering Herd*.[16]

While tame in comparison to her bison encounter, Isabel's excursion with the men from the U.S. Fish and Wildlife Service on a trout study also piqued her interest in the workings of nature. She was fascinated by the process of catching the trout and stroking their bellies to extract milt, which was spread over eggs in an effort to increase trout production in the park's hatchery ponds. For Isabel, Yellowstone seemed unlimited in its educational opportunities. Isabel's summer of 1920 stimulated her interest in education and opened a window on her lifetime goals. She observed that park visitors "were on vacation with time to explore, observe, and grope for explanations of the natural wonders around them," and it seemed to her that the conditions in the park were thus "ideal for teaching."[17] She grew fond of national park educational work during this time, so at the end of her season she knew that, one way or another, she would find a way to teach people about the wonders of nature.

Albright believed that the ranger lectures had been very successful and that Isabel Wasson had helped him lay an important foundation for that work. Encouraged by the public's enthusiastic response to ranger talks, Albright invited Isabel to return the following year, but because she was expecting her first child, Isabel declined for the 1921 season. Albright hired another teacher, Mary Rolfe, to take Isabel's place. He later wrote that while Mary was "a fine enthusiastic girl, who tried very hard to please," her presentations were not as well received as Wasson's because (he thought) that they were "considerably more technical" than Isabel's. Being able to translate science into understandable language for park visitors was Isabel's special talent, which apparently set a standard for Albright in his concept of scientific talks.[18]

The 1921 season's educational programs consisted of eighty-three lectures at the Mammoth Hotel, seventy-seven at the Mammoth Camp, fifty-four at the campfire gatherings at the public auto camp, and sixty-six at various other locations in the park.[19] In only one season, Isabel, with her plain-language non-technical talks, had set the template for park ranger talks, followed to this day. For Isabel that summer proved to be crucial as she discovered her personal love of teaching, and it thus set the stage for her to embrace and pursue her life's calling in science and education.

Following the birth of her daughter Elizabeth Fuller Wasson on September 21, 1921, Isabel began a career as a petroleum geologist with the Pure Oil Company. This career choice, avant garde for a woman in the 1920s, captured the attention of the *Oil and Gas News*, which proclaimed her "one of the very few practical woman geologists in the United States." As one of a handful of American women working as petroleum geologists

Isabel examines a rock outcropping in an unknown location, presumably in her early career as one of the few women geologists of the 1920s.
(COURTESY PETER BERGSTROM)

in the 1920s, she worked alongside her husband making geological maps of Oklahoma and exploring remote areas of South America. Her work in Venezuela led to a 1923 headline in Isabel's hometown newspaper, the *Brooklyn Daily Eagle*, and around the nation, which proclaimed, "Brooklyn Woman Braves Jungle To Explore Vast Venezuelan Oil Fields." However, with the birth of her second child, Edward Bassett Wasson on December 5, 1925, she turned her ambitions homeward.[20]

In 1928, she followed the affinity for education that she discovered in Yellowstone and embarked on a teaching career in River Forest, Illinois. The following year, the birth of Anne Harney Wasson increased the Wasson family to five. But even with three children, Isabel continued to pursue her calling in education. She would spend the next fifty years teaching science, giving community lectures, leading bird-watching field trips, and guiding aspiring naturalists. Isabel and Theron divorced in May of 1953, the same year he retired from his position as chief geologist for the Pure

Oil Company. Even with this disturbance, Isabel's unflappable spirit and dedication never faltered as she fostered public and school education in the natural sciences such as geology, zoology, botany, and ornithology and local history. By the 1970s, she had gained a reputation as a renowned educator and helpful mentor in her own community.[21]

In 1975, the community of River Forest, Illinois, planted a tree in honor of the woman they revered as resident, historian, teacher, and friend. Even though she had retired in 1968, Isabel continued to contribute to the school's programs by designing a course about River Forest history for the fourth grade, and lecturing to teachers on the community's history and geology to prepare them for teaching that course. In 1981 the school district extended the community's tribute to Isabel by dedicating the River Forest history room in the Roosevelt Junior High School. Isabel's decades-long associations with leading scientists and educators as well as prestigious scientific organizations, which included the Morton Arboretum, the Chicago Field Museum, and the Chicago Academy of Science, had brought her the acclaim of "living legend" in River Forest, Illinois.[22]

In 1983 at the age of eighty-six, Isabel moved to Plymouth Place Retirement Center in La Grange Park, Illinois. While age had slowed her to some extent, she still maintained an active schedule. At Plymouth Place, she gave lectures and conducted discussions on local history and continued to guide village history tours and bird watching trips. In her quieter moments, she corresponded with her life-long associates, friends, and family.

On February 21, 1994, Isabel Bassett Wasson died at age ninety-seven. But her legacy arguably lives on today, ably represented by each and every park ranger who stands before an inquisitive crowd of visitors in national parks and explains their geology and the mysterious processes of the earth.[23]

❧

Jane Marguerite "Peg" Lindsley Arnold

(1901–1952)

A Girl Ranger!

"Pooh! What's a little trip from Philadelphia to Yellowstone," scoffed Marguerite Lindsley in the August 1924 issue of *Harley-Davidson Enthusiast* magazine. "Lots of men make longer trips all the time and nobody thinks about it, but just because we're girls, they think we have done something wonderful," she argued in the magazine's article describing her cross-country trip to Yellowstone on her 24 JD Harley-Davidson sidecar outfit. Earlier that summer, she had traversed the Lincoln Highway through Des Moines, Iowa; Omaha, Nebraska; and Cheyenne, Wyoming on a seventeen-day journey westward with her friend, Claire Le Valle of Philadelphia. The two girls averaged 180 miles per day and, characteristic of Marguerite's western upbringing, they camped out along their route. From Cheyenne the pair followed the Yellowstone Highway through Cody, and entered Miss Lindsley's wilderness home of Yellowstone National Park through the east entrance. Described as a typical western girl, game and nervy, "Girl Ranger" Marguerite Lindsley proved to be as much as an enthusiast for Yellowstone as she was for her Harley.[1]

Born October 2, 1901, in Mammoth Hot Springs, Wyoming, Jane Marguerite Lindsley[2] became a true child of Yellowstone National Park. Her father Chester A. Lindsley had traveled to the park from New York in April 1894 to visit his brother, Lieutenant Elmer E. Lindsley, stationed at Fort Yellowstone with the Sixth Cavalry. Apparently quite taken with the place and all its natural wonders, Chester secured employment for the summer with the Yellowstone Park Hotel Company.[3] At the end of the season he accepted a position with the Department of Interior and began his service as a civilian clerk for the military administration of Yellowstone on November 1. Less than a year later, in September, 1895, Miss Jenny Maude Bradley came to Yellowstone to reside with her brother, Captain Alfred Bradley, the post surgeon of the United States Medical Corps, who was also stationed at Fort Yellowstone. Shortly after her arrival Maude caught Chester's eye, and in 1898 the two were joined in marriage. As husband and wife, Chester and Maude took up residence in Mammoth Hot Springs, and began their nearly lifetime connection with Yellowstone National Park. Three years later the couple presented Yellowstone with their new daughter and one of the park's most earnest, lifetime devotees— Jane Marguerite Lindsley.[4]

Growing up in Yellowstone during the "old army days" offered Marguerite a front row seat to a different time in America's first national park. With cannons booming at sunrise and sunset, bugle calls, tootling regimental bands, half-mast flags for the death of a president, rousing polo matches, cracking pistol and rifle range practices, and flashing saber drills, Marguerite grew up witnessing the ceremonial splendor of the U.S. Army at Mammoth. Until its destruction in 1909, the deserted pre-army headquarters building known as the Block House, erected high atop Capitol Hill in 1880 by P.W. Norris as a lookout for Indians, was one of Marguerite's many playgrounds. Always adventurous and daring, Marguerite remembered that her most memorable escapade as a youngster was the thrill of trying to stay on a runaway Indian pony.

Assuredly a darling of Wonderland, Marguerite, also known as Peg, received Christmas gifts from all sorts of people whom she befriended as a child of Yellowstone.[5] The Chinese family who ran Chinaman's Laundry in the old McCartney Hotel, located near the mouth of Clematis Gulch, gave her either embroidered handkerchiefs or Chinese nuts and candy. During one Christmas season, pioneer dude rancher and Marguerite's childhood idol "Uncle Howard" Eaton gave her a Navajo Indian turquoise ring. In his letter, he said that it was an engagement ring and teased her that they would be "married on the ice bridge below Lower Falls on the Fourth of July just as soon as he grew up and was old enough" for her. He furthered her fanciful imagination by claiming that the stone was really a diamond that "he had painted blue so it would not be a temptation to such notorious characters as Jesse James!" Marguerite loved the fact that

Marguerite Lindsley takes a friend for a ride on her pony in Mammoth Hot Springs in this family snapshot. (COURTESY BILL ARNOLD)

"Uncle Howard" wrote her two or three times a year and always closed his delightful letters with one of his characteristic signatures such as "Yours to a frazzle" or "I still love you as hard as a mule can kick." One can only imagine how that tickled her.

Her childhood during the golden days of stagecoach travel in Yellowstone National Park was exhilarating. Five-day trips around "the loop" on dusty and bumpy park roads in government coaches pulled by mules, which she proudly claimed outpaced those of the tourist parties, were high points of her summer life in America's Wonderland. For a young girl of thirteen, news of bandits and robbery in the park's interior on July 29, 1914, must have seemed like something right out of the high-spirited days of the Old West! On that day, the second to the last of the park's big stagecoach robberies occurred at Shoshone Point between Old Faithful and West Thumb.[6] The masked road-agent whose partner was supposedly hiding in the timber, relieved eighty-two people in coaches and surreys of nearly $1,000 in cash and $130 worth of jewelry. Marguerite never forgot how this brash highway thievery caused big excitement not only in her home base of Mammoth Hot Springs but throughout the entire park. It is no wonder that all this excitement in her high-adventure world of Yellowstone made going off to school in the city sound boring by comparison.

Because there was not yet a school in Mammoth for the children of army officers and park employees in the early 1900s, Marguerite's mother home-schooled her through the eighth grade, and her curriculum followed the same course of study used in the Livingston, Montana, schools. Marguerite took her final examinations for eighth grade with the Livingston pupils and elatedly reported that she "passed fourth in the county—all thanks to Mother!"[7] Just before she turned fourteen, she entered the preparatory school at Montana State College (today's Montana State University) in Bozeman, where she finished her high school work in just three years. Following graduation from high school, Marguerite became a student of Montana State College, and she took four years of pre-med work, majoring in bacteriology.

Meanwhile her father, Chester, remained at Mammoth Hot Springs, continuing as civilian clerk under the army's administration of Yellowstone until the establishment of the National Park Service in August 1916. Chester's service of twenty years in Yellowstone was likely recognized as a valuable asset, and he was appointed Acting Superintendent in October 1916.[8] As the National Park Service initiated its roles and designed its mandates, Chester assisted with the transition from military administration to civilian management from 1916 until 1919, when Horace Albright assumed command as the park's first NPS superintendent. From 1919 until 1922, Chester Lindsley worked as Albright's assistant. He then served as Yellowstone's postmaster from 1922 until his retirement in 1935, during which time his appointment certificates were signed by four U.S. presidents: Harding, Coolidge, Hoover, and Roosevelt.

While Chester took pride in his accomplishments during the organizational years of the NPS in Yellowstone, one of his proudest moments must have been when newspapers across the country announced that his daughter was the "Girl Appointed Ranger in Yellowstone Park" for the summer of 1921.[9]

While her breaks from school were always devoted to the park that Marguerite called home, the summer between her junior and senior years of college was very different. She was going to work as a ranger and to get paid for explaining the wonders of Yellowstone. In June of 1921 newspapers at faraway locations such as Michigan, Wisconsin, and

Marguerite, here displaying the interior of an old stagecoach, began her duties as a ranger in 1921. She is wearing a uniform of her own design, because the NPS did not yet have a uniform for women. ((COURTESY BILL ARNOLD)

Oklahoma, as well as many closer to home in Wyoming and Montana, announced to the world that Miss Marguerite "Peg" Lindsley had been chosen to teach tourists about Yellowstone, but more importantly that she had been awarded the official title of National Park Ranger.[10]

Taking her oath of office on June 14, 1921, Marguerite became the third woman to hold the title of ranger in Yellowstone.[11] Mary Rolfe, a schoolteacher also hired that summer, was the second woman ranger because she began her employment just one day earlier than Marguerite. Isabel Bassett Wasson had previously earned the distinction of being the first woman ranger in Yellowstone when she was hired by Horace M.

Albright to lecture to park visitors on the geology and wildlife during the summer of 1920. However, because they were only seasonal employees, all of these women (including Marguerite at this time), were considered temporary rangers. Within the next four years Marguerite would become the first woman in Yellowstone and in the National Park Service to attain a position as a permanent ranger—a status that can be considered historic if not iconic.[12]

With her course work in bacteriology and botany at Montana State College as well as her lifetime familiarity with Yellowstone's natural wonders, Marguerite was a perfect candidate to follow in Isabel Wasson's footsteps. Given the task of providing information and explaining the workings of nature, Isabel and Marguerite were among women of Yellowstone who found their vocations in the sciences and education. The initiative toward this life-calling for many women growing up at the time was most likely inspired by the introduction of nature studies into school curricula in the early 1900s.

Nature study as an educational movement in American public schools began in the late nineteenth and early twentieth centuries. Coinciding with the country's concerns for nature conservation, its curricula were zealously promoted by naturalists and scientists such as Anna Botsford Comstock and Louis Agassiz. Nature study in its earliest form encouraged hands-on observation, and promoted appreciation of the natural world for its beauty as well as its value. "Study nature, not books," Agassiz professed. But in addition to cultivating children's perceptions and insights into the natural world around them, nature study programs included the newly separated fields of zoology, botany, physics, chemistry, geology, mineralogy, and geography.

As with the conservation movement, this philosophy that advocated viewing nature as something to be appreciated rather than something only to be utilized attracted more women than men. Often viewed as romantic or sentimental by male detractors, this new model formed a bridge that allowed women to breach the previously male-dominated disciplines of science, and to gain educational opportunities in natural history and science. By the 1920s, women and nature education seemed to be logical counterparts— and Yellowstone—with its developing educational programs, appeared to many women to be the ideal environment for both to advance. For those women who loved the outdoors and an active lifestyle, positions as park

Marguerite loved to share her knowledge of the park's thermal features with visitors. (COURTESY BILL ARNOLD)

rangers or ranger-naturalists not only were dream jobs, but also provided unique opportunities to utilize their science educations.[13]

Described in a newspaper article as an "honest-to-goodness outdoor girl, an expert horsewoman, and a master of the technique of camp life," she did not quite fit the profile of an average American girl. Marguerite once remarked that it must have been a mistake that she was not born a boy. "I love the work of the rangers, and if I were a boy, I would make the park service my life work. It was born in me, I know," she commented to a newspaper reporter. "I have been used to the saddle, to hiking, skiing, and fishing almost from babyhood," Marguerite added. Her intimate connection with outdoor life in Yellowstone, first as a child and now as a guide who provided educational services, showed Marguerite to be as familiar with the park's geysers as city dwellers were with streets and drinking fountains.[14]

Her duties for the summer of 1921 were to assist Milton P. Skinner, Yellowstone's first official park naturalist, with the small museum and information bureau located at park headquarters, and to give guided walks and talks around Mammoth Hot Springs. In her essay "Early Impressions," in the Spring 1934 *Yellowstone Nature Notes*, Marguerite credited Skinner with helping to instill her love of educational work through his enthusiasm and passion for that subject. But largely it was her own fervent love of

Yellowstone and all its natural phenomena that shaped her desire and eagerness to present accurate information to park visitors.[15]

By the 1920s, the days of the stagecoach drivers' yarns about glass mountains that magnified animals and petrified birds perched on petrified cliffs had become as much a part of Yellowstone's past as those long-gone "knights of the lash." The National Park Service believed that the public, while enjoying those yarns, also wanted truthful information about the park, and Marguerite delivered. Even when asked if the dead trees in the Mammoth Hot Springs were ever alive, she resisted telling the questioners that the "trees grew dead," and patiently explained that the trees had been killed by mineral deposits and lack of water. She prided herself in being able to offer visitors factual and scientific information about the park's features, and she was rewarded with their appreciation and respect.[16]

In addition to guiding visitors, Marguerite's lifelong familiarity with Yellowstone found another outlet during the summer of 1922, when she and park photographer Jack E. Haynes were assigned the monumental task of sorting through the hundreds of Yellowstone place names that had accumulated over the past fifty years. Confusion concerning Yellowstone place names dated to before 1895, when historian Hiram Chittenden included an appendix of them in his book, *The Yellowstone National Park*.

Now, in the 1920s, and in an effort to establish order and authenticity for Yellowstone place names, Horace Albright formed a committee with himself as chairman. He appointed Marguerite Lindsley and Jack Haynes, both lifelong park residents, to assist him. The trio spent countless hours listing current place names, followed by many more hours researching them for duplication and relevance.[17] By 1928, when the committee ceased operations, the three had successfully reduced a great deal of confusion surrounding Yellowstone place names by eliminating duplications, restoring some historical nomenclature, and conforming many of Yellowstone's place names to rules of the United States Board on Geographic Names (USBGN). As a result, the 1928 *Ranger Naturalists' Manual* was updated, and Jack Haynes revised his popular *Haynes Guide* to reflect the clarifications. Upon finishing their assignment, the committee submitted more than 500 new place names to the USBGN, and nearly all of them were approved by 1930.[18]

Following her graduation with honors from Montana State College in May 1922 and her second summer working as a ranger, Marguerite

One can only imagine what it must have been like for Marguerite and her friend Claire to travel thousands of miles from Philadelphia to Wyoming on this 24-JD Harley Davidson sidecar unit in 1924. (COURTESY BILL ARNOLD)

continued to pursue her educational goals. "All thru college and until I received my B.S. degree," she wrote, "my fondest hope was to become a doctor of medicine." She tried to get into the School of Medicine at the University of Pennsylvania, but was not accepted. She believed that coming from a small western college and being unknown there probably hindered her chances. However, she did have the qualifications to enroll in the university's graduate program in bacteriology. So, following the completion of her M.S. degree in the spring of 1923, she returned to Yellowstone to resume her work as a seasonal ranger for the summer. She did not even wait for the formal commencement ceremony because her ranger job was waiting for her. Just as she had done for the past two years,

Marguerite spent another blissful summer guiding visitors around the Mammoth Terraces and taking charge of the Information Office.[19]

That fall Marguerite returned to Philadelphia to begin work in bacteriology at Mulford Laboratories. Some clinical research being done at that time concerned the health benefits of *L. acidophilus*, a friendly bacterium that occurs naturally in the human intestinal tract and protects the body against unhealthy organisms. Some clinical studies in the 1920s, with which Marguerite was probably involved, showed that acidophilus supplements could be useful in improving the environment of the intestinal tract and boosting the body's immune system. According to her friend and fellow ranger Herma Albertson Baggley, Marguerite became the first person to put acidophilus into a form other than liquid. Even though her work there was "most interesting and instructive," her enthusiasm for bacteriology waned when spring arrived and with it an urge to return to Yellowstone. "I could almost smell the melting snow and growing things," Marguerite recalled, "[and] feel the thrill of an early morning [horseback] ride." Yellowstone was just too much of an attraction. And the thrill of a ride proved to be exactly how her summer of 1924 would begin.[20]

While she had begun a career on the East Coast with good intentions, she soon realized that the out-of-doors was her natural habitat. Although she worked full-time at the laboratory for nearly eight months, Marguerite had saved very little of her earnings and her sole mode of transportation was a (nearly paid for) Harley Davidson motorcycle with a sidecar. The only way home was to ride it. Her yearning to return to the west proved to be stronger than her reservation about trekking across the country on a motorcycle, so in late May, accompanied by fellow Mulford laboratory employee Claire Le Valle, Marguerite set out for Yellowstone. Weathering seventeen days and 2600 miles of "not favorable" roads along with even less favorable weather—hail, sleet, mud, and washouts—Marguerite labeled it "next to the greatest escapade" of her life. (She would achieve her greatest escapade later that winter.) According to Herma Albertson Baggley, Marguerite undertook that monumental cross-country trip without even informing her parents of her plan. Imagine their surprise when their 22-year-old daughter roared up to their front door in Mammoth Hot Springs on a Harley! Especially because Marguerite and Claire had arrived in the middle of a formal dinner that Chester and Jenny Maude Lindsley were hosting for a group of visiting NPS dignitaries.[21]

"Paint Pot Peg" shows friends the result of her breaking through the crust of a thermal area. (COURTESY BILL ARNOLD)

From Harleys to horses, Marguerite's exploits and adventures became the essence of her identity. One summer (date unknown), during her early days in the park, Marguerite accompanied "Uncle Howard" Eaton on a three-week horseback trip through Yellowstone that included 200 horses and 125 persons, 75 of whom were dudes (tourists). Marguerite offered to guide a group of tourists through the Gibbon Paint Pot area (today's Artists' Paint Pots). Being *the* Yellowstone native and therefore assumed to be in the know about *all* of Yellowstone, she gamely escorted the group on the expedition even though this area was "terra incognita" to her. Not uncommon in those days of few boardwalks and safe walking paths, she broke through the crust of a thermal area and found herself in boiling clay up to her knee. This experience not only gave her third degree burns where the clay got through her boot lacing but also a new nickname, "Geyser Peg." Apparently, because of that incident she acquired more than one new nickname, which was evidenced by a photograph taken of her during the trip and captioned "Paint Pot Peg."[22]

Summer or winter, Marguerite's adventures placed her in the annals of the park's history. During the spring of 1925, Marguerite achieved what she believed was her greatest escapade when she made a ski trip around Yellowstone with Mr. and Mrs. Hans Larsen and Ranger Leon Carter. At that time no woman had traveled around the entire loop on skis, so she and Mrs. Larsen were the first women to take on the challenge. "It had been an ambition of mine since I was old enough to handle skis at all," Marguerite recalled a few years later. She and the Larsens set out from Mammoth on the first of March and skied twenty miles to the Norris Ranger Station on the first day. The following day they had skied fourteen miles when they met Ranger Carter, who accompanied them for the remainder of the trip. Marguerite did not record how many days it took them to complete the 143-mile journey, probably because what really mattered was that her winter excursion had become the most gloriously interesting trip of her life. "Can you imagine geysers, rivers, waterfalls, and lakes in the grip of winter with over six feet of snow on the level in places?" she later gleefully asked an inquiring journalist. Indeed, venturing into Yellowstone on a multiple-day outing in winter, where temperatures routinely dipped below zero and before the advent of waterproof clothing and instant hand-warmers, Marguerite and Mrs. Larsen had indisputably experienced an extraordinary winter trek in the park.[23]

During the summers of 1924 and 1925, Marguerite worked with her father in the post office, but she also interpreted Yellowstone. She had a license to accompany people touring the park in their own cars, if they desired a guide to go along and explain the sights. During one of these summers she also spent nearly two months with one party in Jackson Hole, Wyoming, on the J.Y. Dude Ranch, a place that Marguerite call "nearer to heaven than any other I have found on this earth."[24]

In late December 1925, Marguerite was offered her dream job: the position of permanent ranger who would assist the park service's newly formed educational division. During the summer she was to be in charge of the Government Information Office at Mammoth Hot Springs, where she and a few "ninety-day wonders" (temporary rangers) would assist 200 to 600 visitors per day from 7 A.M. until 10 P.M. The information they most commonly gave was about Yellowstone roads, geology, flora, and fauna. Even though there were many foolish questions and there was the temptation to answer some of them in the same vein, Marguerite believed that it was more admirable to show visitors patience and courtesy. In the same building was a small museum where Marguerite maintained a wildflower exhibit—from twenty to fifty species—that she labeled with both common and Latin botanical names. Other services rendered by the educational division that Marguerite helped with consisted of evening lectures and walking tours given by qualified rangers. During the winter months she would write and edit articles for *Yellowstone Nature Notes*, gather data, and prepare educational material for the coming season. In this new and fascinating job, Marguerite could embark on her walks and talks as well as do research and observe the park's flora and fauna on a full-time, year-round basis. However, as the history of women in Yellowstone as well as in the National Park Service bears out, Marguerite acquired her permanent position just in time.[25]

Following a visit to Yellowstone by Chief Inspector J.F. Garland and E.K. Burlew, Administrative Assistant to the Secretary of Interior, during the summer of 1926, the future of full-time women rangers in Yellowstone became tenuous. Garland and Burlew's report to Secretary Hubert Work on October 4 stated, "It was noted that the daughter of Doctor Conard, a park naturalist, is assigned to duty as a ranger at Camp Roosevelt. We do not believe that a woman is physically suited for the arduous duties of a ranger and that the service, which is already undermanned, suffers by the loss of what a qualified man in her place could perform. It is recommended that women rangers be not employed..." These Department of Interior inspectors were also not pleased that there were "a number of women under the designation of ranger employed at checking stations." They suggested that "these women should be given some other designation."[26]

Raised during the era of Theodore Roosevelt's ideal that masculinity was directly connected to nationalism and achieved through living the "strenuous life," Garland viewed women rangers in Yellowstone as a threat to his perceived image of the National Park Service ranger. Employing Rooseveltian doctrines that professed the spirit of America to be composed of manly, bodily vigor, Garland's old-guard perception of a ranger seemed to be fashioned from the image of the Rough Riders. He vehemently opposed women's being given the title of ranger and appointments in the field, and he openly acknowledged to Park Superintendent Horace Albright that he much preferred the lectures of the "old-time [male] ranger." Apparently Garland had not attended one of Marguerite's lectures at Mammoth Hot Springs.[27]

Fear of creating a feminized America had followed closely on the heels of the passage of the Nineteenth Amendment in 1920. That amendment assured women the right to vote, but the legislation lacked any other mandates in terms of equality. However, for many men in positions of power, it signaled a significant disruption to the previously delineated spheres of men and women. Evidently Garland saw the National Park Service as an agency still struggling for structure and identity. Moreover, he envisioned women rangers as hindering the respectability of this new bureau. Upon his return to Washington, D.C., he began to seriously pursue actions to restrict the duties, responsibilities, and hiring of women rangers in Yellowstone. Unbeknownst to Marguerite at the time, Garland's "woman question" would cause a rippling effect of inequity throughout the NPS.

Concerned, Horace Albright wrote a seven-page confidential letter to NPS Director Stephen Mather on October 14, defending his employment of women in Yellowstone and refuting the opinions put forth by Garland and Burlew. One of his first opinions was that Garland and Burlew had not spent enough time in the park and thus some of their observations were not well informed. Albright found it unfair that Elizabeth Conard's work had been welcomed in 1925 when permanent ranger Scotty Bauman or one of his assistants wanted to take an afternoon off, but was not valued as highly in 1926 when Department of Interior inspectors questioned Bauman about Elizabeth working at the Tower Ranger station. Another concern raised by Garland and Burlew that Albright rebutted was the matter of Elizabeth's living quarters. Even though Albright explained that she never stayed at the ranger station but rather occupied a small cabin near the road camp, that she was always being chaperoned by Mrs. Royen, wife of the road foreman, and that her father had a tent next to her cabin, the issue of housing women in the park from that point on became the NPS stratagem for rejecting women applicants.[28]

Marguerite dodged this issue probably because she was stationed with Albright at headquarters in Mammoth, where she resided with her mother and father. Apparently Albright's detailed report of Marguerite's duties in the museum, editing the ranger manual, keeping a record of changes in the hot springs, and feeding the animals at the "Mammoth zoo" made her look more like a clerk and therefore less of a threat to the ranger image. And it is possible that her already issued permanent status carried some weight when it came to the decision of whether she was to be retained.

In a letter dated November 30, 1926, Park Superintendent Horace Albright wrote to Dr. Conard, the head of the botany department at Grinnell College in Iowa, informing him that he planned to continue using Conard's services for the following summer season, but that employment for Conard's daughter Elizabeth was another matter. Dr. Conard had spent three summers working in Yellowstone as the chief ranger naturalist and both his daughters, Elizabeth and Rebecca, had worked alongside him as ranger naturalists, providing guided nature walks at Camp Roosevelt. The tone of Albright's letter, indicated that he wanted to re-hire Elizabeth, but the word from Washington regarding Garland's "violent prejudice against women rangers except at the gates where they regard them as clerks,' was about to prevent Albright from obtaining any appointments for women rangers for the next year. Albright conceded that he was "going to have a hard time keeping Miss Lindsley."[29]

Conard was surprised by the news and wrote to Albright in late December that he was "still suffering from shock in relation to the Lady rangers." While he sensed that Albright did not agree with the order from Washington, he also feared that Albright was not going to move to retain Miss Albertson and Miss Lindsley. If that were the case, Conard wrote, "it would be foolish for me to proceed to the attack."[30] However, he obviously changed his mind and decided that a battle concerning the interests of "lady rangers" deserved to be fought. As in any political opposition movement, Conard knew that many voices would speak louder than just one, and he gathered an army of colleagues to help.

Conard and others such as Dr. George Fuller at the University of Chicago and Dr. E. Lucy Braun at the University of Cincinnati wrote letters to Washington, opposing the park service's ban on hiring women rangers. Interior Secretary Hubert Work informed Conard that "we are not going to put into effect a hard fast rule that women shall not be employed in the educational work of the National Park Service, but we hope that it will not be necessary to employ women in this activity until some way can be found to give them a different designation than ranger, which has been, for many years, a term associated with vigorous and courageous men of the west." Secretary Work also invoked the pretext of unsuitable housing as a secondary issue for not hiring women. Acting NPS director Arno B. Camerer followed up with nearly the same response. Sexism was alive and well in 1926-1927 in the National Park Service.[31]

Appalled at the National Park Service's position about women rangers, Dr. Conard chose not to return to Yellowstone that year and was not timid in expressing the reason. In his resignation letter to Secretary Work in January 1927, Conard declared,

> A year ago we welcomed with great joy your announcement that the National Parks should be utilized to the utmost for educational purposes. In harmony with that policy, we created in Yellowstone Park the strongest educational service that that Park has ever known.
>
> Now comes an order from...your department removing all women from that service. You will recall meeting my daughter and Miss Lindsley, both of whom did excellent work. Our organization, if this order holds up, is now arbitrarily broken up.
>
> My daughter and I have, for various reasons, withdrawn from the service, with much regret. But I sincerely petition you to so arrange that this anti-woman order may be withheld for one year, so that the two other women [Herma Albertson and Marguerite Lindsley] so necessary to the service may continue.
>
> Meanwhile the injustice and stupidity of this order maybe become evident, and the Superintendents of the National Parks may be left unhampered in carrying out the work which they alone adequately know.
>
> I am very respectfully,
>
>> Henry S. Conard
>> Formerly Head Ranger-Naturalist
>> Yellowstone Park[32]

Albright confessed his disappointment with Conard's resignation in a letter to Dr. Fuller in January 1927, but added a positive note concerning Marguerite, confirming that he had not been "instructed to discharge Ranger Lindsley." Despite conflicts and negative circumstances

The author of a magazine article described Marguerite perfectly as a "boyish-bobbed, slender young woman." (COURTESY BILL ARNOLD)

surrounding the employment of women in the National Park Service during that tumultuous year, Marguerite was allowed to continue unabated in her favorite role as a voice and face of Yellowstone.[33]

Ironically, amid all of this controversy over women rangers, the *Christian Science Monitor* published a lengthy article on Marguerite on January 28, 1927. "Lady Ranger 'Makes Good' in Yellowstone Park Post, Only Girl Among 34 Men...," declared the newspaper's headline. While her title was causing consternation in Washington, her position as a "full-fledged permanent ranger" was making her a celebrity in the news. Obviously impressed by her qualifications as superb horsewoman; botanist, sometime attendant to orphan antelope, elk, and bear cubs; and all-around outdoor woman, the newspaper reporter contended that "Miss Lindsley has shown that she fully deserves the commission which has been conferred on her."

Giving readers a complete image of Marguerite, he described her from head to toe. "Picture a tall, clear eyed, boyish-bobbed, slender young woman," he wrote, "trim in her well-fitting, olive-green uniform with its shining silver badge denoting that she is a member of the Department of Interior, National Park Service, immaculate in her high-necked white blouse and black tie, ranger-like in her highly polished leather boots, it is no wonder that at first she was indistinguishable from the other 34 rangers." And the author pointed out that while Marguerite may have blended in with the olive-green uniformed figures throughout the park, she maintained her own sense of femaleness. "As a concession to femininity she wears a mother-of-pearl ring, the only [item] at the initial glance, to mark her for the Lady Ranger that she is," the reported noted. While Marguerite believed that women should be afforded the opportunity to ski, fish, hike, ride horses, and do any outdoor activity they desired, she also believed that women should not forget that they were women.[34]

Not surprisingly after that article appeared in early 1927, Marguerite received dozens of letters from women seeking her advice on how to become a ranger. Regrettably, by that time, most opportunities for women rangers in the park service had come to a screeching halt in the wake of J.F. Garland's inspection report. While she acknowledged that she did have her dream job as a ranger, Marguerite relayed the dismal outlook for women in government service to her admiring correspondents. "There is no real field for women at the present time in the NPS and it is doubtful that others will be appointed," she wrote to Christine Funk of Arlington, Washington, in April 1927.[35] She explained that of the four women who were on the temporary force last season, only two would be reappointed in the upcoming season, one being a ranger's wife and the other a ranger's daughter. She realistically told another prospective woman applicant that "it is probable that the Park Service may discontinue their [women's] employment and...the ranger staff will be made up entirely of men." Still feeling strongly that women should be treated fairly, Marguerite responded to one letter writer that "she would rather lose her job than see women employed where they are at a disadvantage."[36] And, sympathetically, Marguerite conveyed to all of her letter recipients that she felt privileged to have been appointed a woman ranger.

In addition to featuring Marguerite, the newspaper article observed that there were other women rangers, although temporary, on duty during the summer of 1926. One of those women mentioned in promotion "lady rangers" was Elizabeth Conard, who had held a naturalist position at Roosevelt Camp. The *Monitor* reporter saw Elizabeth as indispensable to her father through the summer as, together, they conducted a daily eight-mile hike explaining nature's quips and foibles to the tourists en route. Obviously that opinion of Elizabeth's work was one that Inspector Garland had not shared a few months earlier. The article concluded with Horace Albright's diplomatically and optimistically stating that "the success of our experiment with women rangers probably will lead to a further extension of this opportunity to young women who know and love nature." Though thwarted in his objective of hiring more women, Albright was clearly committed to keeping the outdoorsy and hard-working Marguerite on his staff.[37]

By the summer of 1927, fair-haired, blue-eyed Marguerite with her ready smile proved to be as much of an attraction to visitors as the museum at Mammoth Hot Springs of which she was in charge. Fellow ranger and lifelong friend Herma Albertson Baggley commented that "Peg" was her ideal of a woman in uniform. "She was one of the most beautiful women in a uniform that I have ever seen," proclaimed Herma. So too did a reporter for a Utah newspaper. "Park Museum Is Attractive—Woman Ranger in Charge of Yellowstone Exhibits," proclaimed his article's headline in the *Ogden Standard Examiner* on June 25, 1927. While the title may have seemed sexist, the special dispatch was quick to tout her vast knowledge of the park. "Tourists planning a trip to Yellowstone Park during the 1927 season should not fail to see the park museum of natural history...the information desk and museum are in charge of Park Ranger Marguerite Lindsley...who has been a resident of the Yellowstone and is thoroughly familiar with the flora and fauna found in the park...and by reason of her... training in botany and zoology, Miss Lindsley is well qualified to explain the various exhibits," revealed the newspaper.[38]

The Mammoth museum, begun by Ranger Milton Skinner in 1920, originally contained specimens of predatory animals such as a mountain lions and several timber wolves that had been purposely eradicated from the park in earlier times, as well as a striking assortment of birds in their natural habitats. In 1927, the museum expanded its collection to include specimens of more common wild animals such as red fox, beaver, antelope, and mule deer. In her professional capacity of generating an understanding of Yellowstone's ecosystem and its workings, Marguerite judiciously explained to visitors that these newest additions to the museum had been collected "by accident" or, in other words, some had died from natural causes while others had become too badly injured to survive and were shot. In addition, Marguerite's skills in botany contributed significantly to the attractive museum exhibit of pressed wildflowers of nearly every variety known to exist in Yellowstone, complete with botanical classifications.

Marguerite's skills in the outdoors were viewed as equally valuable, if not more so, by some observers. She appeared to one journalist as a "heroine" of all ranger activities especially when it came to caring for orphaned animals.[39] While on one of her daily winter outings, Marguerite found Jimmie, a baby antelope whose mother had been slain by a larger animal, shivering and frightened in the woods. She gently picked him up and wrapped him in her coat and trudged home with her bundle. With a little warmth, milk fed from a baby bottle, and tender care, Jimmie soon revived and became Marguerite's pal. Before long she had gathered a little menagerie of orphaned animals, including a bear cub, that all became part of a little zoo in Mammoth. In an era when such human interactions with wild animals were acceptable in national parks, Marguerite's sensitivity and love for all living things made her a popular ranger. While she loved the closeness of her Mammoth pet-like animals, Marguerite was also entranced by Yellowstone's elusive and wild animals, such as coyotes.

One evening Marguerite stood alone on a bridge watching the "golden orb of a gibbous moon rise solemnly" over a great grassy meadow. She watched as mist and steam rose in tiny wisps through the valley and noted how not a sound disturbed the quiet. In an article for *Yellowstone Nature Notes* she revealed with childlike glee that "some primitive instinct of loneliness in the wilderness made me throw back my head and howl at the stillness." She remembered "the hills sent back the sound, [and] then again, all was quiet for a time." One more time she repeated the cry, "trying to imitate the weird and fascinating note of a coyote." Her efforts were rewarded. From the other end of the meadow came the long drawn howl of a mother coyote, and a few seconds later, in chorus, the less trained voices of her two pups. Marguerite called again and another group, perhaps a mile or so away, joined the first and this time the echoes chased each other around the hills for nearly two minutes before all died away and quiet reigned again. Her wild instincts satisfied, Marguerite turned to leave but not before she spied a silvery flash in the moonlight. Belatedly she realized that if she had not moved she might have encountered a curious coyote who was stealthily seeking the imitator of its call. For Marguerite, the call of Yellowstone's wildness was magical and she savored every moment, on or off duty.[40]

Adventurous, educated, and attractive Marguerite had many male admirers through the years, most of which she kept under her hat, quite literally. The inside of her wide-brimmed ranger hat that she donned for her outdoor duties sported the signatures of at least a dozen hopeful suitors. A fellow ranger recalled that one of the naturalists, who later became the president of a college (probably John R. Van Pelt, president of Michigan Technological University) had opined, "she could marry anybody she wanted. She could marry any of us."[41] In all likelihood, all of her male suitors were well aware that marrying Marguerite also meant having the spirit and vitality to keep up with her.

Besides maintaining the information desk, administering the museum, and keeping the flower display fresh, another of Marguerite's duties during the summer of 1927 was to help erect signs for the new self-guided nature

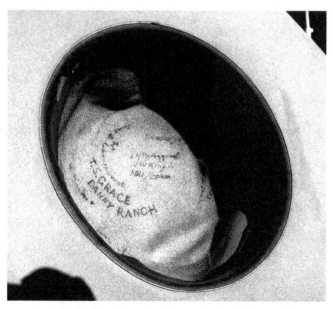

Marguerite's son, Bill Arnold, to this day gets a chuckle out of the number of male suitors that signed his mother's hat in the 1920s. (COURTESY BILL ARNOLD)

trail in Mammoth. To insure that the signs were correctly placed, she incorporated the assistance of one of the rangers stationed at Mammoth, Everett LeRoy (Ben) Arnold, who had come to the park a few years earlier. In one of her weekly reports to Mr. Sam Woodring, the chief ranger, Marguerite wrote that on July 10 she and Arnold rode over the Rangers Nature Trail, where they discussed materials needed for signs, on July 12 she accompanied him to the head of Golden Gate to place a sign, and on July 13 she took a 5:30 A.M. ride over the Rangers Nature Trail accompanied by Arnold and the Chief Ranger. Later that week Ben helped Marguerite place new labels on new museum exhibits in the cases.[42] If that week is any indication of their summer activities, Marguerite and Ben spent a considerable amount of time together and their relationship blossomed. Several years older and looking debonair in his tweed dress overcoat, Ben probably seemed a stable choice for a husband. In all likelihood, it was Ben's aspiration to be a career Yellowstone ranger that cinched Marguerite's choice for a husband.

On April 17, 1928, Marguerite Lindsley married Everett LeRoy (Ben) Arnold in a private ceremony in the home of family friends Dr.

Ben Arnold looked quite handsome in his official NPS ranger uniform in the mid-1920s. (COURTESY BILL ARNOLD)

and Mrs. Sammuel F. Way in Livingston, Montana. Perhaps the location was appropriate, for Dr. and Mrs. (Libby Wakefield) Way had themselves met and married in Yellowstone during earlier stagecoach days, when he was a stage driver and she was the "belle of Yellowstone." According to an undated article in the *Livingston Enterprise*, Marguerite defied the expected convention of the traditional wedding day in her own signature style when she "dressed in a blue gown and wore a corsage of roses."[43]

Following her springtime marriage, Marguerite returned to Yellowstone in a new role as wife, and also assumed the new role of seasonal ranger naturalist. Due to the difficulty of obtaining a full-time duty assignment that would allow her to reside in the same location as her new husband, Marguerite resigned from her full-time position in Mammoth and opted to work only seasonally. Regardless of her title or term of employment, she still fervently pursued her heartfelt mission of helping others to understand the character of the park's unparalleled landscape, to appreciate the flora and fauna that abounded in a predominantly natural habitat, to recognize the value and importance of the park's preservation, and to realize the inspirational splendor of America's Wonderland.

One of the outlets for Marguerite's educational and observational writings was the *Yellowstone Nature Notes*, published monthly or bimonthly, depending on the season, by the National Park Service. During her lifetime, Marguerite authored over fifty articles for the *Nature Notes*. The publication had begun in 1920 as a bulletin that included activities of geysers and hot springs, observations of wildlife, research on geological phenomena, and various historical narratives of importance. Throughout the 1920s, 1930s and 1940s, Marguerite continued to report on her studies and observations of Yellowstone's wildlife and thermal features in her compositions for *Nature Notes* and also made significant contributions to the *Ranger Naturalist Manual*'s continuously revised editions. Her articles ranged from surveys of the hot spring formations at Mammoth to the foraging habits of mule deer in winter to springtime observations that confirmed the seasonal migration of bats in Devils Kitchen to a poem entitled *To a Wild Rose*. In addition to writing informative essays for these publications, she provided sketches that complemented the text and illustrations that graced the covers of many early issues.[44]

During the early 1930s Marguerite was finally able to realize one of her most heartfelt longings—to spend winters "out in the park." According

Marguerite and Ben frequently went exploring into Yellowstone's vast backcounty on horseback. (COURTESY BILL ARNOLD)

to her memoir, she and Ben spent ten wonderful years stationed first at Tower Fall and later at the Northeast Gate. A lover of all of Yellowstone's seasons, Marguerite opined that "the deeper in its unspoiled wilderness we can be, the happier we are." She felt privileged to live immersed in the "real" Yellowstone amongst the animals, birds, trees, and flowers. At Tower Fall they made friends with deer, elk, and antelope and at the Northeast Gate they claimed a family of winter birds as their own, as well as a special furry character, Tippy the weasel. It seemed that Marguerite could never get enough of the wilderness she loved. About this she enthused that "busy summers flew by on swift wings and no winter was half long enough."[45]

On February 11, 1932, she and Ben announced the arrival of son, William (Bill) to their family and began the raising and educating of their own junior ranger. Even with a new addition to their family, Ben and Marguerite continued to live at Tower Fall and continued to love being "out in the park." Just as they had done in the first few years of their marriage, Ben and Marguerite would often saddle up their horses, and head out into Yellowstone's backcountry, leaving baby Bill in the care of family or friends. One of their favorite places to explore was the remote trail less area of the Mirror Plateau. Located just east of their residence at Tower, the Mirror Plateau was and still is one of the least visited areas of the park, and therefore offered the couple sublime immersion into Yellowstone's nature. It was in this area that Ben discovered and filed a report on a little known hot spring area, most likely today's Hot Spring Basin Group. Even as Marguerite embraced her new role as mother, she continued to carry on her work of observing and reporting on Yellowstone's dynamic nature.

In the winter of 1933-1934 Marguerite experienced one of the most momentous episodes of her life. By this period in Yellowstone, timber wolves and mountain lions had been hunted to near extinction and reports of any existing animals were considered doubtful. Ten years after the last wolf was supposedly killed in the park's anti-predator campaign, the wolves of Yellowstone had become mere myths for most people. Late one evening, Ben returned from a patrol on skis to the head of Tower Creek and Marguerite sensed that something unusual had happened. At that time Yellowstone rangers were actively hunting and trapping coyotes, which were believed to be taking a toll on the park's deer and antelope population. Typically, Ben would arrive home with his quarry and tell Marguerite and four-year-old Bill his thrilling tale of taking the "dog." But this particular evening, he came home empty-handed and quizzically toyed with Marguerite's curiosity. "Guess what?" he intoned. After a long silence, which intrigued Marguerite even more, he announced, "I saw four wolves!" In disbelief she skeptically responded, "Oh, not wolves." But, she knew that he must be right. Previously they had found wolf tracks on one of the animal trails near their cabin but kept the discovery to themselves because they feared their news would be cataloged with the all the other doubtful reports.[46]

With Marguerite hanging anxiously on his words, Ben told her that on his way up the creek, he had found the carcass of an old winter-killed elk on which coyotes were beginning to work. On his way back, just as he was approaching a little knoll that shielded him from view of the carcass, he heard the sound of teeth crunching bones. Arriving at the knoll, he peered cautiously over the top. He could hardly believe his eyes. There, in front of him, were four great, dark, hulking wolves tearing and gulping the remains of the dead elk. As they literally plunged into the carcass, pulled back a huge bite, and "wolfed" it down, three coyotes kept a respectful distance in anticipation of their turn to feast. With the two species of canids so close in proximity Ben saw that the wolves appeared three times larger than the slim, grey coyotes and nearly black by comparison. As dusk began to set in, Ben watched as the gorged wolves trotted off unhurriedly down the trail.

"The next day was one of the red letter days of my life in Yellowstone," Marguerite avowed in her article "Yellowstone Wolves" that appeared in the August 1937 issue of *Nature* magazine. "It has always been my highest ambition to observe and study all the animals here in their natural setting," she wrote. Leaving little Bill in the care of his father, Marguerite put on her snowshoes and set out on her own adventure just as the light of the day was beginning to fade. Climbing the steep hill, which was nearly vertical for the last two hundred yards, Marguerite was sure that she would probably frighten away any animal within a half mile with her pounding heart and gasps for breath. As she rested and regained her composure at the summit, Marguerite heard a sound that made her suck in her breath. The sound was that of crunching bones, just as Ben had described it the night before. Peering over the crest of the hill, not more than seventy-five yards from the elk carcass, she saw not one, but four coyotes feasting away on their evening meal. Although she felt a slight sense of disappointment that the wolves were not there, Marguerite soon became absorbed in the antics of the "little wolves." With their uncanny sense for danger, the coyotes would gnaw on a bone for a short while and then put their heads up in the air to make a visual and sound survey. Once or twice one looked directly at Marguerite and she froze to escape notice.

As dusk began to thicken and overtake the evening sky, she was preparing to leave her perch on the knoll when something caught her eye. As she peered through the looming darkness, Marguerite thought to herself, "It couldn't be." But there before her disbelieving eyes, were not one, but two huge black wolves loping along the trail. Even though Marguerite had never seen a wolf before, she had no doubt that these were the animals of her expectation. She gazed in amazement at the peculiar jackknife gait of the wolves, which seemed similar to that of a greyhound and which was totally different from the gliding gait of the coyote. The two wolves went straight to the elk carcass and began tearing out meat and bones and gulping down huge bites. The coyotes withdrew from the immediate scene although they remained in the background watching their big cousins. Like her husband, Marguerite noticed that the dark wolves with their heavy shoulders and forequarters made the coyotes appear much smaller and lighter colored.

Marguerite captured the powerful stance of one of the wolves she observed with this detailed sketch that graced her article in Nature *magazine.*
(COURTESY BILL ARNOLD)

And then while she lay hidden behind the knoll blinking and straining her eyes in the darkness to see every detail of the wolves, Marguerite experienced the pinnacle of the entire exciting episode.

Ever protective of a valuable winter food source, one of the wolves began to survey the nearby area by trotting to the edge of the hill where Marguerite was crouched in statuesque stillness. Not forty feet from her view the wolf stopped and stood broadside. She could see perfectly "how proportionately more powerful he was than any coyote." He had come so close to her that she "could see the black line that runs from the corner of [his] eye back across the face," she vividly remembered. She was so excited

Ben and Marguerite smile fondly at one another while son Bill seems captivated by both his thumb and something just out of the photographer's view. (COURTESY BILL ARNOLD)

and so brimming over with her story, Marguerite did not remember how she got back to the cabin that night.

Watching wolves happily loping along and feasting on winter kill thus became one of Marguerite's most cherished activities in Yellowstone and for her it bordered on the spiritual. Because of their rarity, Marguerite felt honored by the presence of these wolves and she enormously prized her observation of *Canis lupus.* "It will be many a day ere an adventure comes to me," she rhapsodized, "that will eclipse this twilight meeting with the big wolves."

In 1935, the sixty-eight-mile Beartooth Highway from Red Lodge to Cooke City, Montana, was nearing completion and by the following season the new road would serve to open a completely new route to Yellowstone— although closed in winter by snowfall. As automobile travel to the park increased, residents of the two towns had lobbied the U.S. Congress to provide funding for a northeast entrance to Yellowstone. Evidently Red Lodge and Cooke City were not the only prospective towns in the country rallying for additional national park access. In January 1931, President Herbert Hoover signed the National Park Approaches Act, which provided government financing of national park approach roads throughout the country. As a result of the act's passage, the Red Lodge–Cooke City route received one million dollars for the highway's construction, which began in the summer of 1931. Rising above 10,000 feet into the Absaroka Mountains, the Beartooth Highway was touted in the 1930s as a marvel of engineering and, a little over thirty-years later, broadcaster Charles Kuralt would declare that it was "America's most beautiful road."[47]

For Marguerite, Ben, and three-year-old Bill, the opening of the Beartooth Highway in June 1936 began a whole new Yellowstone adventure at the park's northeast entrance. From the perspective, of coping with the isolated post, it seems logical that the NPS would send their most winter-seasoned rangers, Marguerite and Ben to "pioneer the new residence and checking station" at the park's new entryway. According to Bill, the family spent the first winter there without running water of any kind, and they had to melt snow for everything. It was there that Marguerite home-schooled Bill with the Calvert course curriculum through the first grade.[48]

Developed in 1905 by Calvert Day School Head Master Virgil Hillyer, who was a Harvard-educated scholar, the Calvert home-instruction course was first advertised in *National Geographic* magazine. It was offered for the affordable sum of five dollars and was conveniently available by mail order. By the 1930s, Hillyer's Calvert home-school plan had gained world-wide acclaim for delivering education to children in remote locations such as lighthouses on the coast of Alaska and American missionary settlements in Africa. By all standards of the day, Yellowstone's northeast entrance seemed just as remote as some of those faraway places, and home schooling was the only reasonable way for Marguerite to begin her son's education.[49]

As Bill grew up, Marguerite had time to focus on her artwork, and began producing hand-painted note cards and stationery for sale. Her favorite

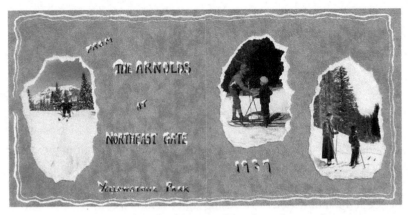

Creating handmade Christmas cards, such as this one depicting a few winter wonderland activities enjoyed by Bill and Marguerite, was one of her special talents. (COURTESY BILL ARNOLD)

subjects to paint were wildflowers and birds. Her close friend and NPS Naturalist Ed Sawyer was a talented bird artist, and often drew sketches of birds for her to paint. At Christmastime, Marguerite handcrafted holiday cards featuring little Bill and the family's winter wonderland at Tower Fall or at the North East Gate. She also developed and promoted the packaging and selling of native Montana and Wyoming wildflower seeds. A journalist for the Gardiner, Montana, *Gateway Gazette* reported that Marguerite's idea had originally "germinated in 1921 and has since grown into an interesting and profitable hobby." According to the newspaper, Marguerite gathered seeds outside the park between Livingston and Gardiner, Cooke City and Red Lodge, and around West Yellowstone. Her son, Bill still remembers being "in on the seed gathering." The timing of the gathering was crucial, as Marguerite had to locate the flower beds and keep a continual lookout so that she could gather the seeds when they matured between early July and the first frost. She packaged the seeds in attractive packets with her original hand-painted designs of the flowers themselves. In all, Marguerite offered forty-three varieties of wildflower seeds. She placed her both her seed packets and her hand-painted stationary on sale at the hotels at Mammoth and Old Faithful, the Haynes Picture Shops at Mammoth and Tower Fall, and at the Pryor Stores at Mammoth and Canyon.[50]

By 1939, Ben had been transferred to Mammoth Hot Springs where he worked for a year before being stationed at Gardiner for the next five

This is one of the last photographs of Marguerite, taken sometime in the late 1940s. Her son Bill is so fond of her expression here that he still carries this photograph in his wallet. (COURTESY BILL ARNOLD)

years, which gave Bill the opportunity to attend classes in Mammoth and Gardiner schools. After spending one more year at Mammoth, Ben was assigned to the East Entrance gate located fifty miles from Cody, Wyoming, in 1947. Marguerite and Ben resided there for the last nine years of Ben's career. Their son Bill attended high school at Cody and after graduating in 1950, he joined the Wyoming National Guard and was immediately sent to Korea.[51]

At the same time that Bill departed for his overseas tour of duty, Marguerite's health began to deteriorate. For several years, she had suffered a series of health problems, most of which were the result of an automobile accident that had occurred ten years earlier. After testifying against a tourist in a park-related court case, Marguerite collapsed and was hospitalized. Her condition at the time was serious enough for the National Guard to give Bill emergency leave and the Red Cross flew him home. It seems that Bill's appearance at her bedside was just the remedy Marguerite needed and her health began to improve. Following his leave to attend to his mother's medical condition, Bill was given a stateside assignment in California. During the winter of 1951-52, Marguerite had several relapses and Bill made a number of trips to Cody to give his mother a sense of caring comfort that only he, as her loving son, could deliver. In April 1952, Bill was released from active duty and returned to Cody where his mother had once again been hospitalized. Somewhere in his travels, Bill contracted malaria and ended up in the hospital across the hall from Marguerite. Within a few weeks, Bill had recovered. Marguerite was not so blessed.[52]

For fifty years of her life, Marguerite survived every challenge she faced, except one. Early in the morning on Sunday, May 18, 1952, Jane Marguerite Lindsley Arnold died. Her funeral was held at 2 P.M. on Wednesday at Christ Episcopal church in Cody, Wyoming. Her son Bill remembers that Yellowstone's east entrance road was opened early for administrative travel so that park rangers and employees could attend. As it still does today, that area of park roadway typically received high amounts of winter snowfall and it often remained heavily snow-packed until late May, because plowing through 8,541-foot Sylvan Pass was a difficult task before the development of today's sophisticated snow removal equipment. Mother Nature may have also played a hand in helping crews swiftly plow the road by providing sunny skies rather than adding more snowfall (the park entrance also opened to the public two days after Marguerite's funeral). In a moving tribute to a beloved colleague, her coffin was borne by six uniformed National Park Service ranger pallbearers. To honor her memory in Yellowstone, Marguerite's husband Ben and son Bill were granted permission to place a small plaque bearing her name and dates on the Mammoth Chapel's outdoor announcement sign in Mammoth Hot Springs. When Ben died two years later in 1954, his name was added to the plaque that now resides on the interior of the sign board at the Yellowstone church.[53]

In the eyes of a family friend, Mrs. Ivy D. Little, Marguerite not only left the land she loved on that lovely spring day, but she also took with her the very breath of Yellowstone:

A breath of Yellowstone left us today
When Peg Lindsley passed away.
Bidding farewell to the land she loved,
To journey on to that home above.

Towering mountains now bow their head,
The whispering forest a prayer has said.
The winding rivers roar "You were mine,"
The trees shed for her their blanket of pine.
Caressing her with a lovely touch,
Seeming to say "Peg we loved you so much."
The girl we claimed for so many years,
The Yellowstone clouds are shedding tears.
Saying "No more you'll ride the Yellowstone
But we'll always claim you as our own."
For the child that dwelled here for so long
The robins and lark have hushed their son
No more to see her riding here,
All were her friends, Elk, Deer, and Bear.
She knew every flower and every tree,
And the Winter land where she loved to ski.
She left in the lovely month of May
When Spring burst forth in soft array,
All seem to say "You left us alone
But Yellowstone will claim her own."[54]

Throughout her more than fifty years of residency there, life in
Yellowstone never left Marguerite at a loss for entertainment and she firmly
believed that the park was the "country's greatest wilderness playground."[55]
For Marguerite it was a place where a young girl's as well as a woman's heart,
soul, and imagination could all take wing and soar above the conventions
of the day. Though her lifetime, Yellowstone provided her with a place
where she could experience intellectual, emotional, and spiritual growth;
and a place where she could develop and boldly put forth her individual
voice. Perhaps, the best summation of her rapture with Yellowstone was
written by Marguerite herself:

> There is no great glory attached to my work. Remuneration is not
> what I should be able to demand in the field in which I was trained.
> There is no particular opportunity for advancement in sight. But it's
> a case of loving the work you are doing—of golden opportunities
> for increasing the knowledge of places and things you like above all

places and things you know. Not satisfaction and content, perhaps, for when we are content ambition cease—merely sustained interest and genuine pleasure. And then this may explain a lot:

"God gave all men all earth to love
But since man's heart is small
Ordained for each one spot should prove
Beloved over all."
That one spot happens to be Yellowstone to me.[56]

Indeed, Marguerite had lived and breathed Yellowstone as if it were a part of her. As a true child of the park, she knew the park better than most of her contemporaries, young or old, and as such her lifetime contributions to the development of Yellowstone interpretation and education were far-reaching and wide-ranging. To be sure, Marguerite's cherished connection to Yellowstone's wildness, beauty, and solace was all-encompassing and ultimately nurtured her to become the confident, self-actualized woman that she had always dreamed of being.

Frances Eva Pound Wright

(1907–1999)

Ranger Jim

"Girl Ranger Makes Spectacular Arrest of Park Bootlegger," proclaimed the *Helena* (Montana) *Independent* on August 12, 1927.

Just two years before that, Frances Eva Pound had been hired as a ranger in Yellowstone. When she was filling out her application for the position in 1925, Park Superintendent Horace Albright recommended that she use her nickname "Jim." Albright's recommendation not only allowed Frances to break through the generally male-dominated field of National Park Ranger, but it also served to "not cause a gender stir in Washington." Known as "Jim," throughout her life, Frances had been given the masculine sounding moniker by her father, who was park ranger Thad C. Pound, when she was a youngster. Seeing his daughter as a daring spirit, Thad identified her with a popular comic strip character of the time who displayed adventurous tendencies. While growing up in Yellowstone she frequently accompanied her ranger father on patrol through the park and later assisted him with his duties at the north entrance gate. From 1925 through 1929, however, Frances "Ranger Jim" Pound, Yellowstone's first female law enforcement ranger, patrolled Yellowstone under her own commission.[1]

Helen Elizabeth Pound declared that the day her beautiful baby sister, Frances Eva Pound, made her appearance on February 13, 1907, was one of the most memorable days of her life. Frances was the third of four children born to Thad Pound and Nellie Grace (Hackney) Pound. Frances's older brother Rupert Earl "Bubs" Pound, was the family's firstborn in 1892 and her older sister Helen followed in 1901. Virginia, the baby of the family, made her debut two years after Frances, in 1909.[2]

Life for Frances began in Park City, Montana, in what Helen described as a stone block five-room "palace" with two bedrooms, a dining room, large kitchen, and a lovely living room looking out on her mother's flower garden. Typical of small town residential areas in the early 1900s, its back yard contained fruit trees, a garden, a coal and wood shed, a tool shed, and a "deluxe outhouse." While they may not have had indoor plumbing, Thad's ingenuity provided the Pound family home with at least one modern convenience. Building an acetylene gas plant in part of the root cellar and piping it into the house, Thad innovatively supplied his home with the first gas lights in Park City.[3]

In 1908, Thad, originally a blacksmith by trade, was appointed deputy sheriff in Billings so the Pound family left their five room "palace" in Park City and moved to the "big city." Billings seemed like a fairy-land to Helen, Frances's seven-year-old sister, with its downtown area of store-lined streets and an enormous two-story school. While the city opened a whole new world for the Pound children, Frances's father Thad nearly had his own world taken away.[4]

Late in the afternoon on September 21, 1910, law enforcement authorities were notified that Benjamin Franklin, a chair-car porter for the Burlington railway, had purchased a revolver and was in pursuit of a man who allegedly robbed him. Earlier that day, Franklin was seen visiting the home of William and Zola Moore, and he left the place in a rage. At the time many observers questioned his claim of truly being robbed because he was a known user of cocaine and they attributed his aberrant behavior to his addictive habit. Authorities were notified when Franklin flashed his gun in the Hart-Albin Company department store as he purchased a belt, presumably a gun belt. When Thad Pound and two other officers entered the store through the First Avenue basement entrance, Franklin left through the side entrance. The lawmen followed and chased him through town. After four blocks, Pound caught up to Franklin on Minnesota Avenue and ordered the suspect to halt. At point blank range, Franklin fired at Pound, hitting the deputy in the left chest, just over the heart. Despite the bullet's penetrating one lung and shattering his shoulder blade, Pound returned fire. From two other shots fired by officers, Willis and Jacobs, Franklin was killed instantly.[5]

The *Anaconda Standard* reported the incident on September 22, noting that Thad Pound was "probably fatally wounded." Newspapers in the surrounding communities monitored Thad's fight for his life in the tense days that followed the shooting. After his being hospitalized for more than week, the *Billings Gazette* announced on October 2 that Thad had made a miraculous recovery and had been "taken to his home by Dr. C.F. Watkins." Although newspaper reports on Thad's condition were positive and optimistic, this incident upset the family's finances. As the eldest child, eighteen-year-old Rupert was forced to give up his plans to attend college, and took a job as a sales representative with J.I. Case Company, an agricultural and construction equipment supplier, to help support the family.[6]

Not deterred from law enforcement, Thad accepted an appointment as United States Deputy Marshal in 1912, and the family moved to Helena. Frances and her siblings found Helena enchanting. Riding the five-cent streetcar out to the then-famous Broadwater Natatorium, they enjoyed roller skating, dancing around the Maypole, and watching dancers in Scottish dress dance the highland fling on the lawn of the state capitol. Those activities colored Frances's childhood through the next three years.[7]

But life for the Pound family once again turned serious during the summer of 1913. Frances's mother Nellie became very ill and, according to Helen, Thad used his vacation to nurse her back to health while caring for his four young children. Shortly after his mother became ill, 21-year-old Rupert, whose job with the Case Company had sent him to various international destinations, also developed health problems and returned home from Argentina. Within the next year Nellie recovered and Thad resigned his position in Helena. It is unclear what prompted his decision, but perhaps the family's two nearly fatal episodes prompted him to consider less stressful and more enjoyable employment.[8]

In 1915, the Pound family moved to Gardiner, Montana. Their first summer in Yellowstone was a family affair as Frances's mother, father and brother all worked for the Old Faithful Camping Company. Thad became the summer manager of Canyon Camp, while Nellie supervised the personnel, and Rupert drove a stagecoach. That fall, Thad secured employment as an army scout, and moved his family into the park at Mammoth.[9]

The United States Army had been in charge of the park since 1886, when corrupt civilian officials and complex administrative difficulties that included vandalism and poaching brought public and governmental demands for park protection to the attention of Congress. The civilian administration supervising the park since 1872 was underfunded, understaffed, and unable to properly safeguard the park's forests, animals, and thermal features. A congressional committee finally made the decision to send in government troops in August of 1886. Captain Moses Harris rode into Mammoth Hot Springs with the Seventh Cavalry, relieved civilian superintendent David W. Wear of his duties, and ordered the construction of the temporary Camp Sheridan. The initial mandate for the army was to restore order and eventually turn the park administration over to civilian command. But, by 1890, it was apparent that the army was in for a long stay, so Fort Yellowstone was established in Mammoth Hot Springs in 1891. Construction of various buildings continued for nearly two decades until the final two structures, the jail and the chapel, were completed during the period 1911-1913. The stone officers' houses and administration buildings from that era continue today to exhibit their commanding presence and serve the park's administrative staff.[10]

The onset of World War I in Europe raised concerns that all army personnel, including those in Yellowstone, might be needed in the war. Partly in response to this, Congress established a new federal agency called the National Park Service in 1916 to relieve the army of its protective duties in several western national parks and to supervise the nation's expanding national park system that now extended from coast to coast. Even with the establishment of this new bureau, a small contingent of the army stayed on at Fort Yellowstone until 1918 to assist with the transition to civilian management. But before that change occurred, Frances and her siblings were treated to some remarkable experiences.[11]

With a sergeant's wife as her teacher, Frances completed her early years of schooling in a converted barracks building at Fort Yellowstone. When not practicing reading and writing, she found excitement in attending the cavalry exercises on the parade grounds in front of the Mammoth Hot Springs Hotel. These military demonstrations were impressive and drew crowds of tourists and residents alike. One of her favorite activities was to sneak into the soldiers' mess hall during breakfast with her little sister Virginia in tow. Here they would listen to the talk, mesmerized by the soldiers' yarns of army life in Yellowstone. One can almost imagine the two impressionable, young girls sitting starry-eyed at a long, benched table, while smartly uniformed men regaled them with story after story of thrilling adventures in America's wonderland. Stealing away to listen to the soldiers' stories became one of Frances and Virginia's most beloved activities during their first years in Yellowstone—until their father found out about their clandestine escapades and forbade them from visiting the soldiers' mess hall.[12]

When it came time for the soldiers to make their final, formal exit down the five-mile road to Gardiner and through the Roosevelt Arch at the park's north entrance in 1918, Frances recalled that there was "not a dry eye in the house." However, not all the soldiers left. Frances' father, as well a number of other army scouts, soldiers, and civil service employees chose to stay behind, and take positions with the newly formed National Park Service.[13]

Changing its administration was only one of the challenges that the Yellowstone officials encountered from 1915 to 1918. Accessible only by horseback after its creation in 1872, Yellowstone was for the most part visited by only the most adventurous travelers. With the building of roads and bridges, and the arrival of the railroad at the northern boundary of the park, stagecoaches and private horse-drawn wagons became the dominant form of transportation for park travelers during the period 1883 through 1915. Pressure from automobile associations, local gateway communities, and other government agencies, led to automobiles' finally being allowed entry into Yellowstone on July 31, 1915. The following year, 1916, proved to be disastrous as the combination of horse-drawn stagecoaches and fuming, backfiring motor cars created chaotic travel scenarios on park roads on a daily basis. In 1917, the old stagecoach drivers hung up their braided whips, took off their jingling spurs, folded up their big-buttoned dusters, and turned the Yellowstone stagecoach roads over to the gear jammers and their internal combustion "auto stages." This change not only revolutionized the transportation system in the park, but also considerably altered the responsibilities of the new National Park Service rangers.[14]

Initially, while Thad was a scout and early ranger, the Pound family lived in a house at the base of the terraces in Mammoth, complete with hot water piped in from the hot springs for the bathroom, and fresh spring water in the kitchen for drinking. But with the new park regulation admitting automobiles, Thad was transferred to Gardiner to administer the north entrance station. Moving into the former soldiers' station there, Frances was thrilled with evidence of prior wild times, such as bullet holes that she saw in the ceiling. But rather than finding a mysterious tale of a whodunit, Frances learned that the holes were the result of resident soldiers using their pistols to exterminate pesky flies. Nonetheless, her life in Gardiner and the north entrance would only get more exiting as time went on.[15]

For many girls growing up in the West in the late nineteenth and early twentieth centuries, the abundance of outdoor activities encouraged behavior that, in essence, rejected conventional female domestic patterns of life. With their interests far afield from the confines of the house and home, western girls sometimes developed close relationships with their fathers. Stimulating and influencing their daughters' interests as well as taking a more active part in their upbringing, fathers thus became novel role models for such girls by the early 1900s. Spending time with her father in outdoor activities allowed Frances to absorb some of his individualism and self-reliance, invaluable qualities that served her well as she matured. One shared activity for Thad and Frances was horseback riding.[16]

As Frances grew up she frequently rode with her father as he patrolled the park boundaries on horseback. In midsummer 1923, that training proved advantageous. Her horsemanship skills garnered an invitation to participate in the dedication celebration of the Howard Eaton Trail on July 19. At the conclusion of the dedication, Frances and her childhood friend, Adelaide Child Nichols, along with several other equestrians, rode silhouetted against the western sky on the crest of Sheepeater Cliff in a picturesque equestrian procession befitting the great western guide. Considered the founder of the western Dude Ranch, Howard Eaton endeared himself to thousands of people who traveled with him through Yellowstone as well as other areas of the country. His friendly western hospitality spread his fame from coast to coast. A classic westerner in manner and speech, Eaton became renowned for many of his expressions, especially his unique invitation to his ranch, "Come over to my ranch, and I'll treat you in a most *hostile* fashion." For many, Howard Eaton personified true western spirit. As Frances rode atop Sheepeater Cliff in tribute to the celebrated western horseman, she felt honored to be a part of one of Yellowstone's most memorable memorials.[17]

For Frances, the summer of 1923 in Yellowstone proved to be filled with events that ranged from participating in the Eaton Trail dedication to experiencing the cordiality of the president of the United States. Learning that President Warren G. Harding was soon to visit the park and that a public reception had been arranged for him at the Mammoth Hot Springs Hotel, Frances's father decided that both of his daughters should meet the country's leader. According to one of her oral histories, Frances recalled there was a line of people waiting to greet the president, but "with my father, you don't stand in line." So with his two daughters in hand, Thad walked directly up to Harding and announced, "Mr. President, I want you to meet two of the most beautiful daughters any man could ever have." The two girls, Frances, age sixteen and Virginia, age fourteen, feeling very privileged, shook hands with President Harding and wished him a pleasant trip through the park. Thad Pound obviously took his role as mentor as well as father seriously. His dedication to his daughters' development was characterized by his active and earnest participation in their education and life experiences, especially those of Frances.[18]

In addition to joining her father in his outdoor patrolling duties, Frances often accompanied him to his station at the north entrance of the park. Thad was responsible not only for collecting the entry fees from visitors but also for relaying and enforcing park regulations for visitors and their vehicles. These regulations included keeping dogs on chains or leashes, sealing all guns taken into the park because hunting was prohibited, and registering both visitors and their vehicles. Yellowstone's mountainous terrain, and rugged dirt roads presented early-day automobile owners with a multitude of challenges that included overheated brakes and tire blowouts. Consequently, visitors entering in their personal vehicles were required to carry at least one, if not two, spare tires, and each vehicle was required to pass a test that would demonstrate that it had sufficient braking power. Frances often assisted her father in conducting these duties, and apparently she made an impression on the park superintendent.[19]

"How would you like to be a park ranger?" Horace Albright asked eighteen-year-old Frances in the spring of 1925. Overcoming her surprise, Frances replied, "well, that's pretty nice, but you know that is not possible." Contrary to her belief that women were not hired as rangers, Albright submitted, "Well I don't know, you've done such a good job, do you think you could get a uniform and be ready by June fifteenth?" With that Frances asked no more questions and dashed off in search of a uniform. Her father was absolutely tickled that his daughter was going to be a ranger and, of course, Frances was ecstatic. But she immediately faced the practical question of, what should a woman ranger uniform look like?

Frances Pound proudly shows off her newly fashioned NPS uniform in 1925.
(COURTESY YELLOWSTONE NATIONAL PARK ARCHIVES)

Apparently, Marguerite Lindsley's riding uniform supplied her with the only model to follow.[20]

Because Frances would be working the entry gate, occasionally carrying a sidearm, and enforcing park regulations as well as being viewed as a National Park Service representative, Albright may have deemed it necessary for her to look "official." Isabel Bassett Wasson and Marguerite Lindsley had previously worked as seasonal ranger naturalists in the park, but evidently they had fashioned "uniforms" of their own creation for their positions in the field. Because there was no specific design for a woman's National Park Service uniform in 1925, Mrs. Albright and Frances's mother created a pattern for Frances in the style of a military riding habit. The Livingston tailor who took her measurements to insure accuracy of the pattern's design found himself quite embarrassed when he discovered that the uniform was to include trousers. Following approval by NPS director Stephen Mather, Frances's design, which featured an A-line knee-length coat with slash pockets and jodhpur-styled breeches, was sent to Philadelphia where her custom ensemble was fabricated in the standard National Park Service forest-green serge material.[21]

Sporting her new coat, pants, boots, and Park Service badge, Frances, now "Ranger Jim," took up her position attending to the duties of Yellowstone's north entrance station in June 1925, just inside the Roosevelt Arch. For that summer and for the next four years, those duties included registering visitors, giving information, and sealing guns. "Sealing guns was an oddity to a lot of people," Frances explained. The procedure included breaking the gun down, putting a wire through the barrel, and sealing it with wax to prevent use. This part of her job caught the attention of a reporter for the *New York Sun* who wrote an article touting her unconventional occupation. The news story's headline proclaimed, "She's Ranger Jim to Pistol Toting Tourists." In addition, the article contained several photographs of Frances demonstrating her prowess in handling guns, a skill she had learned from her father. In addition, her father had also taught her to shoot. Undoubtedly that was a useful skill in her job at the park gate, where she sometimes took in daily receipts of more than $7,000. Because there was no bank in Gardiner to receive the gate money, Frances carried a gun while she was on duty. A woman handling firearms generally garnered stares from park visitors, and even more frequently generated lots of questions. One of the first inquiries that Frances remembered getting was "Are you real employee of the park?" She also recalled that her father was once asked, "What did [Frances] do as a woman?" Other questions ranged from the merely curious, "Do you work here all the time?" to the blatantly judgmental, "Why did they hire women for a job like that?" But, as she was her father's daughter, resourceful and quick-witted, Frances always had lots of answers for quizzical tourists.[22]

Upon occasion she did more than merely answering questions; she assisted with arrests and also made one of her own. Her first experience with an arrest fortuitously came under her father's guidance. An announcement came over the park radio one afternoon for officials to be

Just outside the Roosevelt Arch at the north entrance to Yellowstone, Frances exhibits a trophy sized elk antler rack. Note the W.A. Hall store visible in the background. (COURTESY YELLOWSTONE NATIONAL PARK ARCHIVES)

on the look out for two armed and dangerous bank robbers who were believed to be heading toward Yellowstone National Park. When two men arrived at the gate matching the description of the lawbreakers, Frances's father calmly instructed her to register them just like any other visitor. Once they were inside the station, Thad ordered the men to "put their hands up." As the men obeyed the order, Frances noticed that their raised hands were just inches away from a shotgun sportingly hung in the elk antler trophy mounted on the wall just above their heads. Not saying a word, nor looking up, she relieved the two men of their weapons. To her relief, she found out later that the shotgun was not loaded. This experience probably helped give her a backbone of steel when it came to dealing with wrongdoers of any kind, and surely came into play during the late summer of 1927—when she encountered bootleggers in the park.[23]

On that eventful August day in 1927, Thad had taken the evening off so that he and Frances's mother, Grace, could steal away together for a lovely sunset drive. Frances, working the north entrance gate by herself, watched as a car with "official park access" pulled through the gate and went into town. When the car returned to gain entry into the park, Frances, "Ranger Jim," motioned for the car to stop. Following her suspicions of liquor smuggling into the park, she asked the driver if she could check the back seat. Just as she suspected, she found "every kind of booze imaginable." She subsequently arrested three park employees and held them until her father returned. Impressed by "Ranger Jim's" intrepid act of law enforcement, Superintendent Horace Albright claimed that the capture of these law breakers was "the most important arrest of the season." One of the people she detained was the driver for Yellowstone Camps manager Vernon Goodwin. While Frances knew that she had done the right thing at the time, she later admitted that she felt a little self-conscious that she had arrested Goodwin's driver. Even though "Ranger Jim's" action left him without a chauffeur for the remainder of the season, Goodwin apologized to Frances for his driver's error in judgment, and commended her for professionally handling the incident. The newspaper publicity following that event made anyone seeking entry into Yellowstone with dubious motives aware of the careful eye of "Ranger Jim."[24]

However, some of the "characters" who graced Yellowstone's North Entrance gate were not so easily detected. One summer day in 1927, while working the gate with her father, Frances watched as a strangely dressed man came up to the Roosevelt Arch. Frances noted that his unusual garb included a Navajo-style jacket in wild colors, blousy-military style khaki pants, leather puttees, mustard-colored socks, and shoes that matched the socks. He probably thought that he looked like a typical westerner who would be mostly unnoticed, but she watched the man wandering back and forth around the Arch, continually looking around like he was watching for someone. After some time she inquired of her father: "Who do you suppose this character is?" An astute judge of "characters" of all types, including government men, Thad responded without any question, "I think he's an officer" of some kind. No surprise to Frances, her father was absolutely correct. Colonel Edmund W. Starling, chief of the

Secret Service for five presidents, finally made his way into the station and introduced himself. Discovering that Thad had previously been a deputy sheriff, Colonel Starling engaged Frances' father in convivial conversation about the trials and tribulations of careers in law enforcement. Colonel Starling, as it turned out, was on a scouting mission for the upcoming visit by President Calvin and Mrs. Coolidge. However, Starling advised both Frances and her father that the president's visit was to be held in the strictest confidence. Eagerly Frances expressed to the Secret Service chief her hope to meet the president. "Don't worry about that," avowed Colonel Starling.[25]

Several weeks later, President and Mrs. Coolidge arrived at the entrance gate with their multitude of Secret Service cars in tow, but Colonel Starling was nowhere in sight. Nevertheless, Frances and her father briefly greeted the Coolidges before the entourage proceeded on to the Mammoth Hot Springs Hotel, where Harry Child, Yellowstone's hotel concessioner magnate, held a grand reception for the couple. Several days later, Frances received a telephone call from Colonel Starling. "I have already cleared you at Headquarters," he asserted. "I want you and Peg [Marguerite Lindsley] to meet me at Old Faithful Inn, tomorrow morning at 7:30. I'll let you meet Cal." Colonel Starling made one more stipulation before hanging up the telephone, "I want you both in uniform," he commanded. Learning that Colonel Starling had secured rooms for both her and Peg at the Old Faithful Lodge for that evening, the two elated girls hopped into Peg's car and drove from Mammoth to Old Faithful. After meeting Colonel Starling at the lodge and getting settled in, Frances and Peg went to the outdoor amphitheater for the NPS evening program. Frances noticed that Mrs. Coolidge, who was also in attendance, enjoyed the program immensely and joined in all the songs.

Following the program, everyone went back to the inn and danced, including Mrs. Coolidge and the Secret Service men. Returning to the Old Faithful Lodge at the conclusion of the dance, Frances and Peg polished their boots and hung up their uniforms in preparation for their early morning appointment, and went to bed. But, with excited anticipation, both women were too keyed up to sleep much.

At 7:30 the next morning, Frances and Peg waited anxiously at the desk of Old Faithful Inn as Colonel Starling came down the stairs in his "outfit," as Frances called it, complete with his puttees and mustard-colored shoes. "All right, follow me," he ordered. Upon reaching the third floor room where the president was staying, Colonel Starling knocked on the door and announced, "Cal, I've got some company for you. I want you to meet somebody." Much to Frances's surprise, when Colonel Starling opened the door, there stood the president of the United States in his pants with suspenders and an undershirt. He casually invited the girls into the room and they began their visit. One of the first things he asked Frances was whether or not she thought women should be in the National Park Service. Without batting an eye Frances replied, "Definitely! I think we need women and need them badly!" She explained that people coming to the park wanted to learn about the park and they wanted someone who could also talk to their children; in Frances's opinion, women were the best candidates for the job.

Frances and the president discussed a variety of topics that ranged from conservation to the importance of the national parks, to traffic through the park, to availability and quality of accommodations for the touring public. He then turned to Peg and asked her about the park's museums. On a personal note, the president inquired whether the two female rangers enjoyed their work, asked what were Frances's duties at the gate and what were Peg's tasks at the museum, how long had they been in the park service, and of course, what they did in the winter.

Within a short time, Mrs. Coolidge returned from her morning excursion to the roof of Old Faithful Inn, where she watched a sunrise eruption of Old Faithful Geyser. Frances and Peg conversed for a short time with Grace Coolidge, who wanted to know if the girls, as rangers, got much of a chance to be out in the park. Frances later described the president's wife as a "beautiful person." At the conclusion of their visit, Peg presented the first lady with a pin from the Pi Beta sorority chapter of Montana State University, one of Peg's alma maters. Grace had been one the founders of the Beta chapter of the Pi Beta Phi at the University of Vermont, where she attended classes from 1898 until 1902. The gold pin in the shape of an arrow symbolized the international organization's motto, "Friends and Leaders for Life." Frances recalled that Mrs. Coolidge was "thrilled to death" with Peg's meaningful gift. Concluding their visit at Old Faithful with Frances and Peg, President and Mrs. Coolidge departed for the Yellowstone Lake Hotel.

The next morning the scene at the Lake Hotel was chaotic at best. The president was missing! For several hours Secret Service personnel scoured

President Calvin Coolidge's entourage traveled through
Yellowstone with secret service men walking along for extra
protection as visitors gathered to catch a glimpse of the president.
(COURTESY YELLOWSTONE NATIONAL PARK MUSEUM COLLECTION)

the landscape checking everything and everyone. Probably thinking that he would not be missed, President Coolidge had gone off early in the morning to a particular cove to indulge in one of Yellowstone's famous pastimes, fishing. Fortunately, he had taken two Secret Service men with him, but the agents had failed to relay the president's whereabouts to the rest of the security team before departing. Apparently unaware of the rapid passing of time (fishing sometimes has that effect on people, including presidents of the United States), he returned to the hotel about six hours after his departure, completely satisfied with his jaunt. He had caught enough fish to treat the entire entourage to fresh trout for dinner that evening. Frances, who was back in Mammoth by this time, would have given anything to see the Secret Service men on their toes!

On the last day of the president's stay at the Canyon Hotel, Frances and Peg each got another call from Colonel Starling. Apparently taken by the two young lady rangers, he extended yet another opportunity for them to join the social gathering with the presidential party. "This is their last stop in the park [at Canyon Hotel], so we thought you'd like to come by," invited Colonel Starling. Everyone who beheld its colossal, sprawling architecture considered the massive Canyon Hotel one of the most exquisite hotels in the country, including Frances who believed it to be "one of the most beautiful places anybody could ask for." Frances and Peg were delighted with Colonel Starling's invitation and graciously accepted. After informing them that he had made reservations for them at the Canyon Lodge, which was across the canyon from the hotel, Colonel Starling once again emphasized that Frances and Peg were to appear in uniform.

That evening the two young ladies, attired in their green serge jackets and pants, were treated to a magnificent formal dance in the hotel's massive lobby. Probably entertained by the music of the then-famous Gene Quaw orchestra, everyone danced away the night. Frances and Peg, who by this time had become acquainted with the Secret Service men, danced with them too. Sometime during the course of the evening, Grace Coolidge sought out the pair of female rangers and told them that she was thrilled to know that women were part of the National Park Service. The presidential party departed the following day and business in Yellowstone returned to normal for the rest of the summer.

Upon the park's closing at the end of summer 1927, Frances worked through the winter as clerical and stenographic support in the Chief Ranger's office. In addition to filling in for Superintendent Albright's secretary, she assisted with producing the annual reports of the park's summer activities. Winters in Yellowstone were not as exciting as a presidential visit, but they offered a few memorable moments. One night while driving home to Gardiner at the end of her Mammoth work day, in her Buick Roadster, Frances looked down the road and noticed what appeared to be someone walking in the dark, cold evening. As she got closer she realized it was a bison, and that he had stopped in the middle of the bridge to graze on hay that apparently dropped off a wagon earlier that day. Unlike today, it was quite unusual to see a buffalo on the roadway between Mammoth and Gardiner in the 1920s because they were mostly corralled at the buffalo ranch, which was almost forty miles away in the Lamar Valley. But there he was, "icicles from top to bottom and blowing steam, of course" and blocking the road. Frances waited patiently for a bit, occasionally racing the motor only to have the bison roll his eyes in her direction implying "this is mine, and you'll have to wait." After half an hour, Frances decided she had been patient long enough and kicked the "old butterfly cutout" on the muffler that was accessed from the floorboard of her roadster, and raced the engine. "It sounded like a cannon going off," she recalled. "He jumped! Sort of half stood up, pivoted, and went off the other end of the bridge and up the side of the bank." With her path clear and fearing that the buffalo might double back, Frances made a record run to the ranger station. That sort of contact with motorists and bison would become increasingly more common as the years passed.

In the fall of 1929, Frances and her sister Virginia decided that nine months of winter had become tiresome, and they started planning a vacation. Just as they began to plot their winter getaway, they received an invitation to visit Santa Ana, California, from a family whom Nellie had helped one summer, when the family's father had a heart attack while visiting the park. With a place to reside for an extended stay, Frances and Virginia wasted no time in securing two one-way train tickets to Los Angeles. Perhaps playing and staying in California a little too long, and partly because of the onset of the Great Depression, Frances and Virginia ran out of sufficient funds to return home. About her inability to come back to Yellowstone, Frances later recalled that "when you don't have a lot of money and you're not going to ask your Dad for money, you're going to stay and get a job, and then you'll come back." With that thought in mind, they both found jobs and began saving. The nation's financial instability apparently made Frances and Virginia leery of giving up secure incomes to return to Yellowstone and they resolved to stay in California. Knowing that their mother had dreamed of living in California and their father had recently retired, the two sisters continued saving until they had enough to buy a house. Shortly afterward, Thad, Nellie and youngest daughter, eleven-year-old Ruth, joined Frances and Virginia on the West Coast.

One thing having led to another, life went on for Frances in California until World War II broke out. Frances became involved with the American Red Cross during the war, and taught first aid to automobile club workers and law enforcement staff members. Just before the war ended, she met and married Owen Wright. On October 13, 1946, Frances gave birth to Suzanne Marie and began a new role as a mother. As her daughter attended school, Frances became an active participant in the Parent Teacher Association, where she served in several different capacities. Growing up and working in the outdoor environs of Yellowstone proved advantageous for Frances as

France Pound Wright (in wheelchair) and daughter Suzanne (back row center) were special guests for the park's 125th anniversary celebration in 1997. (COURTESY OF BOB FUHRMANN)

she used stories of her youthful park experiences to enrich and enlighten her young protégées during her ten-year role as a Girl Scout leader.[26]

Although she remained in California for the rest of her life, Frances "Ranger Jim" frequently returned to Yellowstone many times. Probably her most memorable visit occurred in 1997 when Frances was ninety, and she and daughter Suzanne were invited to be honored guests at Yellowstone's 125th anniversary events. During the celebration she treated a contingent of park rangers, cultural resources personnel, and other staff members to an entertaining repertoire of her reminiscences. For many park personnel in attendance, her colorful narratives added a fascinating allure to Yellowstone's vast cultural history, while filling in some gaps in the park's written historical record. Amusing everyone, including herself, Frances "Ranger Jim" Pound Wright told her most cherished stories and memories of Yellowstone days to the park staff with laughter and merriment.[27]

Frances Eva Pound Wright, "Ranger Jim," died on December 27, 1999, at the age of ninety-three,[28] but not before she passed down her most treasured possession. While attending the 125th celebration, she bequeathed her 1925 custom-tailored uniform to the park's museum collection. With this donation, which adds a material historical component to her rich oral histories in the Yellowstone Archives, Frances preserved for all time her legacy as one of the pioneering women rangers in Yellowstone.

Herma Geneva Albertson Baggley

(1896–1981)

Girl Guide for Dudes

Fielding questions about Yellowstone's flowers, animals, and geological features, building a two-mile nature trail, writing a much needed book on the park's plants, and heading up the National Park Service Women's Organization, Herma Albertson Baggley genuinely characterized the pioneer spirit of a 1920s woman. Following her "try out" in nature work during the summer of 1926 and her seasonal position as a park naturalist from 1927 through 1930, Herma gained a status with the National Park Service in 1931 that few women of the day were able to wrangle: permanent ranger. Her graduate degree in botany from the University of Idaho along with her acquired expertise on the park's natural environment, more than likely helped her to transcend the male-dominated national park ranger sphere, and to become Yellowstone's first full-time female ranger naturalist. Bolstered by education and practical experience, Herma established her own trail to success with her passion for outdoor life, her zeal for providing factual, scientific information on Yellowstone's big nature, and her perpetual resolve to be a conscientious conservationist of the national parks.

Herma Geneva Albertson, was born on October 11, 1896, to Clifton and Ruthella Albertson, and the first of that couple's three surviving children. Herma's brother Burton J. was born on December 26, 1901, and sister Ruthella Marjorie was born on September 12, 1907.[1] Growing up in a rural farming community located in the northwest corner of Iowa, Herma developed a hobby of collecting flowers at an early age as she gathered colorful blooms for May Day celebrations. Upon finishing eighth grade, presumably in the two-story wood-frame schoolhouse that doubled as a public gathering place in the nearby town of Inwood, Herma and her family moved to Idaho in 1910 to join her father. Clifton had taken a position operating a store and post office for the Powell Irrigation Project near Arco, Idaho, in 1909.[2]

After living in the Idaho desert for nearly two years, the family settled in Blackfoot in 1911, where Herma attended high school. Her interest in flowers continued, and she recalled that as a teenager she treasured her outdoor excursions near town, "scrambling over lava rocks to locate flowers growing in the crevices." After finishing high school in 1915, Herma taught elementary school for several years in Blackfoot, where she "always managed to give [her] students some nature study."[3]

Living near the mountains of Idaho amplified her longing to learn more about the workings of nature and when, in 1921, she entered the University of Idaho, Herma took as many science courses as the school would allow each semester. It was her summer of 1922 at the Puget Sound Biological Station that persuaded Herma to "follow science in some way."[4]

Her interest in flowers and plants undoubtedly made botany a favored choice. After teaching in the Blackfoot school system for the academic year of 1922-1923, Herma returned to the University of Idaho. Her outstanding scholastic work garnered Herma a position as a student instructor in botany, and from then on her "interest was largely confined to that field." Majoring in botany with a minor in philosophy, she graduated in the spring of 1926 with a B.S., and received highest honors for her scholastic work. According to a draft manuscript of her personal profile and accomplishments that Herma wrote for her sorority Delta Delta Delta ten years later, she and one other girl had "made double honors, the first time anyone had done such a thing at the university." With degree in hand, Herma set out to blossom as a professional botanist.[5]

With Yellowstone and its bountiful nature nearly in her backyard, Herma approached Horace Albright, Yellowstone's first National Park Service (NPS) superintendent, about a position on his educational staff as a naturalist. After hiring Isabel Bassett Wasson, Marguerite Lindsley, Margaret Thone, and several other women through the early 1920s, Albright favored hiring women to give lectures and escort tour groups, because they produced the high-quality informational programs he was looking for. Although many of the seasonal male rangers were college fellows, Albright was convinced that the men on his staff "could not do a lecture if their life depended on it."[6] Ultimately, his goal was to hire qualified rangers who would satisfactorily impart information to the public, male or female. Even though Albright leaned toward employing women, he seemed to be using a high degree of caution in his hiring tactics that summer, and thus submitted an unusual, but unique, proposition to Herma.

> The superintendent said if I was willing to come down from the University for the summer and work as a naturalist, but not have the rating of a naturalist nor the title of a naturalist, live in one of the Old Faithful cabins and be hired by the camps company as a "pillow puncher" [lodge maid] in the morning for my board and room, and work for the park in the afternoon—he would like to try me out.[7]

In a certain sense, Albright was being resourceful with his offer, as he could in effect have a volunteer naturalist for the summer who would be employed by a concessioner.[8] Likewise in accepting his offer, Herma was equally practical, because she could spend her summer following her heart's desire of doing nature work. But most importantly, the summer of 1926 gave Herma the opportunity to "demonstrate to park officials that

Herma Albertson (front row far right) spent her first summer in Yellowstone working with this group of "pillow punchers," otherwise known as maids, in 1926.
(COURTESY YELLOWSTONE NATIONAL PARK ARCHIVES)

a woman, thoroughly interested in nature work, could be as efficient and capable as a man."[9]

Before this time, women had generally entered into the fields of botany and nature study as hobbyists, or as illustrators for their husbands or other male professional scientists. Given that botany in the eighteenth and nineteenth centuries was closely associated with activities deemed acceptable for women—such as gardening, flower painting and flower arranging—it was often relegated to an amateur, popular-science status by male-dominated scientific societies. As scientific research involving plants slowly transformed into a profession, men such as Asa Gray and his naturalist contemporaries strove to raise the status of botany into a professional discipline.

By the end of the nineteenth century, women who had devoted themselves to becoming skilled at identifying unknown plants, mosses, and flowers, and who had previously been welcomed into the field of botany, found that they were being gradually excluded from the discipline as it began to professionalize. Many women continued to work in botany with little or no recognition, but others chose to upgrade their educational status. Armed with educations in various natural sciences, women in the beginning of the twentieth century began to make great strides, advancing into botany and other male-dominated spheres of outdoor scientific work. But as many women realized and discovered, it was still necessary for them to tread softly and find a way of blending into many traditionally male-defined fields, such as that of park ranger-naturalist. Herma seemed to understand this premise, and thus by accepting Albright's offer of a "try out" she began her slow and steady climb to become a professional naturalist in Yellowstone.[10]

During the summer of 1926, Herma worked in the mornings changing sheets, punching pillows, and cleaning guest cabins for the Yellowstone Park Camps Company at Old Faithful, for which she was paid fifteen dollars a month in addition to room and board. In the afternoons, she and her crew worked on developing the Nature Trail at Old Faithful, the first such trail in the area.[11]

Ansel Hall, the NPS chief naturalist since 1923, had put forth the initial concept of a self-guiding nature trail at Old Faithful, but it was up to Herma and her crew to lay out and construct the two-mile loop route to Observation Point and Solitary Geyser. Known for being an enormously creative person, Hall had a gift of getting things done by choosing the right people, providing them with the materials, and leaving them alone to get the job done. Apparently this was his tactic on the Old Faithful Nature Trail. The chief ranger in Mammoth sent Herma a trail crew, and apparently little else. Herma later reported that even though she "knew little about such things and nothing about the trail crews," she formed a team and "together we worked out the trail."[12]

In addition to constructing the trail, Herma and her crew also erected signage so that "an unseen ranger naturalist" could figuratively accompany visitors along the trail and help them to "become acquainted with" many of its wonders of nature. Herma's notes on the trail indicated that she placed as many as 190 natural-history labels or signs along the route, which described trees, flowers, birds, geysers, hot springs, and other natural phenomena. While it is technically unclear who wrote the text for the signs, Herma undoubtedly produced most of it. Her degree in botany and her accomplished writing skill prepared her well for that task.

The detail included on the signs was as engaging as it was informative, and as such, the writing style on the signs appreciably pointed toward Herma as at least one of the authors. Using every-day analogies that anyone could comprehend, Herma and her crew created interpretive markers that translated complicated scientific words into terms that the average person could understand:

WATER BUTTERCUP
(Batrachium conferoides)

Leaves are finely divided like the gills of a fish to permit its breathing under water. This is a true flowering plant that has adapted itself to this strange habitat. Its blossoms are lifted above the water for pollination and as seeds develop this portion of the plant again turns down into the water and distributes itself beneath the surface.

Herma's notes stated that, in addition to the sign identifying the plant, there was a stake at the right side of the trail where a string had been tied to a rock thrown into the midst of the water buttercups, so that they could be immediately located by visitors. This approach of using string, rocks, and stakes to point out plants, burrows, and nests that might be missed by a casual observer was a method that Herma and her crew employed throughout the trail. They also constructed ladders so that visitors could

Herma takes a rest from her trail guiding on the Nature Trail in this
snapshot from her photo album. Note the megaphone she used to deliver
her voice to the multitudes of visitors that trekked along the trail with her.
(COURTESY YELLOWSTONE NATIONAL PARK ARCHIVES)

peer inside the nests of animals such as the pine siskin. Another element
that Herma and her trail crew used was signage with questions to draw
visitors into the learning experience. One sign that hung from the roots of
an upturned lodgepole pine asked, "How deep are the roots of a lodgepole
pine? How far do they spread?" Engaging visitors into thinking about
what they were viewing almost certainly made interpretation seem more
interesting, and possibly explained the trail's popularity through the next
several years.[13]

When she was not punching pillows for the Camps Company or
working on the Nature Trail, Herma served as a relief lecturer in the open-
air amphitheater on banks of the Firehole River, and at the Old Faithful

Lodge. Her first summer of nature work was certainly a busy one, which made it go by far too quickly. At the end of the summer, Herma's gamble paid off. Superintendent Albright and Chief Ranger Samuel T. Woodring, came down to Old Faithful to personally congratulate her on the splendid job she did on the Nature Trail. Albright also invited her to return the following summer as an official ranger-naturalist, for which she would be paid ninety dollars a month. Herma was thrilled that one of her many dreams for the future had come true, her desire to work professionally in the nature field.

Returning to Blackfoot for the winter, Herma tried her hand at what would prove to be her least favorite teaching position—high school science. But before the 1927 spring session of teaching in Blackfoot had concluded, the University of Idaho offered Herma the opportunity to realize another one of her dreams: a graduate degree. Following her completion of an undergraduate degree with honors in 1926, the university obviously saw Herma as a promising young woman, and offered her a graduate fellowship in the Botany Department, to begin in the fall of 1927. Without skipping a beat, Herma exclaimed that she "accepted the offer as quickly as I could run home from the post office, type out an acceptance, and get it into the mail again. That is the extent of my love of teaching high school."[14]

In addition to receiving the invitation for a graduate fellowship, Herma also received a letter of encouragement for her work in the park from the eminent botanist of Grinnell College in Iowa, Dr. Henry Shoemaker Conard. "The work at Old Faithful needs you," he wrote. Embedded in this commentary was a hope that Herma would continue doing research on Yellowstone's plants and follow through with the botany work he had begun. His remark most likely stemmed from the fact that he would not be returning to the park for the summer of 1927. Earlier that year, as detailed in the chapter on Marguerite Lindsley, he had resigned his position as summer naturalist to protest the Department of Interior's new policy that prohibited hiring women.[15]

Despite the ban, Superintendent Albright somehow managed to keep his previous offer to Herma of the opportunity to work as a temporary ranger-naturalist at Old Faithful.[16] Dr. Conard seemed genuinely pleased that Herma would be there to continue researching Yellowstone's unusual plants, even though he was distressed about his own daughter's ineligibility. Understandably, Conard also wanted to insure that his work on the park's flora up to that point would be utilized and not fall into obscurity in the museum's basement. "There should be at the Museum at Mammoth a set of named plants designed for the O.F. naturalists" so that "the main collection can be consulted by so good a botanist as yourself," he informed Herma. The main collection was most likely the herbarium that he had started in 1914-1926, which contained over 700 species of Yellowstone National Park plants. Later, Herma would not only carry on Dr. Conard's herbarium, but also she would use it as a primary source for her book on Yellowstone's plants. Wishing her the best for the season and beyond, Dr. Conard wrote, "Here's hoping you will have a great summer...and you are indeed fortunate to be called back to Idaho University."[17]

Conard was delighted that she also would continue to work on the Nature Trail, which had become nearly as controversial as the women rangers. Another of Chief Inspector Garland's criticisms during the summer of 1926 had been the Nature Trail. He believed that park visitors had "little time to saunter through the woods and follow a trail to find peewees nests, water lilies, and the like," and that he doubted that it would be of interest to "any great number of people." Albright quickly

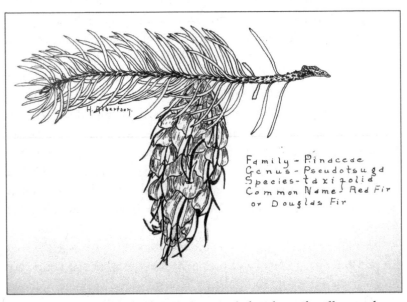

This is just one example of Herma's artwork that she used to illustrate her articles in Yellowstone Nature Notes *and the* Ranger Naturalist Manuals.
(COURTESY YELLOWSTONE NATIONAL PARK ARCHIVES)

countered that the Nature Trail had appealed to so many visitors during the summer of 1926 that it had been "practically worn out." This was one battle where evidence and rationale won out over Garland's unreasonable condemnation of the work of Yellowstone's ranger naturalists and aspiring ranger naturalists. The nature trail remained intact, and Herma assumed charge of it for the summer of 1927. With Dr. Conard's encouragement and Superintendent Albright's support, she must have looked toward the upcoming summer in Yellowstone with a ready and confident spirit.[18]

As Herma prepared for her seasonal position as a ranger-naturalist, she was given yet one more compliment on her abilities. Albright was obviously impressed with her research and writing ability, because he chose to include her seven-page essay "Trees of Yellowstone Park" in the 1927 *Ranger Naturalist Manual of Yellowstone National Park*. In this essay, Herma's blending of facts and poetry showed her talent of weaving scientific observation with insightful nature writing:

> In the deep cool shaded moist ravines of the Park grows the [Engelmann Spruce]; a dark, blue-green, pyramidal-shaped tree of rare beauty and symmetry. In contrast to the Alpine Fir, the needles are sharp and pointed, are distributed all around the branches, leave the branches much roughened when they fall and the cones han[g] pendent from the upper third of the tree. The needles are also square in cross section as compared to the flattened needles of the fir. Surely the Engelmann Spruce is the embodiment of our vision of a perfect Christmas tree. No road is more pleasant to travel, or woodland path more inviting, or mountain stream lovelier, than when winding... thru a dark, blue-green avenue of spruces.[19]

Her interlacing of practicality and prose seemed to be just the sort of writing that Albright had in mind for capturing and satisfying the inquisitiveness of park visitors. Even before she took her position as a ranger-naturalist for the summer of 1927, Herma had begun to make her mark as an able voice of Yellowstone's educational division.

Now an official ranger-naturalist, Herma did not have to work anymore for the camps company because her room and board was supplied at Old Faithful. In her memoir she remarked that she had "graduated to the puphouse," an old one-room army cabin with one window and a door. While the cabin was surely nothing more than basic accommodation, Herma, like most employees who loved to spend their summers in

Yellowstone, did not come to the park for posh lodging. However, this exposure to the inadequacies of employee living quarters was probably the catalyst for Herma's crusade for suitable park housing later in her life.[20]

In addition to rudimentary housing, she was afforded the luxury of taking her meals with the other rangers. She revealed that "during my entire stay at Old Faithful, I was the only woman eating at the ranger's mess, and believe me, I developed a regular man's appetite." Continuing to work on constructing and labeling the Old Faithful nature trail as well as guiding and lecturing, she certainly earned her "regular man's" appetite.[21]

For the next three years (1927-1929), Herma was the only guide on the Nature Trail, and her crowd of interested hikers grew from three to three hundred. "One month during 1928 I guided an average of 200 people each day over the Nature Trail, which was originally built to accommodate 60 people," she recalled. "The largest single party I ever had was 350 persons." The two-mile trail wound its way up the mountain to Observation Point, 500 feet above Old Faithful Geyser, and offered a magnificent panorama of the geyser basin before it meandered through the woods to Solitary Geyser, and then looped around, returning visitors to the starting point. "This," said Herma, "was long enough for dudes in thin-soled high-heeled slippers." Although she had little sympathy for women who tried to tour the park in stylish but improper footwear, she also commended them for being good-natured about the discomforts of the hike. "Sometimes," she admitted, "a person would complain...but for that one person of that type there are a thousand who enjoy the trips and take the small hardships as part of the game." Along the route she revealed the names of birds and animals, called attention to exceptional geological formations, and pointed out interesting sights such as a tree where a grizzly bear's claw marks had recorded his height.

Yellowstone's dynamic nature frequently supplied new discoveries along the trail for both Herma and her groups of curious visitors. While escorting a group on the trail in August 1928, Herma identified a rubber boa snake, *Charina bottae*, which earned her the honor of being the first person to report the existence of that species of boa constrictor in Yellowstone. At the highest point of the Nature Trail was Solitary Geyser, which Herma called "her trail geyser." While her group rested, she explained that Solitary Geyser used to be a mere hot spring, but several years before it had been tapped to furnish water for the Old Faithful swimming pool in the basin just below, and the relief of the pressure converted it into a geyser, which spouted at five-minute intervals.[22]

In this portion of her talk, Herma illuminated for thousands of visitors the consequences of disrupting the delicate plumbing system beneath Yellowstone. In essence, either by design or default, she set in motion one of the National Park Service's guiding principles—educating the public on the necessity of preservation and conservation of the country's natural features. Herma personally believed that people were their "real natural selves only in the out of doors," and that Yellowstone gave them a place where they could be the "interesting, sincere human beings they were meant to be." She, like many other dedicated park service personnel, made it a part of her mission to alert visitors to the importance of protecting as well as enjoying the park, so that future generations could enjoy it too.[23]

For those visitors who might not have had the time or the inclination to hike the nature trail, Herma kept flower exhibits at both the Old Faithful Lodge and the Old Faithful Inn. But keeping them fresh and fragrant was not an easy task, as the flowers had to be "gathered far away," which often required Herma to hike fifteen miles a day. Her duties often included these extra activities, which she graciously accepted, viewing them as "special services that I am privileged to render." One of those special services included gathering wildflowers to enliven the guest rooms and beautify the dining table for President and Mrs. Coolidge during their visit in 1927. Today, of course, flower picking in the park is prohibited, but Herma's world was in a different time.

Superintendent Albright applauded her willingness to handle any job as well as her ability to explain scientific facts in plain language, and considered her "one of the best bets in the park." In the evenings, with her deep focus on the park's plants and flowers, Herma delighted audiences with her lecture "Plant Life of Yellowstone." She never knew who the listeners might be and discovered on more than one occasion that she had entertained curators of Chicago and New York museums. One evening Herma answered numerous questions posed by a dignified looking gentleman, who later introduced himself as the president of Cornell University. Unquestionably, Herma was as enthralled with her work in the park as the visitors were fascinated by her presentations.[24]

As a ranger-naturalist, Herma spent countless hours educating park visitors on what made geysers spout, how to get along amiably with bears, and how to recognize and appreciate hundreds of animals, plants, and birds. One newspaper article featuring Herma reported that through her zeal for education "thousands of park visitors have gleaned more in-depth facts about Dame Nature from her walks and lectures than they would have accrued during an entire semester of study" in a college laboratory. Although Herma amassed considerable knowledge during her summer nature work, she continued to expand her own education at the University of Idaho.[25]

Before her return to the university in the fall of 1927, Herma had become fascinated with the algae in some of Yellowstone's hot springs and pools. She collected a few specimens before leaving Old Faithful, but upon consulting with Dr. Rhule, a professor in the botany department, Herma realized that she needed more samples of algae and hot water from the springs to conduct her experiments. She wrote to Marguerite Lindsley in late September asking if it would be possible for Marguerite to collect samples of algae and bacteria from various hot springs, record the temperatures, and send the samples to the university. In her letter of September 23, Herma noted that she would furnish the collecting bottles and the samples could be sent to the university C.O.D. After obtaining an okay from Superintendent Horace Albright, Marguerite collected samples from Old Faithful and Norris geyser basins and the Mammoth Terraces, and sent them to Herma. As she began her research on Yellowstone's algae, Herma discovered that very little work had been done on that subject and by October she decided to make it her master's thesis topic. Her motivation was that perhaps by studying the algae she could learn more about the differences in plant life between Old Faithful and Mammoth. Through the course of the winter, Marguerite collected and sent Herma samples, and in turn Herma conducted experiments and sent Marguerite letters concerning her findings. Herma also sent Marguerite a composition entitled "The Flowers of Yellowstone" to be considered for the 1928 *Ranger Naturalist Manual*. Marguerite, whose job it was to collect and edit the articles for the manual, commented that she enjoyed Herma's piece very much and believed that it was a "real contribution" to the manual.[26]

Evidently, Herma's proposed thesis on Yellowstone's algae proved to be more involved than she had anticipated, and she chose instead to produce "A Manual of the Axiflorae of Northern Idaho" to fulfill her

"What makes geysers geyse?" . . . every tourist wants to know.

This caricature humorously depicts an interesting collage of Yellowstone tourists in the late 1920s. Herma, in uniform, is portrayed as leading an interpretive lecture on the geysers. (OAKLAND TRIBUNE, SEPTEMBER 22, 1929)

degree requirement. If she were alive today, Herma would probably not be surprised to learn that research on Yellowstone's algae is still being conducted nearly eighty years after she began her study at the University of Idaho.

In the spring of 1929, Herma graduated with her master's degree in botany and returned for yet another summer of nature work in Yellowstone. By that summer, Herma's success as a naturalist had captured the attention of journalist Alma Chestnut, who filed a newspaper article declaring that "Herma Albertson Is One of the Few Women Having the Title of 'Ranger' and Qualified To Tell Tenderfoot Tourists How to Manage Bears or Why Geysers Get That Way." The article, "Girl Guide for Dudes," appeared in the *Oakland* (CA) *Tribune* and the *Miami* (OK) *Daily News Record* on September 22, 1929, and conceivably numerous other newspapers across the country. In the article Herma acknowledged that being a "girl ranger" made her nearly as interesting as the animals and plants. Visitors repeatedly wanted to know where she got her training, what she did during the winter, whether or not the work was hard, and how one obtained such a position. "Foreign visitors to the park particularly are always surprised the find a girl ranger and guide," Herma observed. "A captain in the Czecho-Slovakian army, now connected with educational work, was so impressed with the fact that a mere girl should be given the opportunity to speak in public and mingle with the public as I do serving as a guide, that he expressed his feelings in poetry. What puzzled him most was that I was still feminine." Unfortunately, the poem was written in his native language and Herma never knew the content of what the captain had penned just for her.[27]

Apparently, between the outdoor work and the uniform, the captain expected her to have masculine mannerisms. As one of the few women wearing the official green park service uniform, Herma often found herself a subject of inquiry by women visitors. She learned that many female visitors pitied her having to wear a man's style uniform, which always mystified her. In her mind, they should have envied her. After all, how many women in the 1920s were given the opportunity to pursue their dream job? That fall Herma left Yellowstone for the winter and returned to the University of Idaho to engage in another of her dream jobs: Professor of Botany.[28]

Within the next year, the article "Girl Guide for Dudes" had made its way across the country and appeared in the *Syracuse* (NY) *Herald* on June 22, 1930, just in time for Herma's return to her summer job in Yellowstone. But, this season would be different; she had been transferred from Old Faithful to Mammoth Hot Springs. Herma Albertson had not been on the job in Mammoth long when she tripped and sprained her ankle. Coming to her rescue was Chief Ranger George Baggley, who took her to the hospital in Mammoth and who would later become her lifelong partner.

With her mobility temporarily curtailed, she was placed in charge of the Mammoth information office and museum, where in all probability George and Herma's relationship developed during the early months of the summer. Later in the season, with her ankle healed, Herma resumed her lecture schedule at Mammoth Lodge and Mammoth Hot Springs Hotel, and thus returned to what she loved best about working in Yellowstone— educating the public on the park's nature in the out-of-doors.[29]

Even though she enjoyed teaching at the university and the intellectual stimulation of academia, Herma preferred to work amid the mountains and forests that she now knew so intimately. "The love of my summer work," she wrote, "had grown so strong that I finally resigned from the University... [in] July and took the civil service exam that winter."[30] Even though Herma scored very high on the exams, both written and oral, and qualified for an assistant naturalist position, the narrow-mindedness against hiring women on the ranger force still seemed to hold a disagreeable grip.

In early January 1931, either kowtowing to Washington's resistance to hiring women rangers or being pragmatic, Horace Albright, now Director of the National Park Service, suggested to Herma that her best opportunity for a permanent position would be an appointment as a field clerk or a similar position.[31] Ever respectful of Albright's advice, Herma immediately filed an application to take the civil service examination required for the forest and field clerk position. On January 19 she was informed that her application had been canceled because she did not have the required one year's full-time experience in general clerical work.[32] It seemed that her seasonal tasks in the Yellowstone museum and information office did not devote a high enough percentage of time to clerical duties. Evidently her master's degree in botany did not carry any weight either, when it came to being qualified for clerical employment. Yellowstone Superintendent Roger Toll's response to her being denied the opportunity to take the forest and field exam was to suggest that maybe she could take the stenographic exam because as far as he knew "there is no minimum experience requirement."[33] It seems doubtful that Toll or Albright would have suggested this lower position alternative to the numerous men who had taken the civil service exam and who were also seeking permanent employment in Yellowstone.

Through the next few months, Herma wrote letters to Director Albright, Superintendent Toll, Assistant to the Superintendent Joseph Joffe, Acting Superintendent Guy Edwards, and even Idaho State Congressman Burton L. French in the hope that her persistence on all fronts would pay off. In late February, Albright's office wrote a "strong letter to Yellowstone" recommending that Herma be placed as junior park naturalist, a position that had been created only the year before and was vacant due to the departure of Newell Joyner.[34] In his letter of April 7, Albright informed Herma that he heard that "the superintendent had decided not to accept our suggestion." He seemed genuinely disappointed in this news as he believed that her appointment "would have been the ideal situation." It had become the policy of the National Park Service to "place responsibility in the field" and even though Albright thought the administration of Yellowstone was making a mistake he was not willing to press the issue. Curiously, Yellowstone seemed perfectly willing to reemploy her as a seasonal ranger naturalist for the 1931 season.[35]

While Toll's assistant Joseph Joffe was assuring Herma that they were doing everything possible to get her a permanent position in Yellowstone, either the newly formed NPS education department or the superintendent's office in Yellowstone was busily trying to abolish the junior naturalist position and replace it with a stenographic position. In early April, Herma received a letter from Joffe informing her that they *were* trying to get her an appointment as a junior park naturalist. However, the appointment would be with the understanding that her duties would be "more stenographic and clerical than those of an assistant naturalist." Superintendent Toll followed up with another letter stating that because she passed the examination for assistant park naturalist that it would be necessary for her to advise the Civil Service Commission that she would be willing to accept the lower grade.[36]

On May 8, 1931, Herma received a full time, permanent appointment as junior park naturalist in Yellowstone National Park.[37] After five years of working her way up from pillow-puncher to seasonal guide and ranger-naturalist to permanent ranger-naturalist, she had become one of the few women in the country able to secure any full-time position in the National Park Service. As a result, Herma became the first woman to attain the status of permanent ranger-naturalist in Yellowstone, hired under the civil service program. Up until that time the only other woman to hold a permanent position in Yellowstone was Marguerite Lindsley. Marguerite had been appointed the first woman ranger in 1925, when the only designation for NPS personnel was that of ranger, and prior to the Civil Service exam requirement. Herma valued her and Marguerite's respective "firsts" and, even thirty years later, she took the time to keep that record straight.[38]

Even though Herma had qualified for assistant park naturalist, she welcomed the junior position. "Now that I am in this work," she told a reporter for the *Chicago Evening Post*, "I'm the happiest girl in the world." Now, it seemed, Herma was truly on the path to her dreams.[39]

With the transfer of Assistant Park Naturalist Dorr G. Yeager to Rocky Mountain National Park, Herma temporarily took over his duties

Herma and George Baggley in the 1930s proudly pose in their NPS uniforms.
(COURTESY RUTH ANN BAGGLEY BENNETT)

in addition to working as a general office assistant to Ranger Naturalist Dr. A.H. Povah. She also was charged with the responsibility for the Mammoth Museum library, photographs and slides, and accessioning and cataloging museum items. And she was situated, both physically and professionally, in the perfect position to expand the Yellowstone National Park herbarium in Mammoth that Dr. Conard had begun a few years earlier. As a full time ranger-naturalist, Herma's life was now completely immersed in educating the staff as well as park visitors in the complexities of Yellowstone's nature.[40]

A year earlier, her great fondness for outdoor work had won the attention of George Baggley, the park's first chief ranger appointed under the civil service program. In 1926-1927, George's own love of the outdoors prompted him to enroll in the forestry program at Colorado State College in Fort Collins. But after only one year of studies, he was presented with the opportunity to take the civil service exam in March 1928. Passing the exam, he was offered a job as a ranger with the National Park Service in Yellowstone, which he accepted with the idea that he would return to college that fall. However, like many people who came to Yellowstone for a season, George did not leave and instead began what proved to be a rewarding forty-year career with the NPS. Within a year of his arrival in Yellowstone he was promoted to chief ranger, a job that previously had been held by James McBride (1918-1922) and Samuel T. Woodring (1922-1929), both of whom had transferred from the army to the park service. Hence, his appointment to chief ranger in 1929 and Herma's permanent position as junior park naturalist in 1931 represented the beginning of Yellowstone's organizational as well as interpretive transition from the embryonic Albright era to modern NPS management through the civil service program.[41]

Their career connection was probably the main factor that drew George and Herma together and encouraged their personal relationship. "With a twinkle in his eye and compelling logic in his discourse," George's likable personality won over Herma's heart, and on November 26, 1931, they married at the home of her parents in Blackfoot, Idaho. With this bonding of their affection for one another, George and Herma began a lifetime of pursuing their mutual and personal achievements in the outdoor world they both loved.[42]

During her seven years as a park naturalist, Herma authored and illustrated more than twenty-two articles for the NPS publication *Yellowstone Nature Notes*. Begun in the early 1920s, *Nature Notes* was an informational publication for the benefit of "those interested in the natural history and scientific features of Yellowstone National Park." The reports were originally intended to be distributed through park offices and posted as informative bulletins, but evidently the popularity of the newsletter warranted distribution to a larger audience, so it was offered to anyone who placed their name on a mailing list. Published monthly or semi-monthly, depending on the season, *Nature Notes* also offered park employees the chance to contribute to the greater body of scientific knowledge about Yellowstone by writing compositions about various aspects of its nature. Herma's knack for melding scientific observation with uncomplicated writing in her essays for *Nature Notes* made many of Yellowstone's plants and animals comprehensible to the general public. In December 1932, two of Herma's articles exemplified this ideal. While the content of both chronicles concerned trees, her different approach to each displayed her ability to look at nature with not only a scientific eye, but also with her senses. In her article "Yellowstone Conifers," Herma responded to requests for a guide to evergreens in the park. In a little more than two pages, she provided detailed explanations of how to identify lodgepole and whitebark pines, Englemann spruce, Douglas and alpine firs, and Rocky Mountain juniper. In straightforward language but using scientific names, she pointed out the distinguishing factors for each tree, such as the shapes of needles, features of cones, textures of bark, and the types of branches. In addition she provided principal locations for each of the different trees, so that visitors could utilize the scientific observations that she provided.

In her article "Ghost Trees," Herma explained a different way to view conifer trees. "Late one afternoon during the cold weather of October, I stopped at Emerald Spring," she wrote. "The steam and mist from that violently boiling, erupting spring had been carried to the neighboring trees and frozen into long icicles, which glistened in the setting sun. A musical sound wafted to my ears. Looking and listening more closely I found that the icicles, some eight to ten inches longs, were tinkling in the slightest breeze which stirred the branches. A perfect Christmas tree adorned by Nature!"

Herma was entranced by these "fairy trees" and acknowledged that she "was almost convinced that this was a true fairyland such as only children know." She also noted that while glistening trees in the park were not uncommon, the magic and beauty of these snow and ice enshrouded ghostly forms could only be appreciated by those who took the time to look, listen, and wait for that certain ray of light to shine through the branches. In contrast to her "Conifers" article, where she explained scientific and technical elements of trees, Herma's impression of snow-laden evergreens in "Ghost Trees" illustrated her ability to view Yellowstone's trees, plants, and flowers with philosophical contemplation.[43] Thus, in writing about nature from both scientific fact and personal reflection, Herma provided her readers with an absorbing sense of place in Yellowstone.

During her work as a guide, lecturer, and museum curator she came to feel that there was a growing need for a book on the wildflowers of the park. Year after year, visitors asked her where they could buy a book about Yellowstone's beautiful flowers and plants. The one pamphlet available at the time was wholly inadequate, and Herma began to contemplate assembling a well-researched manual. She felt that the entire field of Yellowstone's flora was open to her— if she could just find the time to work on it. Through the course of several summers, Herma talked with Dr. Walter B. McDougall, a leading plant ecologist and a seasonal ranger in the park about collaborating on such a manual, but with the press of both of their full-time daily duties, there was little time left over for doing research, let alone writing.[44]

In the fall of 1933, Herma talked with Dr. Harold Bryant, Assistant Director of the National Park Service, about the possibility of such a manual's being published by the National Park Service, as previously had been done for Mount Rainier, Glacier, and Rocky Mountain national parks. Bryant returned her enthusiasm for the proposed book and promised to assist with its publication. After securing this needed support for its publication, Herma likely realized that she would have to devote herself to writing full time in order for her book to become a reality. On December 31, 1933, Herma resigned her position as Junior Park Naturalist.

A notice in the January/February 1934 *Nature Notes* expressed the education department's fondness for Herma when they deemed that her "services as an enthusiastic naturalist had been greatly appreciated and... she is much missed." Clearly, Herma had become a respected colleague of the park's educational team regardless of her gender and had been considered a valuable asset to the department. As it did for many women whose husbands worked for the park service, the naturalist department not only welcomed but encouraged Herma's continued "advice and interest in the naturalist work" beyond her resignation.[45]

But, Herma had another reason besides the book venture for her resignation. She and George were preparing to become parents that following summer. Perhaps her resignation was motivated by a potentially fragile pregnancy at age thirty-eight, but she was also aware that while the NPS made certain allowances for women rangers, they would not look kindly on one who was pregnant. Sadly, George and Herma's visions of starting a family were shattered when she gave birth to stillborn twins on July 25, 1934.[46] To work through her heartache, Herma turned her attention to her passion for Yellowstone's plants and flowers and immersed herself in the writing of her long awaited book project.

After nearly three years of hard work by Dr. McDougall and Herma, as well as Director Bryant's tireless effort to push the manuscript through production, the National Park Service announced that "'Plants of Yellowstone National Park,' a 160-page illustrated handbook by W.B. McDougall and Herma A. Baggley...is just off the press." The June 1936, news release stated that "it is to meet the constant demand of...visitors for information to aid in identifying the various species that this handbook has been published," thus affirming Herma's belief in the book's necessity. Ultimately, the success of the handbook came from Herma and her co-author's effort to avoid technical language, therefore making it usable by anyone, regardless of botanical training. Former ranger and friend Marguerite Lindsley Arnold provided line drawings that identified parts of a typical flower as well as shapes and parts of simple leaves, while numerous photographers contributed 115 black and white photographs of various plants. Additionally, Herma and McDougall insured the versatility of the handbook by providing an index that contained common names for the average person, and another index containing scientific names for the trained botanical scholar. The handbook was offered for sale in Yellowstone and through the Superintendent of Documents, Government Printing Office in Washington D.C. for a mere twenty-five cents.[47]

For Herma, the publication of *Plants of Yellowstone National Park* represented the fulfillment of a cherished dream. As her husband's Park Service career kept them on the move and Herma could not be in Yellowstone to guide visitors on a daily basis, she felt a tremendous sense of satisfaction that she had provided the next best thing: an informative manual to Yellowstone's many flowers, trees, and plants. And the timing of the publication of *The Plants of Yellowstone* could not have been more perfect. On the heels of the book's completion, George's career with the National Park Service began to take them to a variety of places around the country and eventually overseas.

In the mid-1930s, George was assigned to Washington, D.C., for nearly eighteen months and then to Denver, to work with the Civilian Conservation Corps (CCC). After spending more than a year in Denver working on coordinating CCC work throughout Colorado, Montana,

Herma and baby Ruth Ann enjoy a day in the sun at Isle Royale
National Park in Michigan in the late 1930s.
(COURTESY RUTH ANN BAGGLEY BENNETT)

Wyoming, Nebraska, and western South and North Dakota, George was offered the position of Project Manager of Isle Royale late in 1936. While Congress had authorized Isle Royale National Park in 1931, it had not appropriated the funds necessary for the acquisition of the land needed to make it an official park. In 1936, Franklin D. Roosevelt, concerned that the island's wilderness areas were in jeopardy, pulled money from an emergency fund and authorized purchase of the land. Beginning in January 1937, George worked to acquire land from private owners, and in April of 1940, Roosevelt officially established Isle Royale National Park. George was appointed superintendent of the newly created park on June 1, 1940, and held that position until November 23, 1946.

After fulfilling her dreams of working as ranger-naturalist and co-authoring a book on the plants of Yellowstone, Herma settled into Isle Royale to prepare for one more dream, to become a mother. On May 29, 1937, Herma and George welcomed daughter Ruth Ann. For the next few years, Herma and Ruth Ann's summer days were filled with sitting on the shore of the island watching commercial fishing boats plying Lake Superior and visiting with the local patriarch, Kneut Kneutson, fondly called the "Commodore" by everyone on the island. Accessible only by boat or float plane, the 45-mile-long and 9-mile-wide roadless island offered Herma, George, and Ruth Ann the luxury of living on island time where days are measured by the natural rhythm of the sea, and the size of the fish Ruth Ann posed with for photographs. As Isle Royale was only a seasonal park, their idyllic island life would come to a close in late October or early November and the Baggley family would travel to Houghton, Michigan, or Denver, wherever George's winter assignment took them. Leaving the island in late fall did not quite coincide with school schedules, so once Ruth Ann reached school age, Herma began her lessons at the kitchen table. In November 1946, George was appointed superintendent of Lake Mead Recreation Area and the family moved from Isle Royale to Boulder City, Nevada.[48]

Moving from Michigan's island of wilderness to the desert of Nevada proved to be a challenge to Herma's gardening schemes, but not to her determination. Even though she had to use a pick to dig a hole to plant *anything* in the fused limestone terrain, Herma made the desert bloom with fruit trees and flowers. The other challenge that she encountered in Nevada was the shortage of available NPS housing. Ruth Ann remembered that for the first few months in Boulder City they lived at the end of the desert on a closed-down military base in a portion of an old dispensary until George could secure a house for them.[49] By the time that the Baggleys relocated to Nevada, George's park service job had moved them around the country for nearly fifteen years and Herma had had a lion's share of dealing with NPS housing issues. In 1952, she decided to do something about it.

Although she preferred plants to politics, Herma decided to take on one more public role with the National Park Service. In accordance with the planning of the Mission 66 program to upgrade park facilities system-wide, Herma and a group of Park Service employees' wives formed the National Park Service Women's Organization on September 9, 1952, at the NPS Superintendent's Conference in Glacier National Park. *Their* interest in the Mission 66 project took aim at the inferior housing that existed in most of the national parks. At the first meeting in Glacier, Bea Freeland, wife of the superintendent of Grand Teton National Park, was elected to head the organization and Herma was elected to be national chair for the housing survey.[50]

Having lived in Yellowstone as well as in several other national parks for over twenty years, Herma was personally familiar with the volume of substandard housing in many areas of the park system, and she resolutely believed that the situation required immediate attention. In her estimation the housing issue was not only handicapping the National Park Service in its ability to attract and acquire new employees, it was crippling the morale of current personnel. In essence, Herma believed that the negative psychological effect of inadequate housing prevented employees from feeling that their sense of worth was equal to those they were serving, and it ultimately reduced their dedication to the work of the Park Service.

Herma organized a group of women to conduct a systematic gathering of employee housing data from all areas of the NPS system over the next eight months. As coordinator and General Chairman, she took on the daunting task of compiling and analyzing the data and generating a report. In June of 1953, Herma presented her findings to Director Conrad Wirth in the *Report of National Park Service Housing Survey 1953*. Her report indicated that ten percent of the agency's field employees were living in tents, twenty percent were in one-bedroom apartments or houses, and forty percent were living in two- or three-bedroom houses or apartments, while the remainder lived in dormitories and trailers. She pointed out that a majority of the park housing structures were old, poorly insulated, lacked closet space, drawers and shelf space, and had makeshift heating systems. Many of the buildings had been built by the CCC in the 1920s and 1930s as temporary lodging designed for summer use, but now the flimsy structures were being used for year-round accommodations. Much of the housing lacked modern utilities such as electricity and running water. Overcrowding and lack of privacy were just a few of the principal problems that Herma identified as affecting the morale and comfort of employees. Throughout the report Herma reiterated that morale and a sense of worth were critical issues in the housing situation. She supported her claim with a testimonial made by one area's declaration that they had experienced a "larger than average turnover in positions due to lack of adequate housing." Herma believed that that statement could have been easily "multiplied many times."[51]

But the NPS Women's Organization did more than produce statistics on housing dilemmas; they offered recommendations. Herma included in her report several model house plans, which reflected standard layouts for basic ranch-style two- or three-bedroom dwellings but offered variations in construction and insulation based on geographic and climatic necessities. While the women had differing opinions on details such as windows and walls, they all agreed that space and privacy were the most overriding issues. The women made it known that they were not looking for luxury, just something comfortable and livable.

By providing statistics and offering solutions, Herma and her group of dedicated women brought park housing to the forefront of the Mission 66 project. The findings as well as the recommendations helped NPS Director Conrad Wirth gain funding in 1955 to begin upgrading housing. With Herma spearheading the housing survey, the NPS Women's Organization had not only identified a critical and urgent park dilemma, but had also succeeded in achieving monumental resolutions.

About the same time that she was heading up the housing survey for the NPS Women's Organization, Herma saw the need to revise *Plants of Yellowstone*. Since the first edition of the book had been published in 1936, many additional species of plants had been identified and named. And many of the plant names that were in use at the time of the original publication had become obsolete. As dynamic as its geological features, Yellowstone's plant life was also continuing to change. Seeing that so much of their plant handbook needed to be revised, Herma and Dr. W.B. McDougall decided to write a completely new book.

In keeping with the aim of the original book and to maintain its usefulness for the great majority of its readers, Herma and McDougall endeavored to make the plant descriptions interesting rather than stereotyped. They strove to furnish professional botanists with an up-to-date checklist of park plants, while avoiding the use of too many technical terms. The revised edition still contained Marguerite Lindsley Arnold's line drawings, but now included some color photographs to replace the black and white images, making it even more useful in the field. The new book, dedicated to Marguerite, who had died in 1952 at the age of fifty, was published by the Yellowstone Library and Museum Association in 1956.[52]

By that time, Herma and George were living in Nebraska. George transferred to Omaha in 1954 where he served as Regional Chief of Operations for the national parks and monuments in the Midwest Region, which included Montana, Wyoming, Colorado, Iowa, Minnesota, Missouri, Kansas, and Nebraska. This move for the family undoubtedly

Ruth Ann, George, and Herma Baggley in a 1954 family snapshot in Boulder City, Nevada. (COURTESY RUTH ANN BAGGLEY BENNETT.)

reinforced Herma's determination to find resolutions for the park service housing dilemma that she had been working on since 1952. As George was transferred in August, they were pressed to get settled into Omaha in order for Ruth Ann to start her senior years of high school. Without readily available housing, George, Herma, and Ruth Ann took up residence in the basement of the home of their friends Frank and Virginia Child. Ruth Ann laughingly said that "she became known at school as the child who lived in Frank Child's basement." To be sure, being resilient and adaptable seemed to be a Baggley family trait that enabled all of them to enjoy the fullness of life no matter what the conditions.[53]

In 1966, Herma accompanied George to Jordan and Turkey, where he provided assistance and advice on making those countries' historic sites

Herma Baggley in 1966. (COURTESY RUTH ANN BAGGLEY BENNETT)

more accessible and useful for tourists. Returning late in 1967, George and Herma resided in Washington, D.C., where she spent four months working with the Smithsonian Institution's Museum of Natural History putting together an exhibit of eighty to one hundred different species of flowers that she had collected during her stay abroad.

In an interview later in her life, Herma confided that she often said to her husband, "If we both had it to do over again, would we go into the Park Service?" She revealed that they both emphatically agreed "that's exactly what we would do." Herma believed that working for the Park Service was one of the most rewarding, although one of the most difficult, jobs she had ever done, but she also felt that it was a fulfillment of something she was destined to do. She mused that while the public contacts were wonderful, something deeper than that had touched her. It was her tremendous love of the natural world and the satisfaction of knowing that she had helped so many people appreciate "this great outdoors of ours."[54]

In 1968, George retired from the Park Service and the couple made their final move to Boise, Idaho. Throughout the next six years, Herma and George spent time traveling the northwest coast of the United States from Alaska to California. In 1974, Herma became ill with Parkinson's disease, which limited their ability to travel. With George by her side, Herma courageously endured her debilitating health issues with "very little complaint." George recalled that living through that experience with Herma was difficult, but confided that it "makes you more patient and understanding of other people's problems." Tenderly he mused that "I am ever so grateful that I could help in her care during those years." Herma Albertson Baggley died August 18, 1981, after a seven-year battle with her illness.[55]

In his 1988 memoirs, George conveyed his deep affection for Herma. Even with his numerous experiences all over the United States and exotic adventures to Antarctica, Argentina, Jordan, and Turkey, he believed that "the most wonderful thing that happened to me was when I found Herma and fell in love with her and we married in 1931. We both enjoyed the national parks so much and she seemed to enjoy the outdoors and we had a wonderful life together for all those years." George joined her in death in 1991 at the age of ninety-two.[56]

Even though Herma A. Baggley long ago departed from this earth her lifelong dedication to education lives on through two university scholarship programs as well a scholarship by her sorority, Delta Delta Delta. Her alma mater, the University of Idaho, today offers the Herma Albertson Botany Scholarship on an annual basis for undergraduates majoring in biological sciences. Colorado State University, where George began his degree in forestry, offers the George F. and Herma A. Baggley Graduate Scholarship on an annual basis to professionals who desire to return to graduate school with a major in forestry, wildlife or natural resources.

In 1999, Herma's daughter Ruth Ann Baggley Bennett bestowed an enduring and poignant memorial to Herma. By placing Herma's name on a brick in the Plaza of Heroines at Iowa State University, Ruth Ann's alma mater, Ruth Ann publicly and eternally honored her mother's accomplishments. In her dedication in the university's registry of the women in the Plaza, Ruth Ann described her mother as "a pioneer in her field" and believed her to be "fearless when it came to breaking ground where women had not ventured before."[57] Indisputably, Herma Albertson Baggley's purposeful quests to achieve her aspirations proved her to be as fearless as she was resolute in the pursuit of her dreams.

Eleanor May Hamilton Povah

(1921–)

Everyone Was Like Family

"Anything but normal" is how Ellie Povah characterizes her life in Yellowstone. The only child of Charles A. Hamilton (1884-1957), owner and operator of Yellowstone's largest general store concession, and May Emma Spence (1899-1955), Eleanor May Hamilton Povah, now nearly ninety, has spent practically every summer since she was six weeks old in the park. From enjoying daily horseback rides as a youngster to managing the Hamilton Old Faithful Store soda fountain at age fifteen to assuming joint command of the entire chain of more than twenty Hamilton Store operations in her mid-thirties, she believes that her life has been anything but ordinary. Long before she was even a twinkle in his eye, her Yellowstone concession pioneer father, had set the stage for her "anything but normal" life.[1]

Ellie's father, Charles Ashworth, the only son of Charles Edward and Alma Lizzie Hamilton, was born in Winnipeg, Manitoba, on November 19, 1884. Charles Edward, who was attorney general and mayor of the province at the time of Charles A.'s birth, moved his family to St. Paul in 1888 where he became British vice-counsel for the district of Minnesota. Without giving it a thought otherwise, Charles E. expected his son to follow in his footsteps and study law. But Charles A., or "Ham" as he would later become affectionately known, had other plans.[2]

As he grew up in St. Paul, where Yellowstone's main railroad line, the Northern Pacific, was headquartered and where official Yellowstone photographer Frank Jay Haynes operated a photography studio, Ham was most assuredly aware of Yellowstone National Park and its booming tourist trade. As leisure travel in the early 1900s became big business, the potential of Yellowstone's money-making opportunities probably appealed to the young and ambitious Hamilton. Earlier in his life he had tested his entrepreneurial skills by selling advertising space on the family's back fence, which was located in one of St. Paul's better neighborhoods. Reportedly his father was not impressed with his son's enterprising idea of covering the vacant fence with a menagerie of garish posters and handbills.

But his father's disapproval apparently did little to dissuade Ham's business desires. Until he could devise another career strategy, Ham enrolled in business college and began his course work with a secretarial court-reporting class. Meanwhile he applied for a job with Yellowstone's hotel company, the Yellowstone Park Association. In the spring of 1905, he was hired as an assistant to L.S. (Daddy) Wells, who was YPA's chief purchasing agent. Without giving it a second thought, Ham packed his things, boarded a Northern Pacific train westbound for Gardiner, Montana, and began what became a lifelong association with Yellowstone National Park. Through the next few summers Ham worked a variety of jobs for the park's hotel company, including as secretary to Harry W. Child, the president, and as an assistant to T.E. Farrow, superintendent of hotels. These positions afforded Ham important business connections and experiences that appreciably contributed to his future in Yellowstone. In 1915, Charles A. Hamilton was offered the chance of a lifetime.

Henry Klamer, who built the first general store in the Old Faithful geyser basin, had died on August 12, 1914. His widow, Mary, ran the store by herself through 1914 and the summer of 1915, but decided to retire at the end of that season. She offered the store to Harry Child. As Harry already controlled the hotel and transportation concessions, he may have been apprehensive about government concerns of monopolistic business dealings in the park, and so urged his son Huntley Child Sr. to buy the Klamer store. Not interested in storekeeping, Huntley immediately suggested his friend Charles Hamilton as a candidate. Ellie has recounted the family story that Harry said to her father, "Ham, why don't you take over the Old Faithful Store." To which Ham replied, "There is nothing in the world I would like to do more than take over the store, but I don't have two nickels to rub together." Not one to take no for an answer, Harry countered Ham's reasoning with an almost unbelievable offer: "Well, if we back you, will you take it over?"

Ellie remarked that her father felt very fortunate to have such generous friends and wasted no time in arranging a meeting with Mrs. Klamer at Old Faithful. Confident of financial backing from Child, Ham accepted her price of $20,000 and wrote her one check for $5,000 as a down payment, and another in the amount of $512.62 for the store's inventory. According to the family narrative, he wrote those checks even though he only had $300 in his personal account. Ellie has stated that he rode at breakneck speed from Old Faithful to Mammoth and secured the promised funds from Child. He then rode another fifty-seven miles to the National Park Bank in Livingston to make a deposit into his account before Mary Klamer cashed the checks he had written earlier that day.[3]

As Charles A. Hamilton began his new business venture in 1916, there were other sweeping changes occurring in Yellowstone. In August 1915 automobiles had been admitted into the park for the first time. The mixture of clanging, sputtering engines and horse-drawn stagecoaches proved to be an uneasy match; the two forms of transportation met with ill-fated results during the summer of 1916. While many people in Yellowstone were not happy about automobiles, Ham saw the historic event as yet another retail opportunity. Even though Harry Child had been given exclusive rights to build filling stations and sell gasoline throughout the park, he was not entirely certain that autos would replace stagecoaches as the dominant form of transportation in Yellowstone, and was reluctant to make the investment into erecting the stations. Younger and perhaps more adventurous, the industrious Ham saw filling stations as a necessity and persuaded Child to go into a fifty-fifty partnership with him. Ellie recalled that Ham wasted no time in installing his first single-pump filling station at Old Faithful in 1916.[4]

Adding to the chaos of 1916, the newly formed government agency the National Park Service (NPS) assumed park administration of the park and relieved the army of its thirty-year duty. The motivation for this change was twofold; to bring all the parks under the auspices of one government authority and to discharge the army from the park in readiness for its participation in World War I. Stephen Mather, first director of the NPS, believed that Yellowstone's concessions would run more efficiently and effectively if they were consolidated into one hotel company, one transportation company, and one camping company. Ellie recollected that Ham was thankful that Mather's consolidation plan did not include the retail store operations, and thus he began plans for expanding his own entrepreneurial reach. The following season he opened two more stores and filling stations, one at Yellowstone Lake and the other at West Thumb.

By the fall of 1917, the United States reluctantly entered the war in Europe. The call for men to serve in the military reached to Yellowstone, and Ham found himself drafted into the army, where he served in the Motor-Transport Corps at Camp Jessup, Georgia. After nearly eighteen months, he was mustered out of the army and "of course rushed back to Yellowstone to get his stores open for the summer season of 1919," Ellie reminisced.

From the outset of his entrepreneurial ventures, Ham relied on family (his three sisters and their husbands) to assist him with the management and daily operation of his growing retail enterprise. Fundamental to his operation were family values of honesty, reliability, and dedication, which eventually became the vital underpinnings of the entire Hamilton Stores' managerial philosophy. His oldest sister Alma Sybil (Syb) and her husband Arden Parks managed the Lake store, while his second sister Pauline (Pearl) and her husband Hugh Samson managed the Thumb store. His youngest sister Eva Victoria (Eve) assisted Ham at the Old Faithful store.

In the spring of 1919, Eve Hamilton suggested to her friend and schoolmate, May Emma Spence, that she should come to Yellowstone and work in her brother's store for the summer. While May and Eve thought it was a grand idea, May's parents were not thrilled to think of their daughter summering in the wilds of Wyoming. Even though Ham had grown up in St. Paul and the Spences knew Ham's sisters, they were not acquainted with the family's only and eldest son, C.A. Hamilton. Coaxed by his sister Eve, Ham made a trip to St. Paul and met May's family. After he was interviewed and cross-examined by the Spences, May was given permission to travel to Yellowstone. For Ham, May's appearance at Old Faithful would change the course of his life.

Thinking she was the prettiest girl he had ever met, Ham was instantly smitten with May. Because he was fourteen years her senior, May was not as immediately taken with him, but she soon came to admire his ambition and drive as well as his gruff character. Nearly complete opposites in temperament, the two got along anyway. May's soft and gentle nature caused her to find Ham's impatience and sometimes brusque disposition amusing rather than annoying. She soon found herself in love with Ham.

They became engaged in the summer of 1920 and were married in the chapel at Mammoth Hot Springs in September of that same year. Following a honeymoon to "the Orient" and an exotic around-the-world tour, Ham and May settled into married life and eventually began a family.

As springtime approached, Ham began preparations to return to Yellowstone to open his store for the upcoming tourist season. May was pregnant and with her expected due date early in June 1921, her parents insisted that she stay in St. Paul for the delivery. "There was no way Grandma was letting her daughter deliver her baby (me!) in the wilderness," remarked Ellie. She laughingly joked, "Good heavens, the Indians might get her." But just six weeks after giving birth to Eleanor May Hamilton on June 2, 1921, May traveled to the park with her newborn baby, and Ellie began what would become a lifetime of summers in Yellowstone.

The Old Faithful (Lower) Hamilton Store was more than just a retail location for the Hamiltons. For more than forty years it served as office, warehouse, and summer residence for Ham, May, and Ellie, until Ellie married. The first floor contained goods to serve the tourists, while the second floor contained a six-room apartment for the Hamilton family. One of the upstairs rooms became Ham's office, where he began a tradition of covering the walls with cancelled checks. Once the walls were completely covered and the amount of checks tallied $1,839,105.60, Ham named his office the "Million Dollar Room," and it became his showcase for business contacts and visitors alike.

Shortly after Ellie was born, Ham and May began interviewing nurses to take over the daily duties of caring for their new baby. They settled on Nana Gutz, who became mother, sister, nurse, and teacher to Ellie for the next ten years. During those years, Nana earned her keep by trying to keep lively Ellie out of harm's way, but she was not always completely successful. When Ellie was two and a half, Nana took her to play with one of the few other children in the geyser basin, nine-year-old Louise Brothers, whose family owned and operated the Old Faithful swimming pool. Louise thought that it would be great fun for Ellie and her to go fishing like the grownups. Together they waded out to a small island in the Firehole River. With twigs and strands of grass they pretended to fish. As she "fished" along the edge of the island, Ellie slipped and fell into a hot pool. The pool was so deep that she was completely immersed in the scalding hot water. Horrified at the peril of her little friend, Louise mustered all of her

The lower Hamilton Store in 1917. (COURTESY YELLOWSTONE NATIONAL PARK)

strength and pulled Ellie onto the riverbank. Knowing that she could not carry Ellie back to the house, Louise ran for help.

Nana raced down to the river, retrieved the screaming toddler, and dashed back to the Brothers' house. In an attempt to relieve Ellie of the burning pain, Nana began tearing off her wet clothes. "But the fabric had cooked into my flesh and my skin came off with the clothing," Ellie recalled. Luckily there were a Yellowstone Park Transportation bus and driver available at Old Faithful Inn, and Ellie was raced to the Mammoth Hospital, unfortunately fifty miles away. The resident park doctor for several years in the 1920s, Dr. Windsor, treated Ellie's totally burned body by prescribing immersion in an oil bath until her skin healed. Nana, utterly beside herself over the accident, sat by Ellie during her entire hospital stay and fed her teaspoons of water to prevent dehydration. Ellie today credits Dr. Windsor's treatment as the reason she was not scarred for life.

Falling into a hot spring proved to be only one in a series of life-threatening events in Ellie's life. When she was about five, she went to Lake to visit her Aunt Sybil. While she was playing outside near Lake Hotel, a bear strolled out of the woods and began walking in her direction. But before he got too close, a car pulled between Ellie and the bear, and the driver snatched her to safety. In surviving two narrow escapes before she was much more than a youngster, Ellie was becoming intimately familiar with the adversities of life, and it was a characteristic that would serve her well.

While her summers were spent in Yellowstone, Ellie's winters passed in Santa Monica, California, where she attended Roosevelt Grammar School. When she was about eight years old, park physician Windsor traveled through California and stopped for a visit with the Hamilton family. When Dr. Windsor inquired about Ellie, Ham replied that she was not feeling well and was in bed. He also suggested that Dr. Windsor might want to take a look at her. Upon discovering that Ellie was suffering from appendicitis, Dr. Windsor made arrangements with a local hospital to allow him to perform the necessary surgery. Nearly six years after saving her from what could have been disfiguring burns from her fall into a hot spring, "Dr. Windsor saved me again," Ellie recalled. Considering all her close calls, it is no wonder that Ellie believes today that she "must have been put on this earth for some reason."

In the fall of 1931, when Ellie was ten years old, her beloved nurse and companion Nana died of a heart attack at Old Faithful. Considering her a member of the family, Ham personally accompanied Nana's body to Livingston and arranged for her to be buried in Mountain View Cemetery. Because her parents were gone for most of the winter, Ellie began attending a Catholic boarding school in Pasadena after Nana's death. As they had done since their honeymoon, Ham and May continued traveling to far-flung and exotic locations. On one of their trips to Africa, May was bitten by a tsetse fly, Ellie remembered, which infected her with encephalitis and caused health problems for the rest of her life.

By the time that Ellie reached high school, May's precarious health had curtailed many of her parents' off-season travel adventures. They began spending more of the winter months in Santa Monica, in a nice, but rented, apartment building while Ellie attended Santa Monica High School. Around 1937, a multistory apartment building on Ocean Avenue called El Tovar came up for sale. Since he was planning to spend more of his off seasons in Santa Monica, Ham decided that he should own a residence rather than rent. He purchased El Tovar and proceeded to build a two-story, twenty-one room, seven-bath penthouse for himself, May, and Ellie. Later, recalling the enormity of Ham's penthouse and her chauffeur-driven rides to high school during that time, Ellie laughingly remarked, "Yes, I had anything but a normal life."

Following her graduation from high school, Ellie went east to Chevy Chase Junior College in Maryland. According to Ellie, its students were considered acceptable companions for the students of West Point Academy in Annapolis, Maryland, and there she made the acquaintance of a young man named Ken, of whom she became quite fond. "But back in those days," Ellie was quick to point out, "you did not have one boyfriend, you had a stable full of guys." However, after meeting Trevor Stewart Povah, a young executive with the Union Oil Company in California who owned a stable full of horses, all of that changed for Ellie.

Horseback riding had been a pastime of Ellie's since she was knee-high to a horse. Once the wranglers at Old Faithful discovered her desire to ride, they took her under their wing and showed her their best techniques, including how to "sit a tight seat" in the saddle. Whenever they had a trail ride going out and a spare horse, Ellie was invited to come along. She declared that she was on a horse nearly every day of the summer when she was a youngster. The wranglers, who had become her best friends, proudly claimed, "your father and mother may have supported you, but we boys raised you."

By taking her on a horseback ride through the hills of Malibu on their first date, Trevor Povah secured a special place in Ellie's heart, and there was no turning back for either of them. She and Trev were married in Santa Monica at St. Augustine by the Sea Episcopal Church on November 28, 1940, when Ellie was just nineteen years old. Her father was not thrilled with his daughter's choice to marry so young. Ellie remembered that it was nearly five years after she and Trev were married that Ham finally figured that maybe their marriage "might work after all."

For those first five years of married life, Ellie and Trev resided in Santa Monica where Trev continued to work for Union Oil, and rose to the position of personnel director. In 1941 Ellie gave birth to the couple's first of four children, Sandra May (Sandy). Evidently Ellie's experience as an only child incited her desire to have a houseful of children, and she began the prospect enthusiastically but not without giving the situation some careful thought. Ellie reminisced that she tried to space them out three years apart so as to have "one housebroken" before she began the process again. Accordingly, second child and first son, Trevor Hamilton Stewart (Terry), was born in 1944.

While Ellie and Trev were starting their new life in California, World War II was severely curtailing life in Yellowstone. Most of the operations and tourist facilities in the park were closed for the duration, including nearly all of the Hamilton Stores.

The end of the war in 1945 finally signaled a recommencement of the good life for the American public. Traveling to and visiting America's national parks, especially Yellowstone, seemed to be on everyone's list. After surviving over a decade of economic depression compounded by nearly five years of severe rationing and war-time travel restraints, singles, couples, and families wasted no time in hitting the road. They began flocking to parks such as Glacier, Yosemite, Grand Canyon, and Yellowstone. Tourism in Yellowstone more than doubled from 85,347 in 1944 to 178,296 in 1945.[5]

Meanwhile, all of Yellowstone's concessioners began scrambling to re-open lodges, hotels, stores, and other visitor facilities, many of which had fallen into serious disrepair during the five-year war closure. An extremely popular facility before the war, the Hamilton Swimming Pool at Old Faithful suffered not only from physical deterioration but also from political wrangling over its continued existence.

Ham had purchased the Geyser Baths from Henry J. Brothers in 1933 when Brothers decided to retire. Upon transfer of the lease from Brothers to the Hamilton Stores, Ham remodeled the old geyser bath buildings and constructed a new huge swimming pool, which he advertised as the "Largest Geyser Water Swimming Pool in the World." The main glass-enclosed pool measured 150' by 50' and included 160 dressing rooms, while the 20'-by-50' kiddies' pool offered the promise of a "life guard always on duty."[6] Following the completion of his improvements in 1934, Ham was granted a ten-year lease for his new pool facility.

In 1944, at the end of that lease, Ham applied for an extension of the pool operating privilege. Much to his surprise, the National Park Service decided that the pool was not in keeping with the agency's mandate to keep the park in a natural state and refused to grant a lease extension. Furthermore, they directed him to remove the pool. However, following the end of the war, the Secretary of the Interior decided that the park concessioners needed to recoup some of the losses incurred through the war years, rescinded the original order, and extended Ham's pool lease for three more years. But there was a stipulation. At the end of three years, Ham would be required to dismantle the building and restore the area. With his extension in hand, Ham focused his immediate efforts on

EVERYTHING YOU NEED FOR YOUR PARK TRIP at

HAMILTON STORES, INC.
Yellowstone Park, Wyo.

General Stores,   Filling Stations,   Souvenir Stores
That Aim To Please You!

General Stores Have a Good Stock of Groceries

Go Swimming in Geyser Water at Old Faithful

LARGEST GEYSER WATER SWIMMING POOL IN THE WORLD!

Main Pool
150 ft. x 50 ft.—Glass Enclosed ●
160 Dressing Rooms, Kept Clean and Neat.
Water, any temperature you wish.

Kiddies Pool
20 ft. x 50 ft.
Safe for the Youngsters.
A life guard always on duty

YOU'LL ENJOY IT!——————————PRICES VERY REASONABLE

Hamilton Souvenir Stores
in ALL Main
LODGE BUILDINGS

●

Take Home a Souvenir.
Send Some To Friends,
We'll Handle the Mailing

Hamilton General Stores
and
Filling Stations

● AT——

OLD FAITHFUL
THUMB of LAKE
YELLOWSTONE LAKE
FISHING BRIDGE

And You Pay No More at Hamilton's Than You Pay at Home

This newspaper advertisement announces that the Hamilton Stores, Inc. can supply "everything you need for your park trip."
(LIVINGSTON ENTERPRISE, JUNE 15, 1939)

restoring the swimming pool to its pre-war state, but he also resolved to fight for the future of the pool.[7]

In 1945, Ham asked Ellie and Trev to come to Yellowstone to help him refurbish and reopen the pool. After being closed for five years, the wooden pool structure and its plumbing were in very bad shape. While supplying the pool with geyser water was as much an economic benefit as it was a novelty, the water contained mineral deposits that coated the pool's wooden pipes. During this idle period, those deposits completely clogged and rotted the pipes. It would take a lot of time and effort to get the pool into working order. This situation proved to be only the beginning of the challenges Ham assigned to Ellie and Trev.

While they worked on refurbishing the swimming pool, Ellie, Trev, and their two children—Sandy aged four and Terry, an infant—resided in two cubicles at the pool's entrance. This arrangement was far from providing the Povah family anything close to "luxury accommodations," as their quarters had neither heat nor running water and the bathroom was down the hall. By the time Ellie became pregnant for the third time, with Eleanor Lynn, they had worked out an arrangement to live in the winter-keeper's cabin.

In 1948, Ellie and Trev assumed full command of the day-to-day operations of the Hamilton Stores. With business escalating at an unprecedented rate, as along with government demands for stricter compliance with NPS regulations, Ham's style of doing business "by the seat of his pants" and running everything "out of a cigar box" no longer worked. Never known as a patient or exceptionally cooperative man, Ham, now in his sixties, became even more difficult to deal with, even for his own family. Even-keeled and tolerant, Ellie and Trev managed to keep the Hamilton Store business afloat and to prosper, in spite of Ham's less than genial behavior. Alongside her husband, Ellie helped to modernize their facilities and guide the company through some weighty political negotiations with the local NPS, and headquarters in Washington. The swimming pool became just one of those debates. The pool contract officially expired on December 31, 1949. By the end of the summer in 1951, Ham finally relented and the pool was razed. Even though he was not a sentimental man, Ellie remembered somberly that the demolition of the pool "broke her dad's heart."[8]

While Ellie and Trev managed the day to day operations, her father continued to keep his finger on the overall pulse. Ever the entrepreneurial expansionist, Ham finally realized his ultimate dream of owning all the park's general stores in 1953 when he purchased the Pryor Stores and filling stations in Mammoth and Canyon from Anna Pryor and Elizabeth Trischman.[9] In expanding his business from a one-man operation to a park-wide system of stores, Ham not only ensured Ellie an enormous legacy in Yellowstone but an enormous responsibility of managing both products and people.

While Ham took care of the nuts and bolts of the business, Ellie's mother May concentrated on giving a family feel to the operation, a trait that she passed on to her daughter, heir to the family business. May's genuine manner of being "just ordinary" to any of the store staff endeared her to many Hamilton employees during her lifetime. However, while she monitored and maintained the emotional health of the stores' employees, May struggled with her own physical well-being. During the summer of

The lower Hamilton store, like the Old Faithful Inn, was ornately decorated with the fantastically-shaped, knotty lodgepole pine limbs that were harvested nearby. (COURTESY LIBRARY OF CONGRESS)

1955, her health began to fail. In her already weakened condition from the effects of the tsetse fly bite years before, she quickly became bedridden and required twenty-four-hour nursing care. On September 8, 1955, May died. Barely skipping a beat, Ellie picked up her mother's torch and carried on the business of supplying care, concern, and consideration to the Hamilton family of employees. Through the next five decades, Ellie took this responsibility to heart, looking after the flock of Hamilton employees as though they were her own children.

Ellie and Trev believed that personal attributes were the keys to good employees. Applicants were advised at the outset what individual qualities the Povahs were looking for. "The type of employee desired by Hamilton Stores, Inc." stated their brochure, "is the person who works with a cheerful disposition; who has the intelligence and initiative to readily adapt himself or herself to new conditions and emergencies; and who can meet the public in a courteous and intelligent manner." Ellie and Trev felt that if an individual was in possession of these traits he or she could be trained for any task. The Hamilton Store employment application endorsed this premise stating "previous experience not necessarily a qualification for positions." Not all businesses could claim that their employment forms exhibit such a sense of welcome to prospective applicants.

Just like Ham, Ellie and Trev were keen observers of loyalty, hard-work, and integrity—and they rewarded their employees on a continual basis. This appreciative attitude kept employees coming back year after year, many for half their lifetimes. Jessie Mockel, the daughter of R.D. Rasmussen who served as Ham's trusted contractor for thirty years, recalled that the Hamilton Stores crews had "such good time." She fondly remembered one evening's excursion where the entire crew of the Fishing Bridge operation enjoyed a boat ride (rowboats tied together and towed by a motorboat) to Stevenson Island where they roasted hot dogs over the flames of a big bonfire and explored the island by the light of a full moon. It was "like one big family," she recalled. Clearly, life at Hamilton Stores included more than hard work.

The family feel of the Hamilton Stores begun by Ham and May and fostered by Ellie and Trev mingled with the magic of Yellowstone and kept employees returning year after year. "Anyone who ever worked in Yellowstone is most grateful for having this privilege," recalled former employee Grace Angvik. Along with memories of bear encounters, bugling elk, dances at various park hotels, cookouts, and hikes, Grace was especially grateful for "having been closely associated with the Hamilton family." Thelma Brandly echoed Grace's thoughts proclaiming that "people who work for the Hamilton Stores return season after season because of the friendly atmosphere." She also believed that it was a special place to work because the "employees are simply a large family working together for a common cause." Of course not everyone who worked for the stores appreciated all elements of the Hamilton family atmosphere. "Miss Ellie," as she was affectionately called throughout her decades as ruling executive, expected a high sense of morality from all of her employees. That included not allowing unmarried employees to be assigned a cabin together and making the second-floor girls' dormitory off-limits to the boys. These rules were strictly imposed, which resulted in a few unhappy employees from time to time. But for the most part it was a rare occasion that anyone protested "Miss Ellie's" policies, probably because the sense of Hamilton amity won over most objections.[10]

This Hamilton Stores camaraderie began at the top with Ellie and Trev treating their managers with respect and a healthy dose of thoughtfulness. Heavy-handed corporate management techniques were never part of the Hamilton management scheme, and it showed. Ellie recalled that "every time I went into a store it was like a 'big embrasso!' Everyone was like family."

Some employees worked for decades. Grace Angvik worked for Hamilton from 1931 until 1934, returned in 1950, and worked until 1983. Inga Thompson Dunn worked for thirty-seven years, and Thelma Brandly for thirty. Ed Daley, who began his employment with Ham in 1929, worked for forty-seven years, and Garfield Helppie, who was the first permanent full-time employee ever hired by Ham, worked for over thirty years, eventually rising to the position of vice president. To be sure, that kind of company dedication was and still is hard to come by.

During the late 1940s and early 1950s, Yellowstone as well as other national parks strove to improve visitor services from hotels to transportation to food service. The National Park Service devised a grand plan that would overhaul everything in all the national parks, including roads, bridges, hotels, stores, and gas stations. In Yellowstone the government provided $55 million in funding, while concessioners were required to jointly contribute $15 million. Begun in 1956 with a projected completion time frame of ten years, the NPS program was dubbed "Mission 66."[11]

On May 26, 1956, Ham personally spaded the first shovel of dirt in the ground-breaking ceremony for the new Hamilton Store at Canyon Village, a part of Mission 66. The store with its 12,000 feet of retail space and equipment would cost the Hamilton/Povah family $650,000. In addition adding retail space to Canyon Village, the Hamilton Stores also built a dormitory that accommodated 100 employees for a cost of $250,000. As a partner in the Yellowstone Park Service Stations, Hamilton Stores shared the $99,000 cost of the new service station at Canyon Junction with YP Company. The construction of all the new Hamilton facilities at Canyon Village was completed in 1956, and they were opened the following summer. However, the opening ceremonies of the new Hamilton Store on July 15, 1957, would be missing one important member.[12]

On May 28, 1957, Ellie's father, Charles Ashworth Hamilton suffered a fatal heart attack at Old Faithful. Appropriately he died in his office, the "million dollar room" where the heartbeat of the Hamilton Stores had resounded for more than forty years. From the time he first came to Yellowstone in 1905 at the age of twenty, Ham had spent every summer of his life except for two in the park. Following a memorial service at Forest Lawn Memorial Park in Los Angeles on June 4, he was laid to rest next to his beloved May.[13]

In Yellowstone, Jack Haynes honored his friend of fifty-plus years with a heartwarming eulogy. In the same chapel where Ham and May had joined their lives together in marriage thirty-seven years earlier, Jack reflected on the persona of the late Yellowstone retail pioneer. "Charlie had a brusqueness about him that was quite interesting," he mused. "He was afraid that you and I might think he was a little sentimental—or soft-hearted; and so he developed an artificial brusqueness that we all knew about, but underneath he was a caring [man]." Mourning the loss of one of his closest friends and business allies, Jack concluded that "You and I will never find a warmer, more sincere, honest, and capable friend than Charles Ashworth Hamilton." Indeed, Ellie and Trev had some big shoes to fill, which Trev did with his famous humor and Ellie accomplished with her gracious warmth.

Trev, who was vice president of the Hamilton Stores and general manager of the Yellowstone Park Service Stations at the time of Ham's death, immediately stepped in to fill the shoes of his father-in-law. On

*The Hamilton Lake store entry way was also decorated with ornate pine wood,
which this 1940s photograph depicts. Sadly this decoration no longer exists.*
(COURTESY YELLOWSTONE GATEWAY MUSEUM YGM.192006.044.1303)

June 3, 1957, Trev was elected president of the Hamilton operations,
a position he would retain until his retirement in 1979. Garfield (Gar)
Helppie, who had been Ham's right-hand man since 1930, was elected
vice president, and Ellie secretary/treasurer. Family friend and business
associate Billy Nichols sent a letter to the Povahs congratulating them
on their new appointments and gave Ellie a cheering note of support for
her standing in the company. "Mr. Povah as President ought to do quite
a job, as long as he has Garfield Helppie for a Vice President," remarked
Nichols, "and if those two can't make a go of it, hand it all to the Secretary-
Treasurer. *She* can run it."[14]

To be sure, Ellie significantly assisted with the company's operations, but
in reality it took all three of them to keep the Hamilton Stores humming
along. After Ham's death, Ellie and Trev faced several serious financial

challenges. One was the hefty mortgage on the new Canyon Village store, and the other was regaining control of Hamilton Stores stock. Using all of their financial reserves, Ellie and Trev managed to buy back all of the company's shares that Ham had willed to his nieces and nephews. With the security of full ownership of the Hamilton Stores, Inc., they plunged into expanding the business with fervor. Ellie took over as buyer for the store's inventories of curios and clothing, which entailed traveling to the shopping-mart meccas of Denver and Los Angeles, while Trev and Gar worked on an enhancement plan for the stores.

West Yellowstone, Montana, became the Povahs' base of operations, both personally and professionally. In the 1950s, Ellie and Trev had purchased Deep Well Ranch on the outskirts of the town and just a few miles from the park's west entrance. They would spend the next several decades making additions and improvements to the small ranch house, and raising their four children. In the summer of 1959 Ellie and Trev began building a warehouse and offices at the edge of town nearly on the park boundary. On August 17, 1959, an earthquake that registered 7.1 on the Richter scale rumbled through an area just outside of West Yellowstone, damaged roads inside the park, altered the character of many of the park's thermal features, and destroyed the partially erected Hamilton warehouse. But throughout her life Ellie had become accustomed to calamities, and as a result she and Trev merely cleared away the rubble and began the warehouse anew.

In 1960 Ellie and Trev expanded their retail ventures outside the park with the purchase of Smith & Chandler, a quaint western mercantile store on Yellowstone Avenue in West Yellowstone. Shortly after they took over that business, disaster struck when a newly installed propane heater developed a leak and the store burned to the ground. They rebuilt Smith and Chandler, with Ellie designing the interior to retain the Old West character of the original store.

In 1967 Ellie and Trev increased their Yellowstone retail holdings once more when Isabel Haynes, the only surviving owner of the Haynes Picture Shops, decided to retire. With no living heir for the House of Haynes, she sold all thirteen park stores to Ellie and Trev on the condition that the Haynes name be removed from the buildings. While Isabel took great pride in the Haynes Picture Shops legacy, she believed that without a descendent to operate the shops it would be more respectful to withdraw the Haynes name from usage and thus indelibly honor her pioneering father-in-law, Frank Jay Haynes; her husband, Jack who died in 1962; and their daughter Lida, who had been killed in an automobile accident in 1952. The acquisition of Haynes Picture Shops elevated Ellie and Trev into owners of the largest privately-owned park concession business in the nation by the mid-1980s, with more than twenty retail operations throughout Yellowstone that hired more than 800 employees during the peak summer season.[15]

In 1979, Trev retired as president of the Hamilton Stores, Inc., and Ellie and Trev's first-born son Terry took over the day-to-day operations. As had Ham, Trev stayed in touch with the store operations and the employees by acting as vice chairman of the company, until his death on April 5, 2001.[16] Within the next year, Ellie, who had remained the active chairwoman of the board of directors, would suffer one more monumental and emotionally charged loss in her life—the Hamilton Stores lease itself.

In 1998 Congress passed the Concessions Management Improvement Act that changed the rights of existing concessioners. It mandated that existing park businesses no longer had a "preferential right of renewal," and that they must bid for contracts against anyone who wanted to put in a proposal. The consequence for Hamilton Stores was that being a pioneering and successful business in a national park for nearly a century no longer carried any overriding advantage.[17]

In September 1999, the Povahs' contract to operate the park-wide Hamilton Stores expired and they were given an extension for three years. The NPS began the process of soliciting bids for the next contract in 2000. In the spring of 2002, Acting Park Superintendent Frank Walker announced that, through the competitive bidding process, Delaware North Parks & Services had been selected to operate the general store concession and that the Hamilton Store contract would expire on December 31, 2002. After surviving the Great Depression, World War II, the 1959 earthquake, the 1974 oil embargo, the 1976 Teton Dam disaster, the Yellowstone fires of 1988, numerous personal crises, and eighty-seven years of annual retail "crapshoots" (as Ellie's son and president of the company Terry once quipped[18]), the famous Hamilton General Stores became relegated to history and ceased operations in 2003.[19]

The passing of the Hamilton Stores, Inc., in Yellowstone represents the end of an era, an era of national park pioneers whose legacies embody more than just commercial enterprises. These stores represent the last vestiges of traditionally family-run businesses whose management and owners treated staff members like they were family.

One illustrative family-type event, supposedly begun to divert weary employees from end-of-season mischief that often began as harmless jokes but sometimes became destructive pranks, was Christmas in August, still an ongoing tradition in Yellowstone. It quickly grew into a special occasion where Ellie and Trev could acknowledge their industrious staff with a big gathering. The event included a family-style Christmas dinner with turkey, stuffing, mashed potatoes, gravy, cranberry sauce, and all the other trimmings. After a round of Christmas carols and gift exchanges, the bosses recognized every employee for their years of dedicated service that ranged from one year to several decades.[20]

In addition to Christmas in August, Ellie and Trev hosted an annual managers' barbecue at Deep Well Ranch, where Trev and later Terry would "roast" various members of the supervisory staff before presenting them with awards for their years of service. In 1999, Del Abelein, manager of the grocery department in the Hamilton Old Faithful Upper Basin Store, was honored at the picnic for his thirty years of service. Like many Hamilton employees, Del began his association with the Hamilton Stores as a college student. In 1955, he worked as a soda fountain clerk and the following year rose to the position of shift supervisor of the soda fountain. After completing college and a tour of duty in the army, Del embarked on a thirty-year teaching career in Shelton, Washington, in 1959. In the summer of 1965 he returned work at the Canyon Village store, but it was not until 1970 that Del began his long seasonal tenure with the Hamilton Stores. After retiring from teaching in 1989 and becoming able to work entire summers, Del progressed to grocery manager in 1992. Upon Ellie's presenting him with a thirty-year service pin at the managers banquet in 1999, Del aged sixty-four, or "two to the sixth power" as he called it, offered her and Trev a profound compliment, "I would love to work...for the Hamilton Stores until I am at least 80...and I would love to receive...a 40-year pin." And probably he would have made it if the Hamilton Stores had continued in business, for Del did not pass away until 2010. At the end of the 2002 season and final closing of the Hamilton Stores, Ellie along with her son Pat and his wife Ginger, personally said goodbye to him with hugs and memorialized the occasion with a "family" photograph.[21]

Like Del, Mike Stevens was a school teacher during the winter months and spent his summers as a Hamilton employee. Working for more than a dozen seasons in the 1980s and 1990s, Mike recalled that being a part of the Hamilton Store family was a most wonderful feeling. He valued highly the warm sense of belonging as much as the worker camaraderie and counted his time at the Hamilton stores as one of his life's most memorable eras. "Ellie," he fondly remembered, "was gracious beyond all expectation."[22]

Indeed, the Hamilton Store story was and is like no other, and before she closed the last chapter of her life, Ellie wanted to make sure that its legacy as well as hers was preserved for all time by bequeathing many of her family's historic treasures to the Museum of the Rockies, in Bozeman, Montana.[23]

"Gift of a Lifetime," proclaimed the September 11, 2009, *Bozeman Daily Chronicle* headline as it announced the large collection of historic items donated to the museum by Eleanor "Ellie" Povah. Museum director Shelley McKamey declared that the donation of over more than 1,200 items was the "most significant collection" the museum has received since its founding by Caroline McGill in the 1950s.

Ellie is thrilled that her family's heritage and treasures have a good home. "It's really the place I wanted it to be," Ellie confided. But there is more to acquiring and preserving a family collection than meets that eye. In addition to bequeathing more than 1,200 cultural objects, Ellie has endowed the museum with $250,000 over a five-year period to ensure that the collection is cataloged, preserved, stored, and exhibited. Just as her father, Charles A. Hamilton, entrusted her with carrying on his legacy in Yellowstone, Ellie has entrusted that her legacy as well as that of the Hamilton Stores be carried on by the Museum of the Rockies.

But, arguably, the real legacy of Ellie Povah resides in the hearts of all of those who lived in the park and worked for her and the Hamilton Stores for so long, and who delighted in Ellie's considering "everyone like family."

Ellie seems to glow in the ambiance of the Deepwell Ranch that she and Trevor purchased and developed near West Yellowstone. (PHOTO BY AUTHOR)

Margaret Mary Meagher

(1935–)

Bears, Bison, and Backcountry

Nearly thirty years after graduate student Herma Albertson signed on for her "try-out" as a volunteer naturalist with the National Park Service in Yellowstone, Margaret Mary Meagher did the same, albeit in nearby Grand Teton National Park. And as it had done for Herma, the experience helped to mark Mary's career path. Mary would eventually become the first woman Ph.D. of wildlife biology in the National Park Service and ultimately emerge as a renowned expert on Yellowstone's most iconic animal, the bison. She began that work in 1959, and continued for nearly four decades. But in 1957, Mary was just being introduced to national park science as one of the first students to participate in a fledgling student conservation program that had been the brain child of conservationist Elizabeth (Liz) Cushman Titus Putman.[1]

As a student at Vassar College in 1951, Liz Titus had enrolled in a new course entitled Conservation of Natural Resources, which encouraged a multi-disciplinary approach to science and was conducted by the school's geology, plant science, and zoology departments. This novel course not only made her conscious of conservation as a field of study, but it also changed the course of her life. In this vein, another influence in Liz's future career was Bernard Devoto's article "Why Don't We Close the National Parks?" published in *Harper's Magazine* in October 1953. In his famous article, Devoto—enraged by the deplorable conditions of all the national parks—strongly criticized Congress for not properly funding the parks and thus making them the lowly "impoverished stepchild of the government."

His proposal to close America's national parks shocked many U.S. citizens, including Liz Titus. Raised in a family who believed that the appropriate response to a problem was doing something about it, she focused on finding a remedy for what Devoto called the "national park crisis."[2] After completing her thesis "A Proposal for a Student Conservation Corps" in 1954, Liz shared her concept with former National Park Service Director, Horace Albright. He liked her plan and encouraged her to visit some of the national parks in the fall of 1955. He recommended that she share her idea to solicit volunteers in parks with various superintendents and staff members to see if it had merit. Several park officials believed it did. Within two years, Liz was setting the stage for the establishment of today's Student Conservation Association (SCA), a CCC-type program that offered national-park volunteer opportunities to young people. Olympic and Grand Teton national parks became the first two national parks to agree to SCA trial projects and Mary Meagher became one of the original participants in Liz's program.[3]

Besides believing that volunteerism was a valuable commodity that could help restore the health of the country's national parks, Liz Titus also believed that parks could offer students (including women) fundamental opportunities and worthwhile work experiences that would help shape their futures. In essence she saw the SCA as a "win-win" prospect for everyone. According to an interview with Liz published in the *Vassar Quarterly*, Mary Meagher was one of only three college women who participated in the SCA's inaugural project during that summer of 1957. It proved to be not only the beginning of Liz's new conservation program, but the beginning of what would become Mary Meagher's lifetime of study in the natural world of America's Serengeti, Yellowstone National Park.[4]

Born on March 13, 1935, Margaret Mary Meagher was the youngest child of Thomas F. and Mary (Miller) Meagher. She grew up in Spokane, Washington, with her older siblings, Patricia and Michael. As a graduate student working on her master's degree in wildlife management, which she began at University of Montana and completed at University of Michigan, Mary experienced an unique encounter with field research in a national park by studying marmots in Grand Teton under the guidance of Liz Putnam's SCA organization. Growing up in the West, Mary had had ample exposure to nature and wilderness, and her work in the SCA programs undoubtedly gave her a window into occupational opportunities for wildlife research in national parks. But Mary soon found that being a woman in natural resource management meant that she had chosen a difficult career path in a male-dominated field. It was a path that she would spend a lifetime negotiating, enduring, and conquering.[5]

Working as a seasonal ranger-naturalist in Zion National Park, Mary was considering going back to school for a Ph.D. when the museum curator position in Yellowstone National Park opened in the fall of 1959. She applied and was hired to fill the vacancy. With her hiring, Mary became only the third woman in the history of Yellowstone to obtain a permanent position there with the National Park Service, following in the footsteps of Marguerite Lindsley Arnold (1925) and Herma Albertson Baggley (1931). She later credited Dave Beal, the park's assistant chief naturalist, for laying that foundation by hiring her. Mary thought her timing was ideal because she believed that the park's previous chief naturalist, David Condon, would not have hired her purely because she was a woman. She commented on one occasion that "to his dying breath, he always referred to me with an appropriate [negative] tone of voice as *that woman.*" While not pleased with his attitude, Mary nonetheless acknowledged his honesty.[6]

After working in Yellowstone for two years Mary saw her job description rewritten to include the duties of park naturalist along with museum curatorial responsibilities, and this gave her some field time in Yellowstone's multifaceted ecosystem. In 1962, with a dissertation focused on Yellowstone's bison, Mary applied and was accepted as a graduate student at the University of California, Berkeley, under the tutelage of Dr. A. Starker Leopold. She worked out a program with the school and the park so she could continue her work as a staff naturalist as well as do dissertation research in Yellowstone and her Ph.D. coursework at the university.[7]

In deciding to attend UC Berkeley, Mary joined the ranks of the National Park Service's and Yellowstone's earliest leaders, naturalists, and wildlife scientists. Stephen T. Mather, first director of the NPS; Horace M. Albright, Yellowstone's first superintendent and second NPS director; Ansel F. Hall, first director of the NPS Education Division; Ben H. Thompson and Joseph S. Dixon, early NPS wildlife biologists; and George Melendez Wright, first chief of the NPS Wildlife Division, were all alumni. And all of these men played instrumental roles in the advancement of science in America's national parks.

In the 1920s, Wright, Thompson, and Dixon were students of university professor Joseph Grinnell (1877-1939), who embraced and taught new ecological concepts of nature and natural systems that linked animal survival to habitat. Scientific ecology at that time was less than thirty years old, but it had evolved from a primitive understanding of nature in the

Mary Meagher (far left) in the company of M. Myers, R. Howe,
Lemuel Garrison, John Good, L. Hadley, and Hugh Galusha
near the cones of Union Geyser in 1960.
(COURTESY YELLOWSTONE NATIONAL PARK MUSEUM COLLECTION YELL35565)

1890s to more complex ideas involving its interconnected systems by the 1920s. Not surprisingly, Grinnell proved to be an advocate for employing ecology-based methodology to wildlife management policies in national parks. George M. Wright was an ardent supporter of Grinnell's ecological theories, especially where they were applied to the parks. But most notably, Wright had the personal finances to sponsor the first scientific assessment of national park wildlife and its habitats. Without Wright's wildlife investigations that eventually served as a scientific marker for Yellowstone, Mary's career path could have taken a distinctly different turn.[8]

Following his mentor's vision for an ecological approach to managing natural resources in national parks, Wright offered to subsidize and conduct a survey of park wildlife in late summer 1928. As a previous NPS assistant naturalist in Yosemite and from his observations in other parks, Wright recognized the need for a methodical survey of national park wildlife. He believed that the information would give each park a better scientific understanding of its wildlife, habitats, and populations. And it was Wright's conviction that this knowledge would provide baseline data that would lead to better informed resource management decisions. Mary would find herself treading in Wright's footsteps forty years later as she struggled to assemble data that would enable the NPS to make rational wildlife decisions. Freed from having to supply funding until Wright proved the validity of the survey, NPS Director Albright readily agreed.

Wright, Ben Thompson and Joseph Dixon began their field research in May 1930 embarking first on an 11,000-mile survey of western national parks. In their research and observations, Wright and his colleagues paid particular attention to rare and endangered species such as Yellowstone's trumpeter swans, adverse affects on nature by the destruction of predators such as wolves, and the causes of injurious encounters between park visitors and wildlife, primarily bears. They produced a 158-page report, published in 1932, that detailed the current condition of park fauna throughout the national park system as well as recommendations for restoring wildlife to a more "pristine state." In response, Albright established the NPS Wildlife Division the following year, with Wright as chief and Thompson and Dixon as staff biologists. Unsurprisingly, with Mather and Albright's focus on education, the newly created division soon became a part of Ansel Hall's Education Division and was headquartered at their alma mater, the University of California at Berkeley.[9] In due time Mary Meagher would see their observations, remarks, and recommendations help formulate the NPS's ecology-based wildlife-management policies, and help institute science as essential in park management.

By 1936, the NPS Wildlife Division employed twenty-seven biologists, all of whom strove to see that park policies considered wildlife, plants, and their combined habitats, not merely tourist facilities and infrastructure. But tragically, the fire of Wright's guiding light was extinguished on February 25, 1936, near Deming, New Mexico. Wright and Yellowstone superintendent Roger Toll were returning from a conference on establishing international parks, forest reserves, and wildlife refuges along the Mexico border, held at Big Bend National Park, Texas, when an oncoming vehicle blew a tire and collided head-on with their car. Toll was killed instantly and Wright died the next day. George M. Wright, the National Park Service's ecological prophet, was only thirty-one years old.[10]

Without Wright's leadership and vision, the Wildlife Division also soon died. Just three years later, only nine of the twenty-seven biologists remained, and in 1940 all were transferred to the U.S. Bureau of Biological Survey. Consequently, two decades later, Mary's entry into Yellowstone science began to disinter some of the same challenges of ecological consciousness that Wright, Thompson, and Dixon had worked on in the 1930s.

At the time of Mary's arrival in Yellowstone in 1959 very limited biological research was being done in the park. Following Wright's death and the demise of the Wildlife Division, Yellowstone and other national parks reverted to their premise that the main function of America's parks was human use and enjoyment. Park wildlife was viewed as a resource for drawing tourists, and management efforts focused on making animals physically or visually available for the public without regard to habitats. Wildlife management in the 1940s and 1950s was conducted largely by ranger-naturalists with limited or no education in ecology or biology. The ranger-naturalist division was also in command of a few wildlife biologists who were allowed only to make recommendations. This system that Mary endured and eventually worked to change persisted into the 1960s and 1970s.[11]

Wildlife management practices prior to Mary's arrival in Yellowstone included the extermination of "bad" animals such as wolves, coyotes, and white pelicans in order to "protect" the "good" animals, such as elk, deer, and fish as well as the erection of roadside "arenas" for easier public viewing of animals. In Yellowstone during the 1940s those arenas included the bison "show" herd corral at Mammoth and another one at Antelope Creek near Tower Fall, and NPS's bear-feeding shows, complete with bleacher seating for hundreds of tourists at Canyon and Old Faithful. These staged animal attractions, especially the bear shows where visitors eagerly watched as black bears and grizzlies ambled out of the woods to gobble up hotel garbage dumped on a cement platform, troubled conservationists who began rallying for change.[12]

Low visitation during World War II offered Yellowstone a prime opportunity to make a few revisions to its wildlife policies. By the 1950s, the bison corrals were dismantled, the bison released into the wild, and the bear shows discontinued. In addition to aesthetics, increases in injurious bear and human encounters triggered a practical reason for closing the bear feeding shows. However, as Mary would find out, the health of Yellowstone's wildlife and its habitats was still not a driving force behind management decisions.[13]

Contrary to what appeared to be a slow return to ecological principles when Mary began her employment, Yellowstone was actually entering into the early stages of the largest park landscape-development plan to date. While Bernard Devoto's 1953 article "Let's Close the National Parks" presented a rallying cry for Liz Putnam to establish a corps of student conservationists, it prompted a different call for the NPS.

Director Conrad Wirth believed that what the parks needed was large-scale development in order to protect fragile areas and wildlife. His counter-intuitive plan, dubbed Mission 66 because it was slated to begin in 1956 and be completed in ten years, called for an NPS system–wide revamping of visitor facilities, roads, and services. He believed that by corralling people into designated areas, other (larger) areas of wildlife habitat would be preserved. In a certain sense, his logic was sound because, after the entry of automobiles, most visitors saw only those parts of Yellowstone viewable through their windshields. The faulty element of Wirth's plan was that there had been no scientific survey of landscapes, wildlife, and individual habitats that would be affected by the massive developments. As Mission 66 progressed, those shortcomings began to emerge and to take precedence. Eventually many of the mission's development plans were curtailed or downscaled in favor of wilderness preservation.[14]

In some ways, beginning a national park science career in 1959, in the middle of a challenging era, was inopportune for Mary. The political and social environment in Yellowstone was distressingly slow to embrace science as a ruling factor and, as she learned later, even slower to accept a woman scientist. But in a way, she was in the right place at the right time. Just as Wright's guiding light of ecologically-based principles began to flicker back to life in the wake of the Mission 66 controversy, Mary's inadvertent timing positioned her to become an influential member of Yellowstone's ecological vanguard who would collectively work to revolutionize park wildlife management and park policies.

At the same time that Mary began her doctoral studies at UC Berkeley in 1962, her major professor Dr. A. Starker Leopold was appointed to the NPS's Special Advisory Board on Wildlife. In the late 1950s and early 1960s, thousands of Yellowstone's elk were slaughtered to reduce the population to what was, at that time, regarded as a sustainable number of animals in the park. This action generated a huge outcry from the local hunting populace who believed the hunting of elk to be a rite of passage and resented what they believed to be the federal government's indiscriminant decision to slaughter six-hundred elk. Television coverage extended that outcry to the American public at large as well as several groups of conservationists. Consequently, the controversy over the elk reductions in the park prompted two major scientific surveys of national park wildlife. One was led by William J. Robbins and it produced a long, detailed National Academy of Sciences Report. The other, headed by A. Starker Leopold, produced the shorter, more renowned Leopold Report. Both of these reports advocated restoration of wildlife habitats and restricting human intrusion, just opposite what Yellowstone had largely been practicing for ninety years. Even though Robbins and Leopold advocated some (apparently temporary) manipulative management to obtain a balance of nature, in essence they revived the spirit of Wright's vision by cultivating national parks as "vignettes of primitive America." Leopold's timely appointment to the Advisory Board began his extensive association with the National Park Service and closely connected him to Mary Meagher's studies in Yellowstone.[15]

Mary began her Ph.D. research in 1963 with the objective to gather, examine, and provide "basic data on the life history, habits, and ecology of bison in the park." Mary's decision to conduct her studies and dissertation on Yellowstone's bison was based on how little scientific research had been done on the park's most iconic mammal. Walter Kittams had been the sole National Park Service ungulate researcher in Yellowstone from 1947, when he transferred to Yellowstone from the U.S. Fish and Wildlife Service in Billings, Montana, until he left in 1958. His only statistics on the park's bison were included in a 1956 reconnaissance report with photos. "Bless him for taking photographs," Mary said later. "I've made good use of his photographs." Mary respected Kittams for being a hardworking scientist, but also recognized that he was a "person who was spread very thin." Her position as museum curator since 1959 facilitated her access to old photographs and scout diaries from the 1880s through World War I, and helped her to assess the early, as well as recent, history of Yellowstone's bison.[16]

While Mary was doing her research, the park's bison population was being reduced just as the elk had been. Shooting the animals was the first method employed, and later park managers used live traps to catch them for shipment to zoos and various other locations around the country. Upon being asked by newly appointed Chief Biologist Glen Cole in the late 1960s to supply the data used to justify reduction programs, Mary discovered that rather than file drawers of supporting documentation,

UNITED   STATES   POST   OFFICE
YELLOWSTONE   PARK   WYOMING

*In the sea of men, Mary stands out as the only female staff member in this
group photograph taken during the 1965 Ranger Conference.*
(COURTESY YELLOWSTONE NATIONAL PARK MUSEUM COLLECTION YELL1981)

which she and others thought existed, there was only Kittams's lone
report from 1956 stating that "I think there is a problem and if there
is a problem, then these should be trial numbers for management
reductions." However, Kittams had also included a cautionary directive
to "evaluate" the population before taking action. Mary's observation
was that there was "no long-term data" on the bison and therefore "no
historical homework" that was being used at that time to make reduction
program decisions.[17]

In 1968, NPS budget cuts eliminated the museum curator's position
and Mary transferred to a research position in the new Resource
Management Division. Most of her research from that point centered on
creating an ecological history of Yellowstone's bison for her dissertation.
She examined early park conditions, numbers and distribution of bison
populations, other wildlife populations, plant and grassland habitats, the
effects of fire, weather, and other environmental factors, and the impact

of human activities upon all of these elements. In the next two years Mary would add considerable data to the park's scientific record of its bison.[18]

She completed her dissertation in 1970 and entitled it "The Bison of Yellowstone National Park: Past and Present," tailoring it to "provide a basis for management and evaluation of the importance of this particular bison population." In her introduction, Mary unassumingly revealed that she hoped her contribution of informative detail on the park's largest mammal would shift the image of Yellowstone's bison from a fabled creature to a natural-world being. As she put it, "the report may make the bison less of a myth, but a far more interesting reality." Her study examined history, population statistics, behavior, and habitat relationships of bison that incorporated her painstaking reading of historic scout journals and ranger patrol logs, and her field research conducted from 1963 through 1968. She documented that the indigenous population of mountain bison had endured even though they had been nearly exterminated by 1902, primarily due to poaching. She also explained that Plains bison were introduced in 1902, mixed with native animals, and within the next sixty years the bison population substantially increased. By the time of Mary's study in the 1960s the Yellowstone bison herd consisted of three main population groups which were identified by their primary habitats— Pelican Valley, Mary Mountain (which included Firehole and Hayden valleys), and Lamar Valley.

Her examination also analyzed the history of the herd's population regulation by both nature and man. She surveyed a multitude of environmental factors, including harsh winters that contributed to natural regulation, as well as manipulative management that included controlling bison populations by removing what was arbitrarily considered an excess. Her conclusion suggested that "the Pelican Valley wintering bison population...had been regulated for many years without interference by man" and so she proposed a theory that all population groups might not need to be controlled. Her dissertation was published in 1973 as a National Park Service monograph. As the only in-depth, long-term scientific study conducted on Yellowstone's bison by an academically trained biologist, this extensive report offered reliable information on bison that could be used both to inform park managers and to educate park visitors.[19]

Mary's completion of her doctoral degree earned her the honor of being the first woman Ph.D. in wildlife biology to gain permanent full-time status in the entire National Park Service system. (Although Margaret Fuller Boos was hired as the first woman naturalist in Rocky Mountain National Park in 1928, and had earlier completed a Ph.D. in geology, she was employed only seasonally.) With accreditation in hand, Mary resumed her observations and studies of the life cycles of Yellowstone's bison.[20]

Unfortunately, she soon began to feel that in some cases even her advanced degree did not seem to win her the respect of which she was worthy. Mary recalled one instance where she was flying around the park conducting a bison count and spied what she thought was a poacher's shack invisible from the ground. Believing this was important, she reported her find to the chief ranger. He coolly informed her that she should "stick to counting buffalo." Later, she unflinchingly remarked, "he was reminding me that rangers know best." That incident alerted her to the fact that most rangers then were not open-minded enough to take advice from a biologist and certainly not from a woman biologist. It was a lesson Mary took to heart. Nevertheless, she continued her study of bison and began producing papers on her findings.[21]

In 1971, she wrote a paper entitled "Winter Weather as a Population Regulating Influence on Free-Ranging Bison in Yellowstone National Park." In the piece, she stated that the present bison population in Yellowstone National Park was essentially wild because it was unrestricted by boundaries or internal park fences, and had not been subjected to regulatory influences from man since 1966. (From the 1920s until the 1960s, a good number of the park's bison were fed hay and raised like livestock, and populations were controlled by removal.) She also explained that her 1963-1968 research supported a hypothesis that the park's original bison population was naturally regulated by the influences of winter. In this essay, which was based on further field research, Mary provided detail to substantiate "the degree to which one environmental factor, severe winter conditions, affected the park's bison population." Her conclusion was that winter weather was a "major population regulating influence on the Pelican Valley bison population." While she was confident in her reasoning, Mary also understood the long-term intricacies of conducting biological research and that it would take time for her to fully comprehend the complexity of environmental and human factors on Yellowstone's bison population trends. She braced herself for more years of observation.[22]

Also in 1971, Mary presented a paper on how snowfall affected bison distribution and population in the Pelican Valley at an Iowa State University symposium. "Bison which winter in Pelican Valley in the interior of Yellowstone Park," she wrote, "are subject to more severe winter conditions that those elsewhere in the park. Snow conditions in this valley appear to be a major factor influencing the regulations of population levels, and determining distribution and use within the valley." Her previous research had shown that the bison in Pelican Valley had historically wintered there and yet the herd persisted. Using the Pelican Valley herd as her case study, Mary compared it to bison populations in the park's other wintering valleys. She demonstrated her breadth of analysis as an ecologically-trained wildlife biologist when she conceded that the "occurrence of severe winter conditions [affecting the bison population in other areas] is partially offset by other habitat factors."[23]

Also in 1974, Mary wrote an article for *National Parks and Conservation Magazine* wherein she provided a capsule history of bison in YNP. In addition to explaining the near extermination of the Yellowstone bison, detailing various past bison management procedures within the park, and addressing environmental factors that affected all three populations (Pelican, Mary Mountain, and Lamar valleys), Mary tackled the difficult issue of brucellosis and the NPS plan to control the animals at the park's boundaries. Known to be carriers of brucellosis, a disease that causes domestic cattle to abort their offspring, Yellowstone's bison were not welcome to range into neighboring Montana, whose ranchers highly prized the state's "brucellosis-free" status for their cattle. Brucellosis in Yellowstone's bison in the 1970s became an increasingly controversial issue that Mary had to contend with for nearly thirty years, and it continues today to be a major political concern.[24] In dealing with it, Mary would author and co-author more than thirty articles, papers, and reports on Yellowstone's bison. And in due course she would also become the co-author of a notable book illustrating Yellowstone's biological timeline, a project that emerged independently from her interest in the bison's habitat.

Mary's years as park museum curator had sparked an idea for examining the history of vegetation changes in Yellowstone that she and ungulate ecologist Doug Houston had begun to ponder in 1970. At the outset they were interested only in documenting landscape change through time by rephotographing a few significant wildlife areas and comparing them with original views of the same places from the 1880s and 1890s. Between 1971 and 1973, Mary and Doug compiled a collection of 320 sets of comparative photographs of various areas of Yellowstone that they neatly mounted on heavy paper and stored away for use as future research tools. In 1982, when Doug used some of the photograph sets to illustrate his *Northern Yellowstone Elk* book, one of his reviewers suggested that "the photograph comparisons were much too valuable to provide only selected views for a monograph about elk." Mary and Doug began again to consider value of their rephotography sets, and they thought seriously about publishing their collection. But their musings about producing a book were put on hold when Doug was transferred to another assignment and Mary's work load increased. After the fires of 1988, the Yellowstone landscape had changed significantly. Mary and Doug saw that as a prime opportunity to include a third view in their photograph sets, which they believed would add further value to the collection. The University of Oklahoma Press agreed, and *Yellowstone and the Biology of Time: Photographs Across a Century* was published in 1998. For Mary, as well as her colleague Doug Houston, the publication of this ecologically significant book more than twenty years after the initial contemplation of the idea must have been a truly rewarding experience.[25]

In 1976, when park supervisory biologist Glen Cole was reassigned to Voyageurs National Park, Mary agreed to take over his position and responsibilities, while continuing with her own research. But because she was a woman, she was not offered the same pay scale. Typical of the times, she accepted a higher level position at a lower pay grade. In the summer of 1978 or 1979 she told Bill Everhart, retired NPS Chief of Interpretation and Visitor Services and author of an entertaining history of NPS life entitled *Take Down Flag & Feed Horses*, that "things have improved, but the Park Service still isn't there yet when it comes to equal opportunities for women." In reality, equal opportunities in America were and still continue to be an ongoing struggle for women.[26]

As with early fighters for woman suffrage, Mary's crusade saw her spending an inordinate amount of time and effort fighting to persevere in her chosen profession in a male-dominated field. She experienced deep battle scars and she rarely enjoyed any pleasure from her hard-won efforts. "I wasted so much time surviving," Mary later lamented, obviously believing that her time could have been put to more productive use. Mary

Meagher has been epitomized since then as a paradigm for the recognition of women's contributions in national parks. Mary contends today that she is being held up as "an example of what women can achieve," in the NPS. She believes that is not an authentic interpretation of her experience. But back in 1976, Mary was young and ambitious and willing to take a chance on the future, regardless of any perceived inequities.[27]

With Cole's reassignment and departure from Yellowstone in 1976, Mary assumed his role in bear management. At that time the role of biologists in the park was merely an advisory one. On-site decisions were handled by park managers, which involved assessing both the scientific data and current politics. In 1978, Mary seemed a bit relieved that she was not in a position whereby she had to make management decisions. She believed that "it would be very difficult to be objective with the data and the recommendations you make based on the data." But in time Mary became more and more concerned over what the data was telling her about the sustainability of grizzly bears. As she became aware that the park's management objectives were more concerned with public acceptance than with what would be in the best interest of park bears, she became an outspoken activist on the side of the bear. That position rarely put her in the good graces of several park administrations.[28]

Mary's unyielding position in the late 1970s and early 1980s was one of rigidly declaring that the natural resources in Yellowstone should take priority over visitor use. Backed by her education in ecological wildlife management principles, Mary, as well as her Yellowstone science colleagues, believed that what the park needed were more scientists and more natural history research, and a lot less concern for alienating the traveling public. Even though the Leopold and Robbins reports in 1963 had advocated modifications to Yellowstone's wildlife management philosophy that encompassed these principles, the wheels of change as turned by NPS bureaucracy moved slowly. Mary was truly concerned that the grizzly bear would not survive in Yellowstone. When conflicts erupted between visitor use and grizzly bear habitat, Mary and her scientific counterparts, who recommended that the park's solution should result in the exclusion of people and facilities, became unpopular with government officials, concessioners, and the traveling public, all three. Having received an education similar to that of her historic mentor, George M. Wright, Mary was, in essence, reviving Wright's ecological philosophy. Wright had advocated for similar modifications thirty years before, when he recommended altering "old practices in the interests of both people and bears."[29] In the end, it would still take nearly sixty years before his advice was heeded in Yellowstone. When much of the commercial development at Fishing Bridge was removed in the 1990s and grizzly bear population numbers began to rise, the ideas of Wright, Leopold, Robbins, and Mary and her Yellowstone contemporaries about managing people instead of animals were vindicated.[30]

Meanwhile Mary's position as Wildlife Division Supervisor consumed most of her time. "All wildlife problems pass over my desk," she later explained.[31] It was her job to talk with scientists and media people from around the country about wildlife issues in Yellowstone. She was also responsible for briefing and giving logistical assistance to the many outside researchers who came to Yellowstone to study, and for the rudimentary beginnings of a permit system, today still in place. One summer she provided assistance to more than 150 researchers, which left her little time for her own research. Although she grew weary of administration, her passion for research never waned, and continued to energize her.

So where did one go when park bureaucracy became overwhelming? For Mary the solution was escaping to the place where her heart and soul found absolute solace—Yellowstone's backcountry. And that is just what she did for more than three decades. The availability of the backcountry had been one of Mary's primary motivations to work in Yellowstone. She adored Yellowstone's primitive wilderness, which she called "irresistible and glorious."[32] In the course of her job and often for her own personal enjoyment, Mary logged countless hours on horseback and cross-country skis. But Yellowstone's backcountry could also be dangerous, especially if one traveled alone, which Mary did a lot. One day while riding far from her cabin, Mary fell and broke her arm. She managed to get back onto her horse and ride several miles out of the backcountry to medical aid. On another occasion she gashed open her head when her horse tripped over a wire and fell on top of her. Living in the backcountry took grit, and Mary proved she had plenty of that. Without that type of grit, few people, women or men, could survive the rigors of life in Yellowstone's backcountry.

Regardless of perils and isolation, Mary delighted in her summertime backcountry residence, an old Yellowstone Park Transportation Company cabin on the Blacktail Plateau located seven miles from

*Exploring Yellowstone's backcountry, Mary and her horse Pilot
stand beside a stone wall at a ridge west of Swan Lake Flat.*
(COURTESY YELLOWSTONE NATIONAL PARK MUSEUM COLLECTION YELL166617-6)

Mammoth. The rustic two-room cabin built in 1931 stood in an open
area of sagebrush next to a babbling creek lined with cottonwoods and
willows. Behind the cabin were a small barn and corral for her horse.
Even though the cabin lacked electricity, it provided Mary with a great
sense of personal comfort from spring until fall. "When I get away from
the office in the evening and drive out to Blacktail, into that grand chunk
of Yellowstone, everything comes together...[and] my worries matter a
lot less," she confided to an interviewer.[33]

In addition to quiet solitude, her seasonal backcountry retreat offered her an exclusive place to observe nearly all of Yellowstone's many species of large mammals, such as bears, bison, elk, and wolves. Her horse was her most earnest companion. Every morning at five A.M. he would rattle the door latch and provide Mary with a most friendly wake-up call. He was rewarded with a handful of oats. Mary remarked that her horse loved company, so much so that he would "plant his front feet on the porch and watch me through the door for hours." Fortunately the porch had been rebuilt around 1978 "with trail bridge planking,"[34] which made the porch sturdy enough so that "it held a horse's weight nicely."[35]

How one handled the backcountry became the yardstick by which Mary measured people—men and women alike. In an issue of *Yellowstone Science*, she praised Linda L. Wallace, a fellow ecologist who had passed away, for her excellent backcountry skills. "Linda was unusual among researchers in the park in her willingness to help the park's people with resource issues," Mary averred. "She made a five-day south boundary trip with rangers Jerry Mernin, Dave Phillips, Tom Olliff, and me to assess methods for evaluating outfitter campsite impact....She pitched in and watched how things were done at cabins and went at it. Backcountry time has long been my setting for evaluating a person, and she passed with flying colors." In addition to that backcountry prowess, Mary also admired Linda's conscientious candor concerning her scientific opinions. "Linda did not tell you what some would think you wanted to hear, she told you what she thought, but she was not a contentious person," Mary recalled. "She was the finest grassland ecologist I will know."[36] Coming from a backcountry expert such as Mary Meagher, that compliment surely would have pleased Linda Wallace.

As 1983 closed, Mary resigned from her administrative and supervisory duties so that she could return to conducting research focused on the ecology of the Yellowstone bison. In 1993, while still working as a full-time research biologist, Mary as well as all of her fellow research colleagues was reassigned to the U.S. Geological Survey Biological Resources Division. She was eventually transferred to the Ranger Division where she continued her bison research in Yellowstone until she retired in 1997.

During her retirement years, Mary's backcountry skills have contributed to others' research, such as that of former Yellowstone National Park archeologist Ann Johnson. One of Ann's missions was to define and assess various land-use patterns in the park. While documented land-use studies in the library can help one intellectually process issues such as "what's on the other side of Mt. Everts?" Ann contends that "to be [physically] up there is invaluable." Indeed, most archaeologists will agree with Ann's premise that "there is no substitute for getting out in the park's backcountry to understand how the resources have been used." Working as a volunteer for the archeology department, Mary shared backcountry knowledge that became a valuable tool upon which Ann drew. "Mary and I talked about how people might have used the land, how animals used it, and how people might have preyed on those animals. Without Mary's time and help," Ann confided, "I would have understood less."[37]

Indeed, the entire Yellowstone science community concurred with Ann's assessment of the value of Mary's wisdom at the 10th Biennial Scientific Conference on the Greater Yellowstone Ecosystem held in October 2010. There Mary received a standing ovation when she was introduced as the A. Starker Leopold Speaker. Her lecture encapsulated her more than forty years of witnessing Yellowstone's wildlife management policies shift from simple range management to ecological process

Mary, along with former park ranger Bob Flather and volunteer
Ray Rathmell, ponder the location of a historic site in Yellowstone.
(COURTESY YELLOWSTONE NATIONAL PARK MUSEUM COLLECTION YELL180308-1)

management. Mary's advice for future Yellowstone researchers carried three short, but astute, points. First, "If it is simple, be careful." Second, "Numbers and computers are great, but don't let them run you." And lastly, "It takes time."[38] Accordingly, time has yet to fully illustrate the wisdom of Mary's salient messages, both spoken and written.

Like many women who struggled in the 1960s, 1970s, and 1980s to create new constructions of women's roles in America, Mary Meagher wrestled with overarching tensions between her own optimistic idealism and demoralizing reality while she determinedly made her place in what was openly acknowledged as a man's world in Yellowstone. Even though today she feels a bit otherwise, through the tenacious pursuit of her science career and her overwhelming determination for her voice to be heard, she *did* become an active participant in the creation of ideologies and patterns that helped to shape women's public, academic, and intellectual roles in Yellowstone as well as throughout the national park system. But, perhaps more notable to her personally, Mary undeniably played an integral part in Yellowstone's advancement of a natural wildlife ideal in national parks. By fostering and doggedly promoting ecological principles Mary was an influential player in moving Yellowstone's management philosophies away from primitive zoo-like concepts and toward viewing the park as a multi-dimensional self-regulating ecosystem.

As this book is written, it is still a common occurrence to see Mary in the park's library and archives, fresh from the field, sporting her own signature style—clad in jeans, boots, and a turtleneck and sweater bedecked with a string of pearls. Still a resident near Yellowstone's north entrance, Margaret Mary Meagher today continues her love affair with field work and research on Yellowstone's complex fauna and flora during her well deserved retirement years.

❧

Endnotes

Introduction

1. "The New Wonderland," *New York Times*, October 23, 1871. For other early references of Yellowstone's first being called Wonderland see Lee Whittlesey, *Yellowstone Place Names* (Gardiner, MT: Wonderland Publishing Company, 2006), 265.

Emma Carpenter Cowan: An Impress that the Years Cannot Efface

1. "Park When Warriors of Chief Joseph's Band Surrounded Them and Opened Fire on Party," (Spokane) *Spokesman Review*, August 21, 1932.

2. Unless otherwise noted, information attributed to Emma Cowan is from Mrs. George F. Cowan, "Reminiscences of Pioneer Life," *Contributions to the Historical Society of Montana*, No. 4 (1903). Memories of her trip west and arrival in Virginia appear on 156-57.

3. Michael A. Leeson, *History of Montana, 1735-1885* (Chicago: Warner, Beers, & Company, 1885), 774; Heister Dean Guie and Lucullus Virgil McWhorter, *Adventures in Geyser Land* (Caldwell, ID: Caxton Printers, Ltd., 1935), 236-37. *Adventures* is a reprint of Frank D. Carpenter's original narrative, *The Wonders of Geyser Land*, a pamphlet published in 1878 by Burnett & Son at Black Earth, Wisconsin. Guie and McWhorter faithfully reproduced Carpenter's original text and supplemented it with a lengthy preface, notes, illustrations, and a series of appendices that added significantly to the accounts compiled by Carpenter.

4. Leeson, *History of Montana*, 1176; Joaquin Miller, *History of Montana* (Chicago: Lewis Publishing Company, 1894), 296.

5. Guie and McWhorter *Adventures*, 25-26.

6. Guie and McWhorter, *Adventures*, 56; Dave Walter, *More Montana Campfire Tales* (Helena, MT: Farcountry Press, 2002), 12.

7. Guie and McWhorter, *Adventures*, 8-14; Theodore Catton and Ann Hubber, Big Hole National Battlefield Administrative History, http://www.nps.gov/archive/biho/adhi/adhi_1_b.htm.

8. Catton and Hubber, http://www.nps.gov/archive/biho/adhi/adhi_1_c.htm.

9. Walter, *More Montana*, 13.

10. Lucullus Virgil McWhorter, *Yellow Wolf: His Own Story* (Caldwell, ID: Caxton Printers, Ltd., 1940), 151.

11. Guie and McWhorter, *Adventures*, 160.

12. Ibid., 163-67.

13. Ibid., 180-86; "More Murders," *Helena* (MT) *Daily Independent*, August 28, 1877.

14. Guie and McWhorter, *Adventures*, 202-203, 208-212.

15. Ibid., 266.

16. Hiram Chittenden, *The Yellowstone National Park* (Cincinnati: Stewart & Kidd Company, 1915), 137.

17. Guie and McWhorter, *Adventures*, 214-16.

18. Ibid., 8; "Territorial News," *Butte* (MT) *Daily Miner*, January 27, 1882.

19. Guie and McWhorter, *Adventures*, 8.

20. Ibid.

21. Guie and McWhorter, *Adventures*, 7, 230.

22. 1900 United States Federal Census, Boulder, MT, http://www.ancestry.com; "G.F. Cowan Dies at Spokane, Wash.," *Helena* (MT) *Independent*, December 19, 1926.

23. Chittenden, *The Yellowstone National Park*, 139; Lee Whittlesey, *Storytelling in Yellowstone* (Albuquerque: Univ. of New Mexico Press, 2007), 88-90. Nearly all of Hiram Chittenden's original signs marking the sites of the Radersburg and Helena tourist party's encounters with the Nez Perce have disappeared through the past century. More than one

hundred years later, the sign marking the Helena tourist party camp near Otter Creek was rediscovered in 2007. This historically significant sign was replaced with an exact replica and the original has been placed in the park museum collection.

24. Guie and McWhorter, *Adventures*, 8; "G.F. Cowan Dies at Spokane," *Helena Independent*, December 19, 1926; "Park When Warriors..."; "Death Claims Pioneer Woman," *Montana Standard*, December 22, 1938.

25. "Sixteen Men Killed and One Man and Two Women Prisoners," *Helena Daily Independent*, August 28, 1877; "The National Park Massacre," *Helena Daily Independent*, August 28, 1877; "The Nez Perces...Nine Pitilessly Butchered," *Chicago Tribune*, August 28, 1877; "A Terrible Experience," *Petersburg Index and Appeal*, September 13, 1877; "Fate of Montana Excursionists," *Pottsville* (IA) *Daily Fair Review*, October 3, 1877; "Park When Warriors..."; "Death Claims Pioneer Woman"; "Pioneer of Helena, Who Had Thrilling Time, Is Summoned," *Helena Daily Independent*, December 21, 1938; "Montana Pioneer, Once Captured by Indians, Succumbs," *Billings Gazette*, December 21, 1938.

Mattie Shipley Culver: Far from Family and Friends

1. Nan Weber, *Mattie: A Woman's Journey West* (Moose, WY: Homestead Publishing, 1997), 11-23.

2. Helena Hayes and Sandford Dody, *On Reflection: An Autobiography* (New York: M. Evans & Company, 1968), 5.

3. Weber, *Mattie*, 27-28.

4. Weber, *Mattie*, 32-39.

5. Weber, *Mattie*, 41-42; R.S.F. Schilling M.D., D.P.H., "Byssinosis in the British Cotton Textile Industry," *British Medical Bulletin* 7 (12): 52.

6. Weber, *Mattie*, 58-69.

7. "Married," *Billings* (MT) *Herald*, October 26, 1882; Weber, *Mattie*, 72-73; Eugene Virgil Smalley, *History of the Northern Pacific Railroad* (New York: G.P. Putnam's Sons, 1883), 401.

8. "Local News," *Billings Weekly Herald*, November 3, 1883; "Local News," *Billings Daily Gazette*, January 10, 1886.

9. *Billings Weekly Herald*, September 1, 1883, "Town Talk," March 28, 1884; *Billings Weekly Herald*, May 31, 1884, June 7, 1884, September 6, 1884; "Gone Up in Smoke," *Billings Weekly Herald*, July 19, 1884; "Town Talk," *Billings Weekly Herald*, January 10, 1885; Weber, *Mattie*, 96.

10. "Local News," *Billings Daily Gazette*, April 7, 1886.

11. *Billings Daily Gazette*, May 1, 1886; "City and County," *Billings Daily Gazette*, June 22, 1887; "City and County," *Billings Daily Gazette*, July 2, 1887.

12. "City and County," *Billings Daily Gazette*, July 28, 1887.

13. Lee Whittlesey, "Monarch of All These Mighty Wonders," *Montana: The Magazine of Western History* 40: 2 (1990), 2-15. For a historic picture of Excelsior Geyser, see Tilden Freeman, *Following the Frontier with F. Jay Haynes: Pioneer Photographer of the Old West* (New York, Alfred A. Knopf, 1964), 384-385.

14. Thomas D. Brock, *Robert Koch: A Life in Medicine and Bacteriology* (Washington, DC: ASM Press, 1999), 117-37.

15. "Leaving for Firehole Basin," *Billings Weekly Gazette*, November 8, 1888.

16. "Wonderland News," *Billings Gazette*, January 10, 1889.

17. "Wonderland: To Be Strung with Telephone Lines," *The* (Billings, MT) *Daily Gazette*, October 30, 1885; *The Weekly* (Billings, MT) *Gazette*, March 7, 1889.

18. "Passing of Ellery C. Culver," n.p., n.d. newspaper clipping, Biography (Culver) file, vertical files, Yellowstone National Park (YNP) Library.

19. Weber, *Mattie*, 98, 113-115.

20. Aubrey L. Haines, *The Yellowstone Story*, rev. ed., vol. 2 (Niwot, CO: Univ. Press of Colorado, 1996), 23, 65; 1900 United States Federal Census, Gardiner, Montana, http://www.ancestry.com; Weber, *Mattie*, 117; "Putting Down a Munchausen," *Salt Lake Tribune*, December 31, 1896; "The Park of Yellowstone: Interesting and Instructive Methods of Advertising the Wonderland," *Decatur* (IL) *Herald*, February 13, 1906, 4; Carl E. Schmidt, *A Western Trip* (Detroit: Herold Press, 1910), 11.

21. Weber, *Mattie*, 118.

22. "Passing of Ellery C. Culver"; U.S. National Homes for Disabled Volunteer Soldiers, 1866-1938, http://www.ancestry.com. Other Yellowstone "old soldiers" who spent their last days at the National Home for Disabled Soldiers in Sawtelle, California, include George W. Trischman, a former park wheelwright and blacksmith and father of Elizabeth and Anna (see their profiles in this book) who died in 1929, and George Whittaker, a former general store operator who died in 1961.

23. Ellery is buried in Section 42, Row Y, Site 4. U.S. Veterans Gravesites, ca. 1775-2006, http://www.ancestry.com.

Anna K. Trischman Pryor and Elizabeth M. Trischman: Coffee, Curios, and the Devil's Kitchenette

1. Social Security Death Index, Before 1951, Los Angeles, CA, http://www.ancestry.com.

2. New York Passenger Lists, 1820-1957, http://www.ancestry.com.

3. U.S. Army, Register of Enlistments, 1798-1914, http://www.ancestry.com.

4. U.S. National Homes for Disabled Volunteer Soldiers, 1866-1938, http://www.ancestry.com.

5. George and Margaret may have had other family connections with Fort Custer. This supposition is based on an obituary for forty-year-old Leo M. Heffner in the *Billings* (MT) *Gazette* on September 14, 1930. The newspaper states that Leo's father William H. Heffner came from Germany in 1869 (two years after George W. Trischman) and settled at Fort Custer. The obituary lists Leo's surviving family, which included three cousins, George [T.] Trisman [*sic*], Anna Pryor, and Belle Cushman [*sic*]). According to the June 5, 1886, *Billings Gazette*, William Heffner married Christina Standgrebe, both of Fort Custer, Montana Territory at the home of Mrs. Frushman [*sic*], presumably Mrs. Margaret Trischman, and Miss Kitty Gleason was a bridesmaid. William and Christina had two children, Conrad John, born September 17, 1887 at Fort Custer and Leo M., born October 18, 1889 in Billings. Ironically, three years after Margaret Trischman had been declared insane, the *Billing Gazette* reported on May 6, 1902 that Leo's father, William H., was being taken to the Warm Springs (insane) asylum. The article also stated that while William and Margaret were not related (hence no family history of insanity), the late Mrs. [Margaret] Trischman and Mrs. [Christina] Heffner are said to have been aunt and niece. Census records for Christina in 1910 and 1920 list her as a widow and using the name Annie C. Heffner.

6. 1900 U.S. Federal Census, Fort Yellowstone, Lincoln, Wyoming, http://www.ancestry.com.

7. Birth date for Harry is listed on World War I Draft Registration Cards, 1917-1918, Yellowstone Park, Wyoming, http://www.ancestry.com. Birth date for Elizabeth is listed on California Death Index, 1940-1997, Los Angeles, and New York Passenger Lists, 1820-1957, April 1, 1937, both in http://www.ancestry.com.

8. World War I Draft Registration Cards, 1917-1918, Butte, Montana, http://www.ancestry.com. Anna, Harry, Elizabeth, and George were all born at Fort Custer, Montana.

9. Date of birth listed on tombstone, Fort Yellowstone Cemetery, Mammoth Hot Springs, WY. Joseph was probably also born at Fort Custer, Montana.

10. "As It Was in Billings 45 Years Ago, from the Gazette, June 1, 1897," *Billings* (MT) *Gazette* June 1, 1942.

11. "She Is Insane," *Billings Gazette*, April 14, 1899.

12. O.G. Warren, M.D., to Timothy F. Burke, June 10, 1899, Folder A-B, Item 81 "U.S. Commissioner Meldrum 1894-1911," Letter Box 38, Yellowstone National Park (hereafter YNP) Archives.

13. "Butchered a Babe," *Livingston* (MT) *Post*, June 8, 1899; "Murdered Her Baby," *Billings Gazette*, June 6, 1899. Based on these newspaper accounts only three other of the five Trischman children were home at the time of Joseph's murder. But because of these reports, the park's history of this incident for several decades has only accounted for four Trischman children, not five. That said, just which one of the children was spared the gruesome nightmare of witnessing baby Joseph's slaying most likely will remain one of Yellowstone's mysteries.

14. "Insane Woman Kills Her Child," *New York Times*, June 5, 1899.

15. "Shocking Infanticide," *Livingston Enterprise*, June 10, 1899.

16. Oscar J. Brown, *Report of the Acting Superintendent of the Yellowstone National Park to the Secretary of Interior* (Washington: Government Printing Office, 1899), 14.

17. "Local News," *Livingston Post*, July 13, 1899.

18. "Corpse, But No Clue," *Billings Gazette*, January 4, 1901, "Local News," *Livingston Post*, January 17, 1901.

19. 1900 United States Federal Census, Helena, Montana, http://www.ancestry.com.

20. Harry enlisted in the army and served as a government scout at Fort Yellowstone from 1909 until 1915. He became a National Park Service ranger in 1916 and later served as assistant chief ranger. Harry retired in 1945 and died in 1950. George T. worked as a miner before serving in World War I. Perhaps his term of service introduced him to the shipboard way of life. He was listed on the 1930 Census of Merchant Seamen as a waiter aboard the *Yukon*, an Alaskan vessel. In 1953, At the age of 63, George T. died on October 28, 1953 in Seattle. Above information on Harry from "Harry Trischman: Lifetime Park Resident Taken," *Helena* (MT) *Independent Record*, March 18, 1950, and on George from http://www.ancestry.com.

21. Aubrey L. Haines, *The Yellowstone Story*, rev. ed., vol. 2 (Niwot, CO: Univ. Press of Colorado, 1996), 181-82.

22. "Wedding at Gardiner Will Be Society Event," *Anaconda* (MT) *Standard*, June 5, 1907; "Gardiner Items," *Livingston Enterprise*, June 8, 1907.

23. Captain Anderson to John W. Noble, March 9, 1891, Doc. 412, Item 2, Letter Box 1, YNP Archives; Ole Anderson to Secretary of Interior, August 20, 1894, Doc. 1828, Item 8, Letter Box 4, YNP Archives.

24. "Specimen Making," *Livingston Enterprise*, April 18, 1896; Robert V. Goss, *Coating Curiosities in Yellowstone: Ole Anderson and the Specimen House* (Gardiner, MT: Goss, 2004), 38.

25. Secretary of Interior [Ethan Allen Hitchcock] to Acting Superintendent [Samuel B.M. Young], May 5, 1906, Doc. 6915, Item 26, Letter Box 13, YNP Archives; Secretary of Interior [Ethan Allen Hitchcock] to Acting Superintendent [Samuel B.M. Young], May 16, 1906, Doc. 6914, Item 26, Letter Box 13, YNP Archives.

26. Anderson assignment of lease, April 30 1908, Folder "190 Expired Ole A. Anderson (Sold to Pryor and Pryor)," Item 60, Letter Box 29; George R. Pryor to Major H.T. Allen, April 10, 1908, Doc. 7888, Item 28, Letter Box 14; Frank Pierce, First Assistant Secretary to Major H.T. Allen, May 12, 1908, Doc. 8180, Item 29, Letter Box 15; Frank Pierce, First Assistant Secretary to Major H.T. Allen May 12, 1908, Doc. 8181, Item 29, Letter Box 15; Frank Pierce, First Assistant Secretary to Major H.T. Allen, June 23, 1908, Doc. 8179, Item 29, Letter Box 15, all in YNP Archives.

27. "Social News," *Gardiner Wonderland*, June 18, 1904.

28. George Pryor to Major H.C. Benson, October 25, 1909, Folder "Pryor and Pryor," Box C-16, YNP Archives.

29. Pryor Store Blueprints, Box C-16; Pryor Letterhead, Box C-16, Folder "Pryor and Pryor."

30. Assignment of Lease (copy), George Pryor, October 19, 1912, Box C-16, Folder "Pryor and Pryor."

31. Lt. Colonel L.M. Brett to Mesdames Pryor and Trischman, August 30, 1913, Folder "380 Privileges, Newsstands 1909 to 1913," Item 73, Letter Box 34, YNP Archives.

32. Lt. Colonel L.M. Brett to George Whittaker, December 19, 1913, Lt. Colonel L.M. Brett to Mesdames Pryor and Trischman, December 19, 1913, Folder "380 Store Privileges 1909-1913," Item 73, Letter Box 34; Whittaker letterhead & Brochure 1913, Folder "George Whittaker," Box C-16.

33. Pryor and Trischman to Secretary of Interior [Franklin K. Lane], June 4, 1915, Folder "380 Store Privileges 1915," Item 73, Letter Box 34; Clerk [Office of Lt. Colonel L.M. Brett] to Mesdames Pryor and Trischman, July 19, 1915, Folder "380 Store Privileges 1915"; Financial Report of Pryor & Trischman 1914, Folder 130, Item 52, Letter Box 25, YNP Archives.

34. Financial Report of Pryor and Trischman 1915, Folder "130 Financial Reports Pryor and Trischman," in Item 53, Letter Box 26, YNP Archives.

35. Robert Shankland, *Steve Mather of the National Parks* (New York: A.A. Knopf, 1951), 120-27; Pryor lease, April 10, 1916, Folder "Pryor and Pryor."

36. Pryor lease, August 18, 1917, Folder "Pryor Stores," Box C-8, YNP Archives.

37. John W. Meldrum to Nellie Jones, January 10, 1917, Doc. 9306, Item 32, Letter Box 17, p. 3, YNP Archives.

38. Ibid., p. 5.

39. Ibid., p. 2.

40. Ibid., p. 1.

41. Pryor & Trischman Annual Reports, 1922, Folder "Pryor Stores," Box C-8, YNP Archives; Horace Albright, *Annual Report of the Superintendent of the Yellowstone National Park to the Secretary of Interior, 1924* (Washington: Government Printing Office, 1924), 31.

42. John W. Meldrum to Nellie Jones, September 8, 1925, Doc. 9304, Item 32, Letter Box 17, p. 2.

43. Pryor & Trischman Annual Reports 1922-27, Folder "Pryor Stores," Box C-8, YNP Archives; Albright, *Annual Report...1925*, 33-34.

44. John W. Meldrum to Nellie Jones, September 8, 1925, Doc. 9304, Item 32, Letter Box 17, p. 2.

45. John W. Meldrum to Nellie Jones, September 8, 1925, Doc. 9304, Item 32, Letter Box 17, p. 1.

46. "Birthday Party in Wonderland For Good Judge," n.p., n.d. newspaper clipping), September 20, 1937, Doc. 9311, Item 32, Letter Box 17.

47. Pryor and Trischman Annual Reports, 1922-1937, Folder "Pryor Stores," Box C-8, YNP Archives.

48. U.S. National Homes for Disabled Volunteer Soldiers, 1866-1938, http://www.ancestry.com. George W. was buried in the Los Angeles National Cemetery, Section 60, Row G, Site 7.

49. John W. Meldrum to Jack E. Haynes, October 16, 1930, Jack E. Haynes to John W. Meldrum, October 20, 1930, Folder 9: 34, Box 9, Collection 1505, Isabel Haynes Papers, Montana State University Library Special Collections, Bozeman.

50. "The Flower Withereth," *Livingston Enterprise*, December 2, 1930; invoice from J.E. Haynes to John W. Meldrum, June 1931, Folder 9: 34, Collection 1505, Isabel Haynes Papers.

51. After he retired from Yellowstone, Whittaker continued his business life in West Yellowstone. He took over active management of a collection of properties that he owned,

which consisted of the Hayward Tourist Cabins, a filling station, a store, a barber shop, and a beauty parlor. George Whittaker lived another thirty years before he died at age 91 on January 30, 1961. Somewhat fittingly, Whittaker died at the same Old Soldiers Home in Sawtelle, California, as had George W. Trischman thirty-two years earlier. For further information on George Whittaker see Robert V. Goss, *Yellowstone's George Whittaker: Soldier, Scout, and Storekeeper* (Gardiner, MT: Goss, 2002), 35.

52. George Whittaker to William Nichols, March 10, 1932, William Nichols Collection, 1928-34, Montana Historical Society Archives, Helena.

53. Pryor and Trischman Annual Report 1932, Folder "Pryor and Trischman Annual Reports 1922-39," Box C-8, YNP Archives.

54. Pryor Stores, Yellowstone National Park, Financial Report, Year Ended September 30, 1934, Folder "Pryor Stores," Box C-8, YNP Archives. Year-end statements for 1933-34 show interest payments being made on notes from John Olsen, Judge Meldrum, Georganna (now using name Georganna Pryor Lockridge), and brother Harry Trischman.

55. "Park Concessions Bought Saturday by Anna K. Pryor," *Livingston Enterprise*, March 20, 1932.

56. Pryor and Trischman Annual Reports 1922-39, Folder "Pryor Stores," Box C-8, YNP Archives.

57. Lease Agreement, June 16, 1941, Folder "Pryor Stores," Box C-8, YNP Archives.

58. Anna K. Pryor to Edmund B. Rogers, Superintendent, July 3, 1946, Pryor to Rogers, July 10, 1946, File "No. 900, Part 3, Public Utility Operations, Pryor Stores," Box C-35, YNP Archives.

59. Anna K. Pryor to Edmund B. Rogers, Superintendent, May 3, 1947, File "No. 900, Part 3, Public Utility Operations, Pryor Stores," and Pryor to Oliver G. Taylor, Supervisor Concessions, January 27, 1948, File "No. 900, Part 4, Public Utility Operations," Box C-35.

60. Pryor to Oliver G. Taylor, Supervisor Concessions, January 27, 1948, File "No. 900, Part 4, Public Utility Operations, Pryor Stores," Box C-35.

61. C.A. Hamilton to Anna K. Pryor September 23, 1952, and Pryor to Hamilton October 7, 1952, File "No. 900-01, Part 6, Pryor Stores," Box C-35; Report on Audit of the Operations of Pryor Stores, Inc., Pryor Stores Annual Reports, 1947-52, Folder "Pryor Stores," Box C-8.

62. C.A. Hamilton to Anna K. Pryor September 23, 1952, File "No. 900-01, Pryor Stores, Part 6," Box C-35.

63. "Georganna Pryor, Anna K. Pryor Daughter, Dies," (Livingston, MT) *Park County News*, November 16, 1961; "Obituaries," Anna K. Pryor, *Livingston Enterprise*, October 29, 1973; California Death Index, Los Angeles, http://www.ancestry.com.

64. J. Rogers Memorandum to Regional Director, Rocky Mountain Region, October 1, 1984, File S7417, "Property Accountability, Disp. of Real Property 1984," Box S-6, YNP Archives.

Ida Christine Carlson Eagle: Mom Eagle

1. Sam (Bud) Eagle, "A Story From the Early Days," *Eagle's Store: 100 Years of Memories* (West Yellowstone, MT: Eagle's Store, 2008), 25.

2. When Ida began her life at the settlement on the park's west entrance, there was nothing much there except for three businesses including Eagle's Store, a handful of residents, and a box car serving as the Union Pacific Railroad depot. The town site was initially called Boundary and, with establishment of a post office, the town's name changed to Riverside in 1908, then to Yellowstone in 1910, and finally to West Yellowstone in 1920.

3. "Mrs. Ida C. Eagle Dies Here," *Bozeman* (MT) *Daily Chronicle*, Tuesday September 23, 1962; Family Group Record, Samuel P. Eagle Papers, 1906-1967, Collection 1263, microfilm, Montana State University Special Collections, Bozeman. Ida had several

siblings. Two sisters, Mrs. Hanna Newman and Mrs. Helen Goss, are evidenced by letters and postcards received by Ida after 1905. According to Wally Eagle's essay in Sam P. Eagle, Jr. and John Edwin Eagle, *West Yellowstone's 70th Anniversary 1908–1978* (West Yellowstone, MT: Eagle Company, Inc., 1978), Ida's youngest sister Elizabeth Carlson married Bill Flynn, who apparently worked as a foreman helping to pave the park roads. But the Carlson family record is unclear as to the whereabouts of Ida's sisters at the time of Susan's death.

4. Patty M.F. Selmes, untitled newspaper clipping, 1891, in Scrapbook 4209, p. 146, YNP Library.

5. "The Yellowstone National Park," *Harper's Weekly* 37 (July 29, 1893), 722. For Fountain Hotel see Lee H. Whittlesey, "Music, Song, and Laughter: Yellowstone National Park's Fountain Hotel, 1891-1916," *Montana: The Magazine of Western History*, 53: 1 (2003): 22-35, and Whittlesey, "'Music, Song, and Laughter': Paradise at Yellowstone's Fountain Hotel, 1891-1916," *GOSA Transactions: Journal of the Geyser Observation and Study Association* 10 (2008): 149-168.

6. Eagle, *Eagle's Store: 100 Years*, 4.

7. Sam Eagle to Ida Carlson, October 1, 1905, Sam Eagle to Ida Carlson, October 20, 1905, Eagle Family Archive, West Yellowstone, Montana.

8. Sam Eagle to Ida Carlson, November 30, 1905, December 16, 28, 1905, January 10, 21, 1906, Eagle Family Archive.

9. Sam Eagle to Ida Carlson, March 14, 1906, Eagle Family Archive.

10. Sam Eagle to Ida Carlson, March 8, 1906; Eagle and Eagle, *West Yellowstone's 70th Anniversary*, 2-20.

11. Sam Eagle to Ida Carlson, April 21, 1906; Eagle and Eagle, *West Yellowstone's 70th Anniversary*, 2-20. The Stuarts' change-of-life plan would result in their settling in West Yellowstone and producing the first baby there, Walter Stuart. Walt would eventually drive visitor snowcoaches in Yellowstone in the 1970s, a job he continued until he was in his seventies.

12. Sam Eagle to Ida Carlson, October 10, 18, 1906, Eagle Family Archive.

13. Katharine Kurland and Lori Zabar, "Furnishing the Arts & Crafts Movement," *Style 1900* 13: 4 (2000): 38-44; Sam Eagle to Ida Carlson, December 28, 1905, January 6, 1907, Eagle Family Archive.

14. Sam Eagle to Ida Carlson, December 5, 10, 12, 18, 22, 1906, Eagle Family Archive.

15. Sam Eagle to Ida Carlson, December 24, 1906, Eagle Family Archive.

16. Sam Eagle to Ida Carlson, January 6, 1907; "The Knickerbocker," *The* [New York] *Morning News*, December 2, 2006, www.themorningnews.org/archives/new_york_new_york/the_knickerbocker.php.

17. Sam Eagle to Ida Carlson, January 15, 1907, Eagle Family Archive.

18. "Willard Hotel," on http://www.nps.gov/history/Nr/travel/wash/dc36.htm; Sam Eagle to Ida Carlson, February 25, March 2, 10, 14, 1907, Eagle Family Archive.

19. Sam Eagle to Ida Carlson, May 13, 1907, Eagle Family Archive.

20. Eagle and Eagle, *West Yellowstone's 70th Anniversary*, 2-11.

21. Forest Service Supervisor to Sam Eagle, March 27, 1908, Samuel P. Eagle Papers; Café Union blurb on envelope addressed to Ida Eagle, May 7, 1908, Eagle Family Archive; author interview with Ida's granddaughter, Kendra Eagle Owen, September 10, 2009, Helena, Montana.

22. Eagle and Eagle, *West Yellowstone's 70th Anniversary*, 2-11; Mark Eagle McPhie, "Eagle Store Building History" in "Eagle's 100th Anniversary Open House," newspaper supplement to *Bozeman Daily Chronicle*, June 15, 2008, 22-23.

23. Eagle and Eagle, *West Yellowstone's 70th Anniversary*, 2-8.

24. Eagle and Eagle, *West Yellowstone's 70th Anniversary*, 1-2, 2-6, 2-20.

25. F.J. Haynes to Mr. S.P. Eagle, March 3, 1910, Samuel P. Eagle Papers; Eagle and Eagle, *West Yellowstone's 70th Anniversary*, 1-2, 2-20.

26. Sam Eagle Jr. to Eagle Wingers, July 21, 1973, Samuel P. Eagle Papers.

27. Eagle and Eagle, *West Yellowstone's 70th Anniversary*, 2-20.

28. Sam Eagle Jr. to Eagle Wingers, July 21, 1973, Samuel P. Eagle Papers.

29. John Nemeth, "Soda Fountain on the Frontier" in "Eagle's Anniversary Open House," 8.

30. "The Liquid Carbonic Company," on www.drugstoremuseum.com.

31. For entire Eagle family genealogy see Eagle Store Family history at www.eagles-store.com.

32. Eva Eagle, "Ida Carlson Eagle," in "Eagle's Anniversary Open House," 13.

33. Author's interview with Kendra Eagle Owen and Margaret Eagle, September 10, 2009, Helena, Montana.

34. Henry C. Eagle, "The Mail Route," in *West Yellowstone's 70th Anniversary*, 1-6.

35. *West Yellowstone's 70th Anniversary*, 2-36, 3-13.

36. McPhie, "Eagle Store Building History," in "Eagle's 100th Anniversary," 22-23; author's interview with Wally Eagle in West Yellowstone, September 12-13, 2009; "Vacationing in Yellowstone," at www.tileheritage.or/THF-ENews08-09.html#yellow.

37. Carol Hoffmann, "Eagle's From the Start," in "Eagle's 100th Anniversary," 5.

38. Eagle and Eagle, *West Yellowstone's 70th Anniversary*, 2-33; Kendra Eagle Owen, "Samuel Peter Eagle," in "Eagle's 100th Anniversary," 12.

39. Joe Glannon, "Sam and Ida's Commitment to Education," in "Eagle's 100th Anniversary," 15.

40. Rose Eagle to Ed Eagle, October [no day], 1934, Eagle Family Archive.

41. Personal memo "From Rose 2-95," copy in possession of author.

42. Author's interview with Charles Anderson, September 10, 2009, Helena, Montana. Sadly, "Uncle Chuck" passed away in May 2010. His bear stories and hearty laugh are very much missed.

43. Author's interview with Margaret Eagle, September 10, 2009, Helena, Montana.

44. Carol Hoffmann, "Eagle's From the Start," in "Eagle's 100th Anniversary," 5. For information about Wally's Feather Duster, see http://flyfishyellowstone-flies.blogspot.com.

45. Delia Eagle Voitoff-Bauman, "Memories of Summer 1961 at Eagle's Store," *Eagle's Store: 100 Years,* 40; Sunni Brown Wilkerson, "The Best Summer of My Life," ibid., 16; author's interview with Margaret Eagle, September 10, 2009, Helena, Montana.

46. Wilkerson, "Best Summer," 16.

47. Kendra Eagle Owen to author, September 12, 2009.

48. Author interview with Kendra Eagle Owen and Wally Eagle, September 12-13, 2009, West Yellowstone, Montana.

49. Ida Eagle to Ed Eagle, September 23, 1934, Ida Eagle to Ed Eagle, November 13, 1934, Ida Eagle to Everybody, February 5, 1935, Eagle Family Archive.

50. Author's interview with Wally and Frankie Eagle, Joe and Kay Eagle, Kendra Eagle Owen, September 12-13, 2009, West Yellowstone, Montana.

51. Susan Eagle Reynolds, "Memories of Eagle's Store," in *Eagle's Store: 100 Years*, 28; Delia Eagle Voitoff-Bauman, "Memories of Summer 1961 at Eagle's Store," ibid., 40.

52. Carl Eagle, "Memories of the 1959 Earthquake," ibid., 37-38; Dick Post, "Eagle's in the Fifties," ibid., 19-20; author's interview with Wally Eagle, September 12-13, 2009, West Yellowstone, Montana.

53. "Mrs. Ida C. Eagle Dies Here," *Bozeman Daily Chronicle*, September 23, 1962.

Willie Frances Crawford Bronner and Jean Crawford Sharp:
Like Mother, Like Daughter

1. Jean Crawford Sharpe, "This Is Me...and This Is What I Remember: A Yellowstone Story 1908-1917" (1985), unpublished manuscript, Yellowstone National Park (YNP) Library, 6.

2. www.findagrave.com/marion.

3. Ibid.

4. 1900 United States Federal Census, Prairie, Arkansas, http://www.ancestry.com.

5. 1910 United States Federal Census, Prairie, Arkansas, http://www.ancestry.com.

6. Sharpe, "This Is Me," 6-7.

7. A.I. Root quoted in *Yellowstone National Park, Wylie Permanent Camps* (Helena: State Publishing, [1904]), 17.

8. For further information on the Wylie Camping Company see Elizabeth Ann Watry, "More Than Mere Coaches and Camps: The Wylie Camping Company and the Development of a Middle Class Leisure Ethic in Yellowstone National Park, 1883-1917," M.A. thesis, May 2010, Montana State University, Bozeman.

9. Sharpe, "This Is Me," 6-7.

10. Robert A. Dellett, "Yellowstone Park," unpublished manuscript [1901], MSS110, H-56-88, Wyoming State Archive, Cheyenne, [2, 13].

11. 1880 United States Census, Bedford, Iowa; 1900 United States Census, Bozeman, Montana, www.http://www.ancestry.com.

12. "A Sudden Death," *Bedford Free Press*, April 29, 1909; "Grim Reaper Is Busy," *Bedford Free Press*, May, 6, 1909; Montana Death Index, Iowa Cemetery Records, www. http://www.ancestry.com.

13. For summer of 1909, see Sharpe, "This Is Me," 4, 10, 5-6, 8.

14. Sarah Christine Peterson, "Yellowstone Park Language," *American Speech*, Vol. 7, No. 1 (October 1931), 21.

15. Peterson, "Yellowstone Park Language," 21-23; Dorothy Cook, "More Yellowstone Lingo," *American Speech*, Vol. 10, No. 1 (February 1935), 75-76; Julie Coleman, *A History of Cant and Slang Dictionaries: Volume III: 1859-1936* (New York: Oxford Univ. Press, 2008), 193-95.

16. For summer of 1913, see Sharpe, "This Is Me," 16, 14, 19.

17. For summer of 1914, see Sharpe, "This Is Me," 23, 21.

18. For summer of 1915, see Sharpe, "This Is Me," 27, 28, 30, 31.

19. Jack Ellis Haynes, *Yellowstone Stage Holdups* (Bozeman, MT: Haynes Studios, 1959), 27.

20. For summer of 1917, see Sharpe, "This Is Me," 36, 35, 39, 41.

21. Mae Urbanek, as told by "Kid" Wilson, "First Auto Travel in Yellowstone Park," *Bits and Pieces*, Vol. 2, No. 2 (May 1966), 21.

22. For Jean's family members see 1930 United States Federal Census, Berkeley, Alameda, California, www.http://www.ancestry.com

23. Oregon Death Index, 1903-98, www.http://www.ancestry.com.

24. www.findagrave.com.

25. Oregon Death Index, 1903-98, www.http://www.ancestry.com.

Beulah Brown: Hostess Extraordinaire

1. "Mayor Tells of Trip Through Yellowstone Park; Meets Ogdenites," *Ogden* (UT) *Standard Examiner*, August 8, 1920.

2. Elizabeth Rigby, "Sanborn Home Will Be Shown in Sedona Tour," (Cottonwood, AZ) *Verde Independent*, April 5, 1962.

3. In 1917, Wylie, Shaw & Powell, Old Faithful, and other independent camping companies were merged into one business enterprise, The Yellowstone Park Camps Company. Stephen Mather, director of the new National Park Service, which took over the administration of Yellowstone National Park in 1916, believed that the public would be better served and the operations could be better managed by one hotel company, one transportation company, and one camping company that was regulated by the NPS.

4. "Mayor Tells of Trip Through Yellowstone Park."

5. "Reminiscences of Other Days," *Democrat and Standard* (OH), September 1, 1903; "Dr. Winslow Brown Resigns Pastorate at Cedar Rapids," *Malvern* (IA) *Leader*, December 26, 1935; 1860 United States Federal Census, Champaign, IL; 1870 United States Federal Census, Jackson, OH; 1880 United States Federal Census, Wooster, OH; 1900 United States Federal Census, Malvern, IA.

6. 1880 United States Federal Census, Pataskala, OH.

7. "Former Spirit Lake Pastor Honored on 79th Birthday," *Spirit Lake* (IA) *Beacon*, July 11, 1929; www.kinfinder.com/Family/SDDescendants/DR01_001.htm.

8. 1900 United States Census, Malvern, IA; "His First Local Sermon Is Heard," *Hamilton* (OH) *Telegraph*, November 14,1901.

9. Iowa Cemetery Records (Original data: Project Administration, Graves Registration Project, Washington, DC), http://www.ancestry.com.

10. "Died," *Spirit Lake Beacon*, February 5, 1904.

11. It is unclear if Dorothy continued on to college. She was married to Walter S. Anderson (1888-1968) and lived for a time in Utah. Dorothy died in August 1976, six months after Beulah. See www.kinfinder.com/Family/SDDescendants/DR01_001.htm.

12. E-mail correspondence with Heather Lyle, University Archivist/Special Collections Librarian, William Howard Doane Library, Denison University, Granville, Ohio. According to the 1920 Denison Alumni Directory Beulah graduated with a Ph.B. in 1909 and she was employed at Muskingum College at that time.

13. Mabel (Sipe) Davis, "Traveling in a Model T Ford," oral interview O.H. 369, October 10, 1979, Youngstown State University, Youngstown, Ohio, transcript, 6; Mabel (Sipe) Davis, "Teaching Experiences," oral interview O.H. 370, November 17, 1975, transcript, 6.

14. *Ogden Examiner*, April 27, 1918.

15. "Ogden Sending Young People to Yellowstone, *Ogden Standard Examiner*, May 29, 1921; "New Teachers in Faculty for High School Next Year," *Ogden Examiner*, June 28, 1918.

16. *The Red Cross Bulletin*, Vol. II, No. 42, Washington, DC, October 14, 1918.

17. "Operation Delays Sailing," *Cedar Rapids* (IA) *Evening Gazette*, August 28, 1918; *Ogden Examiner*, September 30, 1919. While there is no medical confirmation of heredity being a contributing factor concerning appendicitis, the occurrence of two women of the same family being stricken with the malady, does make one wonder if their mother's mysterious illness and sudden death could have been a ruptured appendix. For medical advancements in treatment of appendicitis up to 1939 see, "Statistical History of Appendicitis," *British Medical Journal*, Vol. 1, No. 4087 (May 6, 1939): 928-29.

18. "Mayor Tells of Trip Through Yellowstone Park," *Ogden Standard Examiner*, August 8, 1920.

19. "National Park Pageant Given," *Salt Lake Tribune*, August 28, 1922.

20. Paul Schullery and Lee H. Whittlesey, *Myth and History in the Creation of Yellowstone National Park* (Lincoln: Univ. of Nebraska Press, 2003), 22.

21. Beulah Brown, *My Winter in Geyserland* (n.p., n.d. [1924]), 5. Many of her friends were intrigued by her winter adventure at Old Faithful. So much so, that they persuaded Beulah to write and publish this little pamphlet and offer it for sale in the park gift shops the following year.

22. Beulah Brown, "Winter in Geyserland," *Livingston* (MT) *Enterprise*, February 7, 1923. This article was one of two letters that Beulah wrote to her friend, Lady Mac, during her winter at Old Faithful, which were published in the *Enterprise*. The second letter was published on April 4, 1923 as an article entitled "On Skis in Blizzard." These letters were incorporated into a pamphlet *My Winter in Geyserland* that Beulah published in 1924.

23. Brown, *My Winter in Geyserland*, 6.

24. Ibid.

25. Brown, *My Winter in Geyserland*, 8.

26. "Gardening over a Geyser," *Scientific American*, July 9, 1898, 24.

27. Beulah Brown, "On Skis in Blizzard," *Livingston Enterprise*, April 4, 1923.

28. Brown, *My Winter in Geyserland*, 13.

29. Paul Rubinstein, Lee Whittlesey, and Mike Stevens, *Yellowstone Waterfalls and Their Discovery* (Englewood: Westcliff Publishers, 2000), 140.

30. Brown, "Winter in Geyserland."

31. This account of Brown's and Musser's ski trek is from Brown, "On Skis in Blizzard."

32. Brown, "Winter in Geyserland."

33. Lee Whittlesey, *Yellowstone Place Names* (Gardiner, MT: Wonderland Publishing Company, 2006), 205.

34. Davis, "Traveling in a Model T," interview, transcript, 7. Mabel Davis located and visited with Beulah at Mammoth Camp in the summer of 1924.

35. Mark Barringer, "When Harry Got Taken: The Early Days of the Yellowstone Camps," *Annals of Wyoming: The Wyoming History Journal*, Fall 1997, 2-12.

36. U.S. Passport Applications, 1795-1925, http://www.ancestry.com/; New York Passenger Lists, 1820-1957, ibid.

37. Rufus Steele, "Savage Summers," *The Outlook*, May 12, 1926, 57. For a library catalog reference to Beulah Brown and the Songs of Yellowstone Park Camps see http://www.loc.gov/folklife/guides/BibCampSongs.html. The Yellowstone National Park (YNP) Library houses a number of editions of Brown's *Songs of Yellowstone Park Camps* and *Songs of Yellowstone Park Camps and Lodges*, booklets that range in date from the 1920s to 1950s.

38. During the 1920s, the Yellowstone Park Camps Company slowly evolved from a tent camping operation to a system of lodges with modern kitchens and dining rooms as well as cabin-style accommodations. The name was formally changed to Yellowstone Park Lodge and Camps Company in 1928 when Harry Child took over full ownership. However, the term "lodge" had come into common usage when referring to the Camps Company long before the company's official renaming.

39. Photo in album in Herma Baggley Papers, MSC-7, Box 1, YNP Archives.

40. Linda W. Greene, *Death Valley National Monument: Historic Resource Study: A History of Mining* (Denver: National Park Service, 1981), Volume I, Part 2 of 2, Section III: "Inventory of Historical Resources: The West Side," http://nps.gov/history/online_books/deva/section3d3.htm.

41. Ron Miller, *Fifty Years Ago at Furnace Creek Inn* (Death Valley: Death Valley 49ers, 1977), 7-8; "Miss Brown Directs Inn," *Ogden Standard Examiner*, October 26, 1927.

42. Joseph Gennaro, *75th Anniversary: Furnace Creek Inn* (Death Valley: Furnace Creek Inn, 2001), 9; Miller, *Fifty Years Ago*, 9.

43. State of California, Certificate of Vital Records, Standard Certificate of Marriage, May 2, 1928, YNP Library, Biography (Brown), vertical files.

44. Richard C. Erd, James F. McAllister, and Hy Almond, "Gowerite, A New Hydrous Calcium from the Death Valley Region, California," *The American Mineralogist: Journal of the Mineralogical Society of America*, Vol. 44, nos. 9 and 10 (September-October, 1959), 911.

45. Harry P. Gower, *50 Years in Death Valley: Memoirs of a Borax Man* (Death Valley: Death Valley 49ers, 1970), generally; Richard E. Lingenfelter, *Death Valley & The Amargosa: A Land of Illusion* (Berkeley: Univ. of California Press, 1986), 456.

46. "Lake Arrowhead: Heritage and History," Lake Arrowhead Resort, http://www.laresort.com/lars/aboutus/heritagehistory.htm.

47. California Voter Registrations, 1900-1968, San Bernardino County, 1932, California Voter Registrations, 1900-1968, San Bernardino County, 1936, http://www.ancestry.com/.

48. For further history on Mammoth Cave see Margaret M. Bridwell, *The Story of Mammoth Cave National Park Kentucky: A Brief History* ([Mammoth Cave, KY]: Bridwell, 1968); "Civilian Conservation Corps at Mammoth Cave National Park," http://www.wku.edu/Library/nps/ccc/index.html.

49. Bob and Judi Thompson, *Images of America: Mammoth Cave and the Kentucky Cave Region* (Charleston, SC: Arcadia Publishing, 2003), 23, 75.

50. Ethan Carr, *Mission 66: Modernism and The National Park Dilemma* (Amherst: Univ. of Massachusetts, 2007), 363-364.

51. "New Officers Named by Park Concessions," *Park City* (KY) *Daily News*, January 31, 1962; "Hansen Named President of Park Group," *Park City Daily News*, February 2, 1958; "Brief Items in the Daily Life of Prescott," *Prescott* (AZ) *Evening Courier*, October 9, 1947.

52. "Obituary," *Barren County* (KY) *Progress*, February 19, 1976.

Isabel Deming Bassett Wasson: Ideal for Teaching

1. Belle Preston, *Bassett-Preston Ancestors: A History of the Ancestors in America* (New Haven: The Tuttle, Morehouse & Taylor Co., 1930), 32-33.

2. Ibid.; *Biographical Directory of the United States Congress*, http://www.bioguide.congress.gov http://bioguide.congress.gov; Cornell University, *Guide to Edward M. Bassett Papers, 1892-1948*, Collection: 2708, Biographical Note; Donald A. Krueckeberg, ed., *The American Planner: Biographies and Recollections* (New York: Methuen, Inc, 1983); "Edward Bassett: 'Father' of Zoning," *New York Times*, October 29, 1948.

3. Preston, *Bassett-Preston Ancestors*, 32-33; *National Cyclopedia of American Biography*, Current Volume, Vol. 1 (New York: J.T. White, 1964), 408.

4. Isabel Bassett Wasson, Oral History #00-6, Yellowstone National Park (YNP) Archives.

5. Thomas Chrowder Chamberlin (1843-1928) was a prominent geologist and educator in the American Midwest. While teaching at Beloit College (1873-1882), Chamberlin participated in a geological survey of Wisconsin on a part-time basis in 1873, and by 1876, he had become the chief geologist for the project. His mapping of southeastern Wisconsin led to greater understanding of the stages of the earth's glacial epochs and garnered him national attention. In 1881, Chamberlin was appointed head of the glacial division of the U.S. Geological Survey (USGS). His reputation earned him an offer from the University of Chicago in 1892 to organize a geology department, where he served as professor until 1918. Earlier, as a professor at Beloit, Chamberlin had become acquainted with Rollin Daniel Salisbury (1858-1922). Salisbury enrolled in Beloit in 1878, where he studied geology under Chamberlin. After graduating in 1881, Salisbury served the following year as at Chamberlin's field assistant with USGS. In 1882, Salisbury filled the vacancy left by Chamberlin at Beloit. By 1884, Salisbury had become the chair of the geology department. In 1892, he participated in the Peary Relief Expedition to Greenland and joined the faculty of the University of Chicago. There he organized the department of geography in 1903 and remained in that position until 1918. Allen F. Schneider, "Chamberlin, Salisbury, and Collie: A Tale of Three Beloit College Geologists," *Geoscience Wisconsin*, Volume 18 (2001): 9-20.

6. Isabel B. Wasson, unpublished memoir, "Summer of 1920, First Naturalist Ranger in Yellowstone National Park," September 29, 1975, 1, Manuscripts (Wasson), YNP Archives; Isabel Bassett Wasson, Oral History.

7. Quoted in Lemuel Garrison to Chief, Division of Interpretation, Memorandum, October 25, 1961, in Aubrey L. Haines, "Memorandum of the History of Women in Uniform (National Park Service) in Yellowstone National Park, October, 1961," vertical files, YNP Library; Kiki Leigh Rydell and Mary Shivers Culpin, *Managing the "Matchless Wonders": A History of Administrative Development in Yellowstone National Park, 1872-1965* (Mammoth, WY: Yellowstone National Park, 2003), 97; Wasson, "Summer of 1920," 1.

8. Rydell and Culpin, 97.

9. Rydell and Culpin, 98; Horace M. Albright, *Annual Report of the Superintendent of the Yellowstone National Park to the Secretary of Interior,* 1920, 39.

10. Wasson, "Summer of 1920," 1.

11. "Botsford Family Genealogy: The Line of Joseph I.I.12, Ten Generations 1639-1939," p. 138 on http://www.ancestry.com.

12. Horace M. Albright, *Annual Report...*1920, 39; Rydell and Culpin, 97.

13. Wasson, "Summer of 1920," 2. For additional information on the Wylie Camping Company see Elizabeth Ann Watry, "More Than Mere Camps and Coaches: The Wylie Camping Company and the Development of a Middle Class Leisure Ethic in Yellowstone National Park, 1883-1916," M.A. Thesis, May 2010, Montana State University, Bozeman.

14. Wasson, "Summer of 1920"; F.H. Knowlton, *Fossil Forests of the Yellowstone National Park* (Washington, DC: Government Printing Office, 1921), 11. In later years, the number of reputed layers of petrified forests was expanded to twenty-seven.

15. Knowlton, *Fossil Forests,* 11; Wasson, "Summer of 1920, 2.

16. Wasson, "Summer of 1920," 2; Richard Bartlett, *Yellowstone: Wilderness Besieged* (Tucson: Univ. of Arizona Press, 1989), 291-93.

17. Wasson, "Summer of 1920," 2.

18. Albright to Wasson, October 8, 1921, quoted in memorandum from Lemuel Garrison to Chief, Division of Interpretation, October, 25, 1961, in Aubrey L. Haines, "Memorandum of the History of Women in Uniform (National Park Service) in Yellowstone National Park."

19. Rydell and Culpin, 98-99.

20. "Obituaries," (River Forest, IL) *Pioneer Press,* March 9, 1994, 116, 118.

21. Theron Wasson married Ann M. Hand on May 21, 1959. Cook County, Illinois Marriage Index, 1930-1960, http://www.ancestry.com/. On August 6, 1970, Theron Wasson died in Chicago, *Southern Illinoisan,* August 7, 1970.

22. "Roosevelt Holds Grad Rites for 99," (River Forest, IL) *Pioneer Press,* June 17, 1981; "Obituaries," *Pioneer Press,* March 9, 1994, 116, 118.

23. "Obituaries," *Pioneer Press,* March 9, 1994, 116, 118.

Jane Marguerite Lindsley Arnold: A Girl Ranger

1. Lindsley quoted in *Harley-Davidson Enthusiast,* August 1924, 16; "Home on Motorbike from Philadelphia," *Billings* (MT) *Gazette,* June 17, 1924.

2. Her name appears as Marguerite in nearly every reference, including National Park Service records, except on her transcript from the University of Pennsylvania, where she is listed as Jane Marguerite Lindsley, her birth name. She and apparently her parents preferred using her middle name, Marguerite.

3. Marguerite Lindsley Arnold, "Early Impressions," *Yellowstone Nature Notes,* March-April 1934, Volume XI, Nos. 3-4, 15, Yellowstone National Park (YNP) Library; Jack E. Haynes, *Haynes Guide: Yellowstone National Park* (Bozeman, MT: Haynes Studios, 1936), 136.

4. Aubrey Haines, *The Yellowstone Story: A History of Our First National Park,* rev. ed., vol. 2 (Niwot, CO: Univ. of Colorado, 1996), 458.

5. Childhood friends and events are described in Arnold, "Early Impressions," 15-17.

6. In "Early Impressions,"Marguerite mistakenly identified the location of the robbery as Spring Creek canyon road. There was a stagecoach robbery on the Spring Creek road but it was in 1908, when she was only seven years old.

7. Marguerite Lindsley to Regina Stoltz, November 26, 1927, Arnold-Lindsley Family Archive, copy in author's possession.

8. From October 1916 until November 1917, Chester's title was Acting Supervisor. The designation of superintendent was reinstated in November 1917, when Chester's position

was changed to Acting Superintendent. Haines, *Yellowstone Story*, Vol. 2, 458.

9. Ibid.; *Janesville* (WI) *Daily Gazette*, June 24, 1921.

10. *Ironwood* (MI) *Daily Globe*, June 23, 1921; *Ada* (OK) *Evening News*, June 23, 1921; *Wyoming State Tribune*, June 25, 1921; n.p., n.d. newspaper clipping in Biography (Lindsley), vertical files, YNP Library.

11. In the early 1920s, the only designation for NPS employees was that of ranger. In 1926 that designation when applied to women became problematic.

12. Lemuel A. Garrison, Memorandum from Lemuel A. Garrison to Chief, Division of Interpretation, October 25, About History of Women's Uniform in the National Park Service, vertical files, YNP Library.

13. Louis Agassiz quoted in Sally Gregory Kohlstedt, "Nature, Not Books: Scientists and the Origins of the Nature-Study Movement in the 1890s," *Isis* 96 (September 2005): 325. For further information on the nature study movement, see Anna Botsford Comstock, *Handbook of Nature Study*, 12th ed. (Ithaca: Comstock Publishing Company, 1922), Kim Tolley, *The Science Education of American Girls: A Historical Perspective* (New York: Routledge, 2002).

14. N.p., n.d. newspaper clipping, Biography (Lindsley), vertical files, YNP Library.

15. Arnold, "Early Impressions," 15-17.

16. "Knights of the Lash" was an old-time moniker applied to stagecoach drivers. N.p., n.d. newspaper clipping, Biography (Lindsley), vertical files, YNP Library.

17. While the United States Geographic Board (today known as the United States Board of Geographic Names) existed in 1890, few of Yellowstone's place names followed its rigorous code. The code mandated that names of living persons should not be used, but at the same time instructed that names in common usage should be maintained if possible. Yellowstone created quite a quandary in that respect for the committee, as many sites, such as Norris Geyser Basin, were named after living persons. Aubrey Haines, *Yellowstone Place Names: Mirrors of History* (Niwot, CO: Univ. Press of Colorado, 1996), xii-xiv.

18. Haines, *Yellowstone Place Names*, xv-xvi.

19. Lindsley to Stoltz, November 26, 1927. According to the University of Pennsylvania alumni records, she received her M.S. on June 20, 1923.

20. Lindsley to Stoltz, November 26, 1927.

21. "Home on Motorbike from Philadelphia," *Billings* (MT) *Gazette* June 17, 1924; Polly Kaufman, "Challenging Tradition: Pioneer Women Naturalists in the National Park Service," *Forest and Conservation History* 34 (January 1990): 16, n. 34; Lindsley to Stoltz, November 26, 1927; author's e-mail communication with Bill Arnold, March 29, 2010.

22. Arnold, "Early Impressions," 16; photograph in album in Arnold-Lindsley Family Archive.

23. Arnold, "Early Impressions," 16-17; Lindsley to Stolz, November 26, 1927.

24. Lindsley to Stolz, November 26, 1927.

25. Ibid.

26. E.K. Burlew, Administrative Assistant, and J.F. Garland, Chief Inspector, to the Secretary of Interior, October 4, 1926, Folder 154.32 Educational Division Correspondence Fiscal Year 1926, 1927, Box K-16, YNP Archives.

27. Kaufman, "Challenging Tradition," 11.

28. Horace Albright to Stephen Mather, October 14, 1926, Folder 154.3 Fiscal Year 1927, Box K-18, YNP Archives.

29. Horace Albright to Henry S. Conard, November 30, 1926, Folder 154.3 Fiscal Year 1927, Box K-18, YNP Archives.

30. Conard to Albright, December 26, 1926, Folder 154.32 Educational Division Fiscal Year 1926,1927, Box K-16, YNP Archives.

31. Henry S. Conard to Hubert Work, January 24, 1927; Work to Conard, February 5, 1927; George Fuller to Stephen Mather, January 24, 1927; Arno Cammerer to George

Fuller, February 9, 1927; Arno Cammerer to Mr. Braun, February 9, 1927; all in Folder 154.32, Box K-16, YNP Archives. It is interesting to note the addressee on this last letter. It was a common practice among women throughout history to use initials when writing for a professional purpose instead of their first names, to give a pretense of being male so they would be taken seriously. This seems to have been the case when E. Lucy Braun wrote to Cammerer complaining about the exclusion of women as rangers as Cammerer addressed his response to Mr. Braun.

32. Henry S. Conard to Hubert Work, January 24, 1927, Folder 154.32, Box K-16, YNP Archives.

33. Horace Albright to Dr. George Fuller, January 26, 1927, File 154.3, Box K-18, YNP Archives.

34. "Lady Ranger 'Makes Good' in Yellowstone Park Post," *Christian Science Monitor*, January 28, 1927; Marguerite Lindsley to Christine Funk, April 1927, Arnold-Lindsley Family Archive, copy in author's possession.

35. Lindsley to Funk, April 23, 1927.

36. Lindsley quoted in Polly Kaufman, *National Parks and the Woman's Voice: A History* (Albuquerque: Univ. of New Mexico, 2006), 82.

37. "Lady Ranger 'Makes Good.'"

38. Herma (Mrs. Geo. F.) Baggley oral history [1962], Reel XXXV, transcript, p. 21, National Park Service Harpers Ferry Center, Harpers Ferry, WV.

39. "Lady Ranger 'Makes Good.'"

40. Marguerite Lindsley, "Coyote Replies to Imitation Call," *Yellowstone Nature Notes*, September 30, 1927.

41. Herma (Mrs. Geo. F.) Baggley oral history, transcript, 23.

42. Marguerite Lindsley, Personal Memorandum for Mr. Woodring, July 18, 1927, Arnold-Lindsley Family Archive, copy in possession of author.

43. "Arnold-Lindsley," n.d., *Livingston* (MT) *Enterprise*, in Biography (Lindsley), vertical files, YNP Library.

44. *Yellowstone Nature Notes*, May-June 1952, YNP Library. This issue was dedicated to Marguerite Lindsley and contained a sampling of the many articles that she wrote for the publication.

45. Marguerite Lindsley Arnold, "Yellowstone Women: A Native Speaks," unpublished memoir in Biography (Lindsley), vertical files, YNP Library.

46. Information about Ben and Marguerite's wolf sighting, unless otherwise noted, is from Marguerite L. Arnold, "Yellowstone Wolves," *Nature*, August, 1937, 111-112.

47. United States Department of Agriculture, Forest Service Rocky Mountain Division, *Chief Joseph Scenic Byway & Beartooth All-American Road: Interpretive Plan* (Washington, DC: Government Printing Office, 2009), 1, 14.

48. Author's e-mail correspondence with Bill Arnold March 29, 2011.

49. "Calvert School History and Philosophy," on http://homeschool.calvertschool.org/about-calvert/historyphilosophy.

50. "Collecting and Selling of Rocky Mountain Wild Flowers Is Unique Hobby," *Gardiner* (MT) *Gateway Gazette*, August 1, 1940; author's e-mail correspondence with Bill Arnold, March 29, 2011.

51. Author's e-mail correspondence with Bill Arnold, March 29, 2011.

52. Ibid.

53. "Funeral Services for Mrs. Arnold Held Wednesday," *Cody* (WY) *Times*, May 22, 1952; "Mrs. Ben Arnold From Yellowstone Dies At Age of 50," *Cody* (WY) *Enterprise*, May 22, 1952; "Park Resident Dies in Cody," *Billings* (MT) *Gazette*, May 20, 1952; "Funeral Services Held for Park Ranger's Wife," *Billings Gazette*, May 22, 1952; "Park Entrance to Open Friday," *Cody Enterprise*, May 22, 1952; author's e-mail correspondence with Bill Arnold, March 29, 2011.

54. Ivy D. Little, "Tribute to Marguerite Lindsley Arnold," (Livingston, MT) *Park County News*, May 29, 1952.

55. Marguerite Lindsley Arnold, "Yellowstone Women: A Native Speaks."

56. Lindsley to Stolz, November 26, 1927, 3.

Frances Eva Pound Wright: Ranger Jim

1. Carol Shively, "Ranger Jim," in *People, Land, & Water*, March/April 1999, 57-58. Unlike today, when the NPS has separate divisions of personnel, the term ranger in the 1920s encompassed a number of duties, which included interpretation, fire-fighting, wildlife management, and law enforcement. But not all rangers carried firearms. Because Frances wore a firearm while on duty, technically she would have been considered a law enforcement ranger.

2. According to various family histories of the Pound family, Frances' great-grandfather was Elijah Pound, father of Thaddeus Coleman Pound and Albert Elijah Pound. Thaddeus C. Pound's son was Homer Loomis Pound, father of the poet Ezra Loomis Pound. Albert E. Pound's son was Thaddeus Chad Pound, father of Frances Eva Pound. If this family pedigree is accurate, it makes Frances a second cousin to Ezra Pound.

3. "Helen Elizabeth Pound Talcott," *History of Park County, Montana* (Livingston: Yellowstone Gateway Museum, 1984), 465.

4. Ibid.

5. *Anaconda* (MT) *Standard*, September 22, 23, 1910; *Billings* (MT) *Gazette*, October 2, 1910, January 4, 1911.

6. "Helen Elizabeth Pound Talcott," *History of Park County*, 465; *Anaconda Standard*, September 22, 23, 1910; *Billings Gazette*, October 2, 1910, January 4, 1911.

7. "Helen Elizabeth Pound Talcott," *History of Park County*, 465.

8. Ibid.

9. Frances Pound Wright oral history, July 11, 1981, transcript, p. [23], File 62-3, Yellowstone National Park (YNP) Archives.

10. Kiki Leigh Rydell and Mary Shivers Culpin, *A History of Administrative Development in Yellowstone National Park, 1872-1965* (Yellowstone National Park: Yellowstone Center for Resources, 2006), 27-30, 60-61.

11. Aubrey Haines, *The Yellowstone Story: A History of Our First National Park*, rev. ed., vol. 2 (Niwot, Colorado: Univ. of Colorado, 1996), 289-91.

12. Wright oral history, 1981, transcript, p. [4], [10-11].

13. Frances Pound Wright quoted in Shively, "Ranger Jim," 58.

14. Richard Bartlett, "Those Infernal Machines in Yellowstone," *Montana: The Magazine of Western History* 20 (Summer 1970), 16-19.

15. Wright oral history, 1981, transcript, p. [1].

16. Teresa S. Neal, *Evolution Toward Equality: Equality for Women in the American West* (Lincoln, NE: iUniverse, 2006), 32-57.

17. Wright oral history, 1981, transcript, p. [27]; Howard Eaton quoted in Jack E. Haynes, *Haynes Bulletin*, St. Paul, Minnesota, December 1923, 2-3.

18. Wright oral history, 1981, transcript, p. [8].

19. Ibid., [13].

20. Horace Albright quoted in Wright oral history, 1981, transcript, [5]; "Frances 'Ranger Jim' Wright Dies at 93," *Pasadena Star News*, December 30, 1999.

21. Wright oral history, 1981, transcript, [5]; Janette Williams, "A Lone Ranger Recollects Yellowstone," *Pasadena Star News*, August 10, 1997; "Frances 'Ranger Jim' Wright Dies at 93"; "Ranger Jim Was First 'Lawman' in Yellowstone," (Livingston, MT) *Park County Super Shopper*, August 15, 2000.

22. *New York Sun*, undated newspaper clipping in Wright oral history File 62-3; Wright oral history, transcript, [13], [18-19].

23. Wright oral history, 1981, transcript, [13-14]; Frances Pound Wright, Oral History, August 26, 1997, File 99-1.

24. Wright oral history, 1981, transcript, File 62-3, [14-15]; "Girl Ranger Makes Spectacular Arrest of Park Bootlegger," *Helena* (MT) *Independent*, August 12, 1927.

25. The accounts of Coolidge's visit through that of the Pound family's move to California are from Wright oral history, transcript, File 62-3, [5-6], [7-9], [22], [12-13], [19-20].

26. Shively, "Ranger Jim," 58.

27. Wright, Oral History, 1997, File 99-1.

28. Social Security Death Index, http://www.ancestry.com/.

Herma Albertson Baggley: Girl Guide for the Dudes

1. Clifton and Ruthella had a total of six children. According to the family Bible, Clara Lillian was born January 7 and died on April 21, 1906; Ralph Walrath was born December 12, 1899 and died April 28, 1900; and Leonard Clifton was born December 26, 1903 and died April 15, 1905. The cause of death of these children was not recorded.

2. 1910 U.S. Federal Census records indicate that Ruthella, and children Herma, Burton, and Ruthella M. were living in Richland, Lyons County, Iowa. Clifton does not appear on a Federal Census that year. "Aged Bingham Resident Dies," (Idaho Falls, ID) *Post-Register*, September 30, 1955, reported that Clifton was in Idaho in 1909.

3. Doris Minney, "Naturalist, Omahan Co-Authors Book on Yellowstone Flowers," *Omaha World Herald Magazine*, July 22, 1956.

4. Begun in 1904 by zoology professor Trevor Kincaid (1872-1970) and botany professor Theodore C. Frye (1869-1962), the Puget Sound Biological Station offered informal summertime, open-air, field study sessions on the subject of marine biology near the remote port of Friday Harbor in the San Juan Islands. In 1930 the Biological Station became part of the new University of Washington Oceanographic Laboratories.

5. Herma Albertson Baggley, "I was born...," Folder "Correspondence 1927-36," Box 4, MSC 7, Herma (Albertson) Baggley Papers, Yellowstone National Park (YNP) Archives.

6. Horace Albright quoted in Robert V. Hine and John Mack Faragher, *The American West: A New Interpretive History* (New Haven: Yale Univ. Press, 2000), 452.

7. Herma Albertson Baggley, quoted in Bill Everhart, *Take Down Flag & Feed Horse* (Chicago: Univ. of Illinois Press, 1998), 115.

8. This may have been one of the first instances of the National Park Service utilizing a concessioner employee for volunteer duties. Since that time there have been thousands of professionals as well as students who have come to Yellowstone to work for concessioners, but with the dual motivation of following their passions in botany, geology, or history by doing volunteer duty for the National Park Service.

9. Roger Toll, *Monthly Report of the Superintendent*, June 1931, Memorandum for the Press #31, YNP Library.

10. For more on this subject, see Elizabeth B. Keeney, *The Botanizers: Amateur Scientists in Nineteenth-Century America* (Chapel Hill: Univ. of North Carolina Press, 1992); Marcia Myers Bonita, *Women in the Field: America's Pioneering Woman Naturalists* (College Station: Texas A&M Univ. Press, 1991); Kim Tolley, *The Science Education of American Girls* (New York: Routledge, 2003); Eugene Cittadino, "Ecology and the Professionalization of Botany in America, 1890-1905," *Studies in the History of Biology* 4 (1980): 171-198.

11. Baggley, "I was born..."

12. William C. and Merrie H. Winkler, "Ansel F[.] Hall," in *National Park Service— The First 75 Years: Biographical Vignettes*, http://www.nps.gov/history/history/online_books/sontag/hall/htm; Herma Albertson Baggley quoted in Everhart, *Take Down Flag*, 115.

13. [Herma Albertson Baggley], "The Nature Trail," manuscript, Box 1, MSC 7, Herma (Albertson) Baggley Papers, YNP Archives.

14. Baggley, "I was born..."

15. Dr. Henry S. Conard to Herma Albertson, April 18, 1927, Folder "Correspondence 1927-36," Box 4, MSC 7, Herma (Albertson) Baggley Papers, YNP Archives.

16. In a 1962 oral interview with Herb Evison, Herma claimed that she was paid as a laborer for three years, which may explain how Albright could keep his promise. However, her name appears listed as a ranger-naturalist in the *Ranger Naturalist Manual* and the *Nature Notes* for 1927, 1928, and 1929.

17. Conard to Albertson, April 18, 1927.

18. Garland quoted in Polly Kaufman, *National Parks and the Woman's Voice: A History* (Albuquerque: Univ. of New Mexico, 2006), 79; Albright quoted, ibid., 81.

19. Herma Albertson, "Trees of Yellowstone," *Yellowstone Ranger Naturalist Manual* 1927, 105-112, in Box 1, MSC 7, Baggley Papers; *Yellowstone Ranger Naturalist Manual* 1927 in YNP Library.

20. Herma Baggley quoted in Everhart, *Take Down Flag,* 115.

21. Roger Toll, *Monthly Report of the Superintendent,* June 1931, Memorandum for the Press #31, p. 2.

22. "Girl Guide for Dudes," *Oakland* (CA) *Tribune,* September 22, 1929, 26; Herma Albertson, "A New Genus for Yellowstone," *Yellowstone Nature Notes,* Volume V, No. 9 (September 1, 1928): 6-7.

23. Roger Toll, *Monthly Report of the Superintendent,* June 1931, Memorandum for the Press #31, p. 2.

24. Albright quoted in "Girl Guide for Dudes"; Joseph H. Mader, Jr., "Special to the Chicago Evening Post," draft manuscript, no date [1931], copy in possession of author, 4.

25. "Girl Guide for Dudes."

26. Herma Albertson to Marguerite Lindsley, September 23, 1927; Lindsley to Albertson, September 30, 1927; Albertson to Lindsley, October 5, 1927; Lindsley to Albertson, October 14, 1927; Albertson to Lindsley, October 21,1927; Albertson to Lindsley, October 30, 1927; Lindsley to Albertson, November 3, 1927; Albertson to Lindsley, November 15, 1927; Lindsley to Albertson, November 23, 1927; Albertson to Lindsley, December 2, 1927; Lindsley to Albertson, January 13, 1928; Albertson to Lindsley, January 25, 1928; Lindsley to Albertson, February 7, 1928; Albertson to Lindsley, February 23, 1928, copies of letters in possession of author.

27. "Girl Guide for Dudes"; Mader, Jr., "Special to the Chicago Evening Post."

28. Roger Toll, Monthly Report of the Superintendent, June 1931, Memorandum for the Press #31, p. 2; Baggley, "I was born..."

29. Ibid.

30. Ibid. The National Park Service had been put under the jurisdiction of the Civil Service Commission in 1927; see Denise S. Vick, *Yellowstone National Park and the Education of Adults,* copy of Ph.D. dissertation, YNP Library.

31. Horace M. Albright to Herma Albertson, January 13, 1931, copy in author's possession.

32. J.G. Teicher, District Manager, U.S. Civil Service Commission, to Herma Albertson, January 19, 1931, copy in author's possession.

33. Roger W. Toll to Herma Albertson, April 2, 1931, copy in author's possession.

34. Horace Albright to Herma Albertson, February 26, 1931, copy in author's possession.

35. Horace M. Albright to Herma Albertson, April 7, 1931; Roger W. Toll to Herma Albertson, April 1, 1931, copies in author's possession.

36. Joseph Joffe to Herma Albertson, April 7, 1931; Roger W. Toll to Herma Albertson, April 9, 1931, copies in author's possession.

37. J. Alwood Maulding, Chief, Division of Appointments, Mails, Files Department of the Interior to Miss Herma G. Albertson, May 8, 1931, copy in possession of author.

38. Herma (Mrs. Geo. F.) Baggley, Reel XXXV, oral history interview with Herb Evison [1962], transcript, p. pp21-23, National Park Service Harpers Ferry Center, Harpers Ferry, WV.

39. Mader "Special to the Chicago Evening Post," 4.

40. Baggley, "I was born..."; Roger Toll, *Monthly Report of the Superintendent,* June 1931, Memorandum for the Press #31, p. 2.

41. George Baggley, Oral History, 77-3, March 6, 1977, YNP Archives; narrative by George Baggley, 1988, vertical files, History-YNP-Employees (Baggley), YNP Library.

42. Everhart, *Take Down Flag,* 16.

43. *Yellowstone National Park Nature Notes,* December, 1932, 51-54.

44. Dr. Walter B. McDougall received his Ph.D. from the University of Michigan in 1913, and taught at the University of Illinois and the University of California. He served as a ranger-naturalist for the National Park Service in Yellowstone during the summers from 1929 until 1934. He became a renowned botanist, pioneer writer about and teacher of ecology, and he was one of the earliest advocates for allowing natural fires to burn in park forests. Dr. McDougall died on Christmas Day 1980 at the age of 97.

45. Baggley, "I was born..."; *Yellowstone National Park Nature Notes,* January-February, 1934, 1.

46. *Idaho Death Index, 1911-51,* Blackfoot, Idaho, ancestry.com. The twins were buried in Grove City Cemetery in Blackfoot, Idaho.

47. United States Department of the Interior, Press Release, June 9, 1936, Herma A. Baggley Papers, YNP Archives; W. B. McDougall and Herma A. Baggley, *The Plants of Yellowstone National Park* (Washington, DC: United States Government Printing Office, 1936), 1-2. Color photography did not appear in commercial form until the 1950s, consequently the only photographs available for the book were black and white.

48. George Baggley, Oral History, 77-3, March 6, 1977, YNP Archives; Narrative by George Baggley, 1988, Vertical files, History-YNP-Employees (Baggley), YNP Library.

49. Author's interview with Ruth Ann Baggley Bennett, June 20, 2010, Mill Creek, Washington.

50. Ethan Carr, *Mission 66: Modernism and the National Park Dilemma,* Library of American Landscape History (Boston: Univ. of Massachusetts Press, 2007), 89-92, 167-69; Kaufman, *National Parks and the Woman's Voice,* 113-115.

51. Herma A. Baggley, *Report of National Park Service Housing Survey, 1953,* Herma A. Baggley Papers, YNP Archives.

52. Doris Minney, "Naturalist, Omahan Co-Authors Book on Yellowstone Flowers," *Omaha World Herald Magazine,* July 22, 1956; W.B. McDougal and Herma A. Baggley, *The Plants of Yellowstone National Park* (Yellowstone Park: Yellowstone Library and Museum Association, 1956), iv-vii.

53. Author's interview with Ruth Ann Baggley Bennett.

54. Herma (Mrs. Geo. F.) Baggley, oral transcript, 20-21.

55. George Baggley, Oral History, 77-3, March 6, 1977, YNP Archives; Narrative by George Baggley, 1988, Vertical files, History-YNP-Employees (Baggley), YNP Archives; Herma A. Baggley Papers, Biographical Note.

56. Narrative by George Baggley, 1988, Vertical files, History-YNP-Employees (Baggley), YNP Library.

57. Iowa State University, College of Liberal Arts & Sciences, The Plaza of Heroines, http://www.las.iastate.edu/plaza/

Eleanor Mae (Hamilton) Povah (1921–): Everyone Was Like Family

1. Unless otherwise noted, information is from author's interview with Ellie Hamilton Povah at Deep Well Ranch, West Yellowstone, Montana, August 28, 2008, and Gwen Petersen, *Yellowstone Pioneers: A Story of the Hamilton Stores and Yellowstone National Park*

(San Diego: Oak Tree Publications, 1985), 29, 30, 61, 64, 72, 73, 96, 99-101, 105-106, 108.

2. Sir Bernard Burke, C.B., LL.D., *Genealogical and Heraldic History of the Colonial Gentry* (London: Harrison & Sons, 1895), 832-33.

3. Robert V. Goss, *Serving the Faithful in Yellowstone: Henry Klamer and the General Store in the Upper Geyser Basin* (Gardiner, MT: Goss, 2003), 48. For further information on Mary (Henderson) Klamer and her three sisters, Helen (Henderson) Stuart, Barbara (Henderson) Lyall, and Jenny (Henderson) Ash, who all were involved in early Yellowstone tourist services, see Robert V. Goss, "Yellowstone's First General Store: A Legacy of Jennie Henderson and Her Family," *Yellowstone Science* 13: 2 (Spring 2005): 16-28.

4. Daniel Mark Barringer, *Selling Yellowstone: Capitalism and the Construction of Nature* (Lawrence: Univ. of Kansas Press, 2002), 78.

5. Aubrey Haines, *The Yellowstone Story: A History of Our First National Park*, rev. ed., vol. 2 (Niwot, Colorado: Univ. of Colorado, 1996), 479.

6. "Everything You Need for Your Park Trip," *Livingston* (MT) *Enterprise*, June 15, 1939.

7. Richard Barlett, *Yellowstone: A Wilderness Besieged* (Tucson: Univ. of Arizona Press, 1985), 198-199; "Press Release June 15, 1949," File "Operators," Box C-1, Yellowstone National Park (YNP) Archives.

8. Bartlett, *Wilderness Besieged*, 175, 194.

9. Haines, *Yellowstone Story*, Vol. 2, 365.

10. Grace Angvik and Thelma Brandly, quoted in Peterson, *Yellowstone Pioneers*, 100-101; author's interview with former Hamilton Stores employee Mike Stevens, March 26, 2011.

11. Aubrey L. Haines, *Yellowstone Story*, rev. ed., vol. 2, 374.

12. File C58, "Buildings, Ham's Stores, 1953-59," Box C-30, YNP Archives; Peterson, *Yellowstone Pioneers*, 105.

13. "C. A. Hamilton Taken by Death," (Butte) *Montana Standard*, May 30, 1957.

14. William M. Nichols to Mrs. Trevor S. Povah, Mr. Trevor S. Povah, and Mr. Garfield Helppie, July 2, 1957, Folder "Business Correspondence 1957," Box 35, Yellowstone Park Company Collection, YNP Archives. William M. "Billy" Nichols began working for Harry Child's Yellowstone hotel company as a clerk in 1907. He married Harry's daughter Ellen Dean Child that same year and worked his way up through the company to the position of vice president by 1915. When Harry died in 1931, Nichols succeeded him as president of the company. Nichols suffered a heart attack on July 28 and died on August 6, 1957.

15. Haines, *Yellowstone Story*, rev. ed., vol. 2, 365; Bartlett, *Wilderness Besieged*, 194.

16. "Obituary for Trevor S. Povah," *Bozeman* (MT) *Daily Chronicle*, April 8, 2001.

17. National Parks Omnibus Management Act of 1998 (Washington, DC: Government Printing Office, 1998), 2-18.

18. Terry Povah quoted in *Lakeland* (FL) *Ledger*, September 23, 1988.

19. For a parallel situation involving Verkamp stores in Grand Canyon National Park, see "Grand Canyon Shop Closing After 102 Years," *Park County Shopper*, April 22, 2008.

20. There is a conflict as to which concessioner actually started the "Christmas in August" celebration. See Leslie Quinn, "Savage Christmas: The Best of Times," *Yellowstone Science* 9 (3)(2001): 2-5.

21. Del Abelein, "My 33 Years with Hamilton Stores: Part 3, 1992 through 2002," [3], December 29, 2005, manuscript in author's possession; "Retired Shelton Teacher: Abelein Is Honored After 30 Yellowstone Seasons," *The Shelton-Madison* (WA) *County Journal*, September 23, 1999; Del Abelein, "My 33 Years with Hamilton Stores," p. [9].

22. Author's interview with Mike Stevens, former Hamilton employee, Gardiner, Montana, May 3, 2010.

23. Gail Schontzler, "Gift of a Lifetime," *Bozeman Daily Chronicle*, September 11, 2009, 1.

Margaret Mary Meagher (1935–): Bears, Bison, and Backcounty

1. Polly Welts Kaufman, *National Parks and the Woman's Voice* (Albuquerque: Univ. of New Mexico Press, 1998), 129; see also Herma Albertson Baggley chapter above.

2. Bernard Devoto, *Harper's Magazine*, October 1953, 49.

3. Nina S. Roberts, "Women in Natural Resources," *Vassar Quarterly*, Vol. 101: 3 (Summer 2005), 1-2.

4. Roberts, "Women," 4.

5. Kaufman, *National Parks and the Women's Voice*, 129; interview with Margaret Mary Meagher by Dorothy Hyuck, Yellowstone National Park, July 26, 1978, transcript, 4, Dorothy Hyuck Collection, National Park Service Harpers Ferry Center, Harpers Ferry, WV.

6. Denise Vick, "Yellowstone National Park and the Education of Adults," Ph.D. dissertation, University of Wyoming, 1986, 201; Mary Meagher quoted in "The Biology of Time," *Yellowstone Science* 5: 2 (1997), 12.

7. Meagher in Hyuck interview, pp. 7-8; "Questioning Greater Yellowstone's Future: Climate, Land Use, and Invasive Species," *The 10th Biennial Scientific Conference on the Greater Yellowstone Ecosystem Agenda and Abstracts*, October 11-13, 2010 (Yellowstone National Park, WY: 2010), 11.

8. Information on Wright's work from Richard West Sellars, *Preserving Nature in the National Parks: A History* (New Haven: Yale Univ. Press, 1997), 95, 96, 87; "George Melendez Wright, Scientist and Visionary," http://www.nature.nps.gov/georgewright/index.cfm.

9. Ansel Hall (1894-1962) was the first Chief Naturalist of the NPS. In addition, Hall was responsible for organizing the Education Division (today's Division of Interpretation), and became an instrumental figure in developing ranger-led interpretation in national parks.

10. Susan Shumaker, "Untold Stories from America's National Parks," companion volume to a film by Ken Burns, *The National Parks: America's Best Idea*, http://www.pbs.org/nationalparks/media/pdfs/tnp-abi-untold-stories-pt-09-wright.pdf, 186.

11. Sellars, *Preserving Nature*, 149-203.

12. Alice Wondrak Biel, *Do (Not) Feed the Bears: The Fitful History of Wildlife and Tourists in Yellowstone* (Lawrence: University of Kansas, 2006), 50-53.

13. Ibid.

14. Sellars, *Preserving Nature*, 98, 204-66.

15. Sellars, *Preserving Nature*, 195-200, 246-249; W. J. Robbins et al., "A Report by the Advisory Committee to the National Park Service on Research, National Academy of Sciences–National Research Council, August 1, 1963"; A.S. Leopold, et al., "Advisory Board on Wildlife Management appointed by Secretary of the Interior Udall, March 4, 1963"; Mary Meagher, "A. Starker Leopold, 1913-1983," in *National Park Service—The First 75 Years, Biographical Vignettes*, http://www.nps.gov/history/history/online_books/sontag/leopold.htm.

16. "Other Perspectives: Excerpts from Oral History Interviews, 'Mary Meagher, park curator/naturalist 1959-1967; biologist 1968-1997,'" *Yellowstone Science* 8: 2 (2000), 21-22.

17. Margaret Mary Meagher, *The Bison of Yellowstone National Park*, NPS Monograph (Washington, DC: Government Printing Office, 1973), v; "Other Perspectives: Excerpts from Oral History Interviews..."

18. Meagher, *The Bison*, 1; Vick, "Yellowstone National Park and the Education of Adults," 201.

19. Margaret Mary Meagher, "The Bison of Yellowstone National Park: Past and Present (Ph.D. diss., University of California, Berkeley, 1970); Meagher, *The Bison*, 1, 110.

20. Kaufman, *National Parks and the Woman's Voice*, 169.

21. Bill Everhart, *Take Down Flag & Feed Horses* (Chicago: Univ. of Illinois Press, 1998), 84.

22. Margaret Mary Meagher, "Winter Weather as a Population Regulating Influence on Free-Ranging Bison in Yellowstone National Park," in *Transactions of the National Park Centennial Symposium*, National Park Symposium Series, No. 1 (Washington, DC: Department of Interior, 1976): 29-38.

23. Margaret Mary Meagher, "Snow as a Factor Influencing Bison Distribution and Numbers in Pelican Valley, Yellowstone National Park," *Proceedings: Snow and Ice Symposium* (Ames: Iowa State University, 1971), 63-66.

24. Margaret Mary Meagher, "Yellowstone's Bison: A Unique Wild Heritage," *National Parks and Conservation Magazine: The Environmental Journal* 48: 5) (1974): 9-14.

25. Mary Meagher and Doug Houston, *Yellowstone and the Biology of Time: Photographs Across a Century* (Norman: Univ. of Oklahoma Press, 1998), xiii.

26. Meagher quoted in Everhart, *Take Down Flag*, 84.

27. Ibid.

28. Meagher in Hyuck interview, transcript, 16.

29. George M. Wright, Joseph S. Dixon, and Ben H. Thompson, *Fauna of the National Parks of the United States: Fauna Series No. 1, May 1932* (Washington, DC: Government Printing Office, 1933), 84.

30. Schwartz et al., "Temporal, Spatial, and Environment Influences on the Demographics of Grizzly Bears in the Greater Yellowstone Ecosystem," *Wildlife Monographs* 161: 1 (2006): 1-68; Sue Consolo Murphy and Beth Kaeding, "Fishing Bridge: 25 years of Controversy Regarding Grizzly Bear Management in Yellowstone National Park," *Ursus* 10 (1998), 385-393; Mark A. Haroldson, Charles C. Schwartz, and Kerry A. Gunther, "Grizzly Bears in the Greater Yellowstone Ecosystem: From Garbage, Controversy, and Decline to Recovery," *Yellowstone Science* 16: 2 (2008)13-24.

31. Meagher quoted in Everhart, *Take Down Flag*, 85.

32. Everhart, *Take Down Flag*, 85; Meagher in Hyuck interview, transcript, 45.

33. Meagher quoted in Everhart, *Take Down Flag*, 86; Mary Meagher, "Memorandum: Upper Blacktail Patrol (Mary's) Cabin," Structures, Vertical File Collection, YNP Library, 3-4, 7.

34. Meagher quoted in Everhart, *Take Down Flag*, 86.

35. Mary Meagher, "Memorandum: Upper Blacktail Patrol (Mary's) Cabin," p. 3, Structures, vertical files, YNP Library.

36. Mary Meagher, "Passages," *Yellowstone Science* 19: 1 (2010), 5.

37. Tami Blackford and Tom Olliff, "The Groundwork for a Career in Yellowstone's Past: A Yellowstone Science Interview with Archaeologist Dr. Ann Johnson," *Yellowstone Science* 18: 1 (2010): 22.

38. Mary Meagher, A. Starker Leopold Speaker, 10th Biennial Scientific Conference on the Greater Yellowstone Ecosystem, Mammoth Hot Springs Hotel, Yellowstone National Park, Wyoming, October 12, 2010.

About the Author

ELIZABETH "BETSY" WATRY is a researcher, author, speaker, and independent scholar specializing in 19th and early 20th century cultural history of the American West. Her primary research interests are in tourism and women's history. She holds an M.A. in History from Montana State University and is the co-author of *Images of America: Yellowstone National Park; Images of America: Livingston (MT)*; and *Ho! For Wonderland: Travelers' Accounts of Yellowstone, 1872-1914.* Betsy first visited Yellowstone at the impressionable age of eight and became fascinated with its long cultural history. Her lifetime passion and ambition to research and write about the park's yesteryears has been the wellspring of inspiration for all of her books. When not doing historical research, Betsy enjoys photography and hiking in Yellowstone's remote backcountry. Her latest book project is *Dining in Yellowstone: A Cookbook of Historic Menus.*

ALSO BY ELIZABETH A. WATRY

Images of America: Yellowstone National Park
Images of America: Livingston (Montana)
Ho! For Wonderland: Travelers' Accounts of Yellowstone, 1872-1914